Martin Luther King Jr. and the Image of God

Martin Luther King Jr. and the Image of God

RICHARD WAYNE WILLS SR.

OXFORD

UNIVERSITY PRESS

Oxford University Press, Inc., publishes works that further
Oxford University's objective of excellence
in research, scholarship, and education.

Oxford   New York
Auckland   Cape Town   Dar es Salaam   Hong Kong   Karachi
Kuala Lumpur   Madrid   Melbourne   Mexico City   Nairobi
New Delhi   Shanghai   Taipei   Toronto

With offices in
Argentina   Austria   Brazil   Chile   Czech Republic   France   Greece
Guatemala   Hungary   Italy   Japan   Poland   Portugal   Singapore
South Korea   Switzerland   Thailand   Turkey   Ukraine   Vietnam

Published by Oxford University Press, Inc.
198 Madison Avenue, New York, New York 10016
www.oup.com

First issued as an Oxford University Press paperback, 2011

Oxford is a registered trademark of Oxford University Press

Library of Congress Cataloging-in-Publication Data
Wills, Richard W., 1956–
Martin Luther King Jr. and the image of God/Richard Wayne Wills Sr.
p. cm.
Includes bibliographical references and index.
ISBN 978-0-19-530899-0 (hardcover); 978-0-19-984396-1 (paperback)
1. King, Martin Luther, Jr., 1929–1968.
2. Black theology.   I. Title.
BX4827.K53W55 2009
230'.61092—dc22   2008034409

9 8 7 6 5 4 3 2 1

Printed in the United States of America

History is made up of living men whose work is handed over defenseless to our understanding and appreciation upon their death. Precisely because of this, they have a claim on our courtesy, a claim that their own concerns should be heard and that they should not be used simply as a means to our ends. History is meant to bear witness to the truth of God, not to our achievements, so that we must avoid any thought that we already know what they have to say and be prepared to hear something new.

Karl Barth, Protestant Theology in the
Nineteenth Century

Acknowledgments

Books are never written apart from the substantial assistance and support of others. To that end, the writing of this book represents a collective effort for which I shall forever remain grateful. I am indebted to a very significant circle of scholars, colleagues, and mentors who proved second to none in their assistance and encouragement. Charles Marsh is to be thanked for his extraordinary role as adviser and mentor during my studies at the University of Virginia. His timely publication of *The Beloved Community*, in addition to his ongoing work with the Project on Lived Theology, has been a model of immeasurable value. James Childress and Charles Mathewes are to be highly regarded for their mastery of the classical thinkers and for their constructive guidance in the discipline of theoretical and practical ethics and religion in public policy. My friend and colleague Corey Walker, now on the faculty of Brown University, is to be thanked for his generosity of time and insight. My conversations regarding the weighty theological concepts considered in this work benefited from his scholarly read in the area of African American religious studies. Wende Marshall's insights also proved invaluable; she is to be thanked for her thoughtful reflections as an anthropologist and theologian.

Beyond the circle of UVA faculty, mention must be given as well of professors, scholars, and colleagues who facilitated this process in a less formal but equally meaningful sense, including Frank Eakin, who first pointed me in the direction of the Rotunda, William

MacDonald, Wallace Best, Larry Bouchard, Robert Franklin, Henry and Ella Mitchell, Ralph Luker, Martha Simmons, Clayborne Carson, Stephen Ray, and Julian Bond for their gifts of insightful conversation and, at times, much-needed encouragement. The completion of this manuscript has also benefited greatly from the wisdom, expertise, and incredible competence of Mamie Woo McNeal, who graciously assisted by assuring that the document was properly formatted and reproduced in preparation for its submittal to the publisher. Among all else, she helped me remain on schedule with my self-imposed and often unreasonable deadlines. My heartfelt thanks and sincerest gratitude must also be extended to Editor Theo Calderara and the wonderful staff at Oxford University Press for extending the courtesy and space required following the recent passing of my father, James R. Wills. The extent of their professionalism and forbearance cannot be overstated.

Finally, I must acknowledge the remarkable faith and fortitude of my family, who, with prayer and presence, have consistently sustained and inspired the completion of this work in wonderfully thoughtful, and at times surprising, ways. In addition to my parents and siblings, this book and the years of research that preceded its writing could not have been successfully undertaken apart from the treasured companionship of my wife, Sheila, and our children, Richard, Whitney, Michelle, and Reginald. Their day-to-day love made possible the translation of the rigor of writing into a labor of love. They have invested as much as, if not more than, I to assure this moment. To them I dedicate this work.

Contents

Prologue

As one reared under the iron heel of Jim Crow, Martin Luther King Jr. often contemplated how American society would look from a socio-political perspective minus systemic racial injustice and whether, in fact, this type of sweeping social transformation was indeed plausible. As such, his chief theological inquiry was anthropological in nature, delving into questions as to whether or not humanity could conceivably overcome the stubborn societal realities ushered in by the institution of slavery. If so, how should society then proceed from "what is" to what "ought to be"? King's brooding inquiry, in essence, explored humanity's capacity to desire and achieve that which represented the best and broadest interest of the "American dream" for all "God's children."

Although he assumed a local social activist stand from Atlanta's prominent Ebenezer pulpit, "Daddy King" seemingly could not satisfactorily convey the broad theological analysis of the human condition that his son sought, nor could he offer a comprehensive prescription for society's modification, should such a prospect exist. This, of course, is not to say that King's early experiences and encounters were negligible. The childhood influences offered by his community, church, and home would, in fact, provide an orientation that was suggestive of the "friendly universe" he later hoped to experience. Equipped with a glimpse of this self-assured possibility and securely positioned in the activist tradition prompted by his father's indelible impression, King would wrestle with the complexities of human progression—and the lack thereof—for the next eleven years as a student of philosophy, religious studies, and systematic theology. He would gradually adjust his findings in the years ahead and according to the events that followed.

To date, much of the King scholarship provided by theologians, historians, and political scientists such as James Cone, Taylor Branch, and David Garrow has, in essence, argued that King is best described as the product of their unique disciplines' bent and tends to emphasize the particularity of their individual intellectual claims. Perhaps the best instance of this diversity of opinion is discovered in Garrow's attempt to gather the various literary "fragments" together in his ambitious three-volume project entitled *Martin Luther King, Jr.: Civil Rights Leader, Theologian, Orator.* If there is a recurring theme throughout his multifaceted work, it is to be found in the various contributors' attempts to profile and claim King in *their* terms. Garrow himself discounts L. Harold DeWolf's Personalist assertion and others of similar mind, as he seeks to join Cone in establishing the prominence of King's relation to the black church.

The difficulty, of course, with narrowed presentations such as these is that while they are extremely helpful and necessary in terms of their particularities, they invariably must, by the very nature of their focused presentation, fall short in their ability to convey a more thorough assessment of King's life and the interrelatedness of his rich theological framework. While scholars may attempt to argue the school of thought that *appeared* most prominent, King ultimately was not a composite of these competing ideologies; instead, his thoughts represented a careful blend of several intertwined concepts. Therefore, to attempt a segmentation of King's life and thought into neat ideological and categorical pigeonholes, apart from this broader recognition of his tendency to *mediate* ideas, is to misunderstand and to inevitably run the risk of misrepresenting him.

Such is the case in instances where King is presented as one who divorced himself altogether from liberal theological thinking in an attempt to reclaim the firmer foundation of theological fundamentalism. In hasty renderings of King's *fundamental* theological profile, it has been argued that King abandoned liberalism as a result of its impotence (its unwillingness to translate meaningful social principles into equally meaningful social practice) and that any earlier suggestion of King's allegiance to liberalism during his student years was no more than a superficial attempt to appease his university instructors.[1] This profile of a "convictionless King" tends to oversimplify King's critical role as theologian. As a skilled mediator of theological concepts, it is clear that King avoided that which he considered "theological extremes." To say that he avoided the extremes, however, is not to conclude that King forsook Christianity because of the church's failure to support the principles of social gospel in

Birmingham and elsewhere, or to suggest that he would have embraced aspects of fundamentalism simply to appease his father. While obviously disappointed by liberalism's "appalling silence" and waning support, King nevertheless continued to embrace aspects of the ideology's affirmation of humanity's hopeful future.

King's concern with an *extreme* liberal view was that it lacked sufficient realism, and as a result, he tempered the theologically naive position with that of his own personal reflection and aspects of Reinhold Niebuhr's more sobering description of human nature. This, however, is not to imply that King rejected all liberal ideas. A closer read of King reveals that while he may have rejected liberalism's naïveté concerning the human condition, he did not dispense with its underlying optimism altogether. In his address to the Montgomery community at the conclusion of the 1965 Selma-to-Montgomery march, King raised a series of rhetorical questions that posed "how long" it would be before justice and community were realized. His optimistic response was "not long." Essentially, he maintained that human society could progress, although he rejected the liberal notion that it would do so on the wings of *human inevitability*. For King, this logic was too closely allied with arguments posited by gradualists who vehemently criticized him for unduly rushing the social process, arguing instead for the allowance of more conventional methods of change at a much more moderate pace. If, therefore, liberalism offered an unbridled celebration of human possibility, King offered its overstated ideology a reconstituted theological anthropology sufficiently mediated to take into account the reality of human evil without negating its euphemistic hope for dramatic progression.

What makes King additionally difficult for the casual reader to decipher is that he represented an eclectic theological mix that was developed under the auspices of a more general strand of historical literary criticism. His intellectual venture represented a composite of evolving theological thought, with comparable traces of his anthropology dating back to doctrinal positions developed during the fifth century. We must, therefore, rethink the tendency to place King in competing camps of theological thought when, in fact, the various profiles of him represented nuanced subheadings of this larger stream of thought. While King arrived at what would undoubtedly be considered a nonorthodox anthropology, in no way did he endorse an entire school of liberal ideas uncritically and he rarely appropriated any concept, liberal or neo-orthodox, in its original form. Ideologically, King aligned himself with, and was drawn to, a *methodology* of biblical interpretation that consistently served to identify and intersect corresponding truths located across varied fields of study, thus distinguishing his commitment to a *process* rather than a particular *position*. Lewis V. Baldwin provides an insightful assessment of King's political astuteness that readily speaks to the comparable manner in which he mediated theological positions:

> The powerlessness of African-Americans in a complex and hypocriti-
> cal land—in a nation claiming to be the citadel of freedom while
> denying civil rights to its citizens of color—led King to combine what
> might be termed "conservative," "liberal," and "radical" elements in
> his politics. The situation he addressed proved in many respects so
> ambiguous, even anomalous, that he, given his high intellect and
> integrity, had to be politically flexible, adjusting his thinking and
> activities toward the changing realities on the racial scene.[2]

Undoubtedly, King's political fluidity was a reflection of the mediating skills he developed as a theologian and further substantiates the thoroughness of his commitment to the methodological process. Ideologically, King, by his own admission, was not wed to the Democratic or Republican creed. His commitment was to the overarching promise held forth in the ideals of a liberal pluralistic democracy, and thus he pledged his support to the political party that best embodied its principles and the interests of his civil rights cause. Similarly, it could be said that King was neither a committed liberal nor a neo-orthodox theologian, but rather, that he positioned himself in an overarching process of theological discourse that encouraged the critique and appropriation of an array of positions based on their ability to withstand the scrutiny of intellectual and scientific investigation, with a sense that "all truth is God's truth." One might assume that King was a committed liberal by examining his theological stance, but what I believe is critical is that he would not have considered himself so, no more than he would have considered himself a devout Democrat simply because he may have voted along those party lines in a given election. Though he clearly stood well within a liberal strand, King was certainly much more fluid than he has so often been depicted to date. It is this mediating quality—and by this I simply mean his commitment to a methodological process that sought intersecting truths—that makes the issue of competing categories a somewhat mute matter. King, in the spirit of Enlightenment thinking, was less interested in protecting dogma and much more interested in arriving at a theological blend that rang true, given the then vast advances in the sciences and technology.

This seems to make sense, especially when one considers the degree to which the dogmas of his day failed to address the centrality of his concern. For example, where earlier pseudosciences and Biblicism tended to denounce racial equality and desegregation on the basis of biological and theological evidence pointing to inferiorities that were considered racially inherent, the advent of twentieth-century advances disputed these earlier arguments, paving the way for modern interpretations and a wave of subsequent appeals for modified social practices. It is therefore not at all surprising that King, who incidentally entered the Montgomery scene upon the *Brown v. Board of Education* wave, expressed little or no apprehension in abandoning concepts that previously proved too thin, if not altogether mistaken. As a mediating theologian, King assumed the task of attempting to create from what was, what theologically could be, even at the risk of being labeled "unorthodox" and/or "liberal." This was a small price to pay when one considers that King did not see himself as writing for himself, but on behalf of his generation, his nation, and ultimately his "world house."

It is not surprising, then, that much of his theological pondering would be anthropological in nature. After all, it was already understood by young King, via his black church tradition, that "God can do anything but fail." Boston's Personalism assured him of the abiding presence of his "Cosmic Companion." These so-called informal and formal introductions to God would be translated from theoretical knowledge to actual encounter in the kitchen of his Montgomery parsonage. King, therefore, was not in a quandary about God's loving capacity for creation; the looming variable was with respect to his lofty questions concerning *human capacity*. While human failure was ever apparent, to what degree could human beings succeed in their long march toward the—not perfect—but *more* perfect union? King drew upon the usefulness of an ancient Christian tradition to bring new meaning to his old dilemma. He commenced his modern inquiry with an analysis of the relationship between *image of God* and civil rights, and he did so not unaware of the extent to which *image of God* language had been employed by abolitionists, sectarian Protestants, and social activists of the preceding century.

This book, therefore, examines the theological idea of image of God as Martin Luther King Jr.'s ethical basis for civil rights considerations and explores the several implications of an image of God ideology as they related to issues of justice, community, and power, with the intent to claim King's theological promise for contemporary discussions in systematic theology and religious ethics. The focus, in previous years, has been placed on some of the more obvious aspects of King's theological legacy such as his treatment of agape, his embrace of Personalism as a theological framework, and the Christological and ecclesiological nature of his radical involvement. My contention, however, is that the contributions in these areas of concern, though each extremely helpful in its own right, do not adequately speak to the ethical basis underlying humanity's pursuit of social justice, and therefore, each ultimately falls short of clarifying that which was foundational to King's thinking and acting, his theological anthropology.

As such, this work illuminates the extent to which the introduction of a textured study of King's anthropology by viewing his theological explication of *image of God* in contrast to other theologians, and through the lens of its implied praxis, is acutely overdue. Hence, it advances a fresh consideration of King's theological anthropology, with the sincere hope that "something new" shall indeed be heard.

PART I

Historical Explication

1

The Historical Context

Martin Luther King Jr.'s use of *imago Dei* language existed on the
edge of a historical dialogue and quest for human and civil rights, and
must therefore be viewed from within the rich traditional context from
which he spoke and acted. He participated in and gave new expression
to a theological concept that existed as early as Augustine and later
found application in the fertile soils of the Mississippi Delta as late as
the nineteenth century, as evidenced in the writings and speeches of
abolitionists and antislavery proponents. It is clear that King ultimately
developed the particulars of his theological outlook from within the
historical context of this Western world defined by its rigid forms of
institutional slavery. This chapter, therefore, shall speak to the more
immediate historical discourse developed during the antebellum and
post-antebellum periods, in an attempt to initially explore the unique
manner in which image of God language found reintroduction and
gained currency during a specific period in the development of Western culture and under specific circumstances, with which King saw
himself successively linked. While part II broadens the analysis so as
to view this more immediate conversation within the earlier theological context of classic Christian thought from which the language is
ultimately derived, informed, and shaped, the primary purpose of this
chapter shall be to substantiate King's use of image of God language
as his primary appeal for civil rights. This chapter will serve to clarify
how we understand King's appeal in relationship to the civil rights
activists and abolitionists who immediately preceded him.

Although some historians may have disputed whether or not the social activism of the 1950s and 1960s was, in fact, linked in some linear fashion to the abolitionist activity of the eighteenth and nineteenth centuries or whether writers mistakenly created an illusion of connectedness,[1] King, in no uncertain terms, saw himself as the grandson of those who were enslaved. He considered himself uniquely engaged in the continuum of his foreparents' struggle for freedom—be it a struggle that was considered in linear or circular terms, or some combination of the two. By no means did King see his civil rights cause as a modern-day social movement that was somehow divorced from the history of America's reign of racial oppression. The language of so-called difficulties and dark days that he often employed to describe the social climate during the 1960s was not somehow detached from the language used in the 1860s. King indicated his awareness of the relationship between the situation of his modern day and that of his ancestors who labored under the iron heel of slavery in a 1963 speech when he wrote, "Lincoln had hoped the slavery issue could be relegated to secondary place, but life thrust it into the center of history. There segregation, the evil heritage of slavery, still remains."[2] It was the lingering remnant of this "evil heritage" that King sought to redress and correct. As King imagined God and contemplated what it meant to have been created in the image of God, his questions and conclusions were undeniably diffused through the lens of his personal social experience and the historical attachments that defined it. In a very real way, King felt himself connected to the lingering heritage of slavery. His theological formation, therefore, was attached to a specific worldview that had been shaped by specific social realities. As such, King's dual interest in theology and civil rights cannot be read or understood apart from his social context and its dire historical attachments. His life reflected, echoed, and sought to continue their freedom struggle.

That is not to say that conditions were not improved by King's day. Americans of African descent had clearly experienced marginal progress by the first half of the twentieth century. The vestiges, however, of failed social construction, better known as Reconstruction, remained evident to King in and through the oppressive demands of Jim Crow in the South and the more subtle forms of racial redlining and discriminative practices in the North. Although King returned to the South to address the overt forms of racial discrimination evidenced there, he was not unaware of the extent to which the challenges of his home were discovered throughout the nation in a less obvious and more understated fashion. In a 1962 address to the National Press Club, King did not fail to point out that although segregation existed in the South in overt and glaring forms, it also existed in the North in hidden and subtle forms. His was a reminder that housing and employment discrimination were often as prominent in the North as they were in the South and that the racial issue confronted in America was not a sectional but a national problem.[3] The social ills that attended his childhood experience were not simply local and regional; they permeated the national body and as such called forth in him the need to determine the cause of illness while attempting to administer the social antidote with hopes of hastening the cure. As King, therefore, challenged unjust laws and oppressive social practices, he consciously did so in a manner reminiscent of and intentionally linked to the abolitionists' former heralds for social justice. King certainly provides every indication that he engaged the civil rights movement with that historic backdrop in mind. As an avid defender of life's downtrodden, he wrote, thought, and acted out of that specific historical context. He remained ever mindful of the political, economic, and theological debates that eventually drew slavery, at least as a formal institutionalized system, to its end. As did the activists of the preceding century, King would courageously confront and contend with the lingering vestiges of that institution the remaining years of his life. He did so with an understanding of slavery's lengthy and significant history.

Preserved and perpetuated through succeeding centuries by one ideological form or another, the robust hope for freedom imagined by and for those in the colonized New World was complicated by the anomaly of slavery. In fact, the growing ambivalence over the slave question in America followed a rather comparable and consistent history that paradoxically wrote slavery into the societal equation as one of its justifiable and, in some sense, necessary aspects. Inspired by Plato's conceptual contrast of the human body's material subjection to its rational soul, Aristotle developed a philosophic justification for slavery that "would help shape virtually all subsequent proslavery thought."[4] This duality of thought, which justified the human subjugation of some while promoting the human freedom of others, would later become a defining element in "Roman law (the code of Justinian), which ruled that slavery was the single institution contrary to the law of nature but sanctioned by the law of nations. . . . This was the official view of Christian churches from the late Roman Empire to the eighteenth, or even 19th century."[5] The paradoxical relationship of these two diametrically opposed conditions of the human situation were alluded to in Locke's eighteenth-century attempt to reconcile egalitarian conceptions of freedom with society's ubiquitous acceptance of slavery. David Brion Davis notes, "Because John Locke made natural liberty the center of his philosophy, he had to place slavery outside the social compact, whose purpose was to protect all men's unalienable rights."[6] Locke's humanist philosophy further illustrated the degree to which this dichotomous coexistence of human enslavement and human progression was not historically viewed as an intolerable social norm, at least not until the latter part of the eighteenth century. Davis writes:

> In the mid–18th century, when black slaves could be found from
> French Canada to Chile, there was nothing unprecedented about New
> World chattel slavery, or even the enslavement of one ethnic group by
> another. What was unprecedented by the 1760's and early 1770's was
> the emergence of a widespread conviction that New World slavery
> was deeply evil and embodied all the forces that threatened the true
> destiny of the human race.[7]

This development of an abolitionist tradition, of which King considered himself an heir, loomed large on the horizon of the mid–eighteenth century as planters, politicians, and even preachers debated the fact and fate of the enslaved.[8] In an attempt to define the most significant causes of slavery's decline in the Western world, some authors have highlighted the growing intolerance associated with the blatant inhumanities characteristic of that slave society; while others have drawn attention to the rise of industrialism and conflicting international market interests. A number of historians, however, have pointed to the Revolutionary War (1775–1783) and its attendant ideas of freedom as the watershed event most responsible for the dramatic development of abolitionist sentiment. Indeed, by the late eighteenth century, the national political debate found resonance in the countless longings of the enslaved, as American politics fast-forwarded its focus on the meaning of freedom so as to expedite their liberation from the Commonwealth. After all, more than a Eurocentric longing, freedom represented a human longing. The language of justice could readily be applied to all forms of injustice. At long last, individuals of goodwill had conceived of a free democracy that was inclusive of all. The enslaved, and those who advocated their freedom, were infused with new hope by the nation's independence movement from England. The language of liberation captured the essence of their longings too. It was therefore hoped, and perhaps even expected, that the fight for American freedom would at some point translate into a fight on behalf of all suffering humanity. As such, the national mood and move toward independence were undoubtedly viewed by some as a hopeful pioneering toward a universal freedom that was divinely destined and God-ordained. The agenda may have had American independence as its focal point, but beyond that center, those suffering from the egregious injustices committed against them would eventually be ushered in. Vincent Harding vividly captures this longing when he writes:

> As democratic dogma and revolutionary rhetoric filled the colonial
> legislatures and reverberated through the Continental Congress

and were proclaimed in local communities seeking justification for armed rebellion for the sake of Independence, many black people took careful notice. Was it so hard to grasp that the ideas of no taxation without representation, the equality of all men under God, and divine right of humankind to freedom and self-government had some direct reference to their own lives? Indeed, in the fall of 1774, word spread among them that the Continental Congress had formally approved a resolution pledging the colonies to forsake the African slave trade altogether.[9]

Though certainly unintentional, the events that played out on the world stage directly influenced and served as a convenient case study for the enslaved, who were also in search of life, liberty, and the pursuit of happiness. Patrick Henry's "Give me liberty or give me death" rang with great resonance and thereby heightened the enslaved community's sense of social awareness and hopeful expectations for emancipation. The prominent rumblings of freedom in their midst and in the world signaled a universal shift in the moral compass. For the plantation populace who had become enlightened by the firsthand accounts provided by indigenous émigrés of the Haitian revolt, and the growing domestic discussion about the inevitability of an American Revolution, the idea of their personal freedom and the experience of a more just existence seemed altogether plausible. It was as though the language of independence, the willingness to launch a freedom revolution, and Haiti's successful overthrow of forced colonization were all suggestive of a growing sensitivity to the cries of the oppressed. A global freedom movement was at work that would eventually advocate their cause against all odds as well. It was certainly no coincidence that King took note of a similar dynamic still at work in his own time. Notwithstanding the opposition to change, King gleaned great hope from the newfound freedoms he witnessed. Just as King drew great inspiration and determination to further the cause of civil rights in America from the reports of Asian and African countries that gained independence from colonial dominance in his day, so the enslaved became energized by the hopeful liberation pursuits of their neighbors. If injustice anywhere threatened the hopes of justice everywhere, the furtherance of freedom anywhere also bolstered the hope for freedom everywhere, especially in a land guided and governed by the democratic principles of "liberty and justice for all."

Confirmation, or so they thought, came in the 1774 decision handed down by the Continental Congress. The recurring question was with respect to how effectively this conviction in the *principles* of freedom and equality rooted in human nature would *pragmatically* apply to the particular condition of slaves and freed persons of African descent. To what extent would the inspired language of "We the people" represent the inclusion of African people and their freedom aspirations? Would the spirit of freedom that spanned ecclesiastical reformations and social revolutions also provide sufficient theological and sociopolitical grounds for the dismantling of slavery's egregious legacy? If the thwarting of social and religious freedoms should be challenged and resisted in the instance of American life, a comparable effort should be explored and extended in terms of African life, or so it seemed. That the enslaved should not experience a similar kind of liberation appeared untenable, given the uncompromising and unquestionable actions that were being taken to secure American independence. As such, the activists prepared and unapologetically presented arguments for the dismantling of the slave institution on the same moral and theological grounds. After all, the enslaved, despite the claims of pseudoscience and skewed Biblicism, were not property objects to be bartered and bargained for. As far as they were concerned, the enslaved were not intended by some divine scheme to function as slaves. Contrary to Aristotle's conclusions with respect to social ordering such that some were created to serve, none were deserving of that level of human mistreatment and abuse. In some instances, the holder's livestock received better treatment than the enslaved. The enslaved were not the victims of some divine ordering, nor were they a pitiable remnant of some subhuman species as many assumed. Rather, they were fellow members of the human household with all the dreams, hopes, and aspirations espoused by their holders. Although most were unwilling to acknowledge it, the universal truths eloquently expressed in the founding documents applied to the voiceless, powerless plantation labor force as well. Historian Ira Berlin illustrates the degree to which these kinds of antislavery sentiments sought to make that connection:

> The turmoil of the war marked only the beginning of the
> slaveholder's problems. The invocation of universal equality—
> most prominently in the Declaration of Independence—further
> strengthened the slave's hand. The insistence on the universality
> of liberty overflowed the bounds of the struggle for political
> independence. How can Americans "complain so loudly of attempts
> to enslave them," mused Tom Paine in 1775, "while they hold so
> many hundreds of thousands in slavery?"[10]

The rising sentiment on behalf of the enslaved and their advocates became self-evident to those who not only did not share their misguided enthusiasm but instead determined to do all in their power to discourage, diffuse, and destroy it. As far as the abolitionists were concerned, the governing politic of the fledgling democracy correctly embraced a sociopolitical position attuned to the universal ring of freedom. It was expected that slavery should also be considered an egregious affront, sufficiently reprehensible under all circumstances and in the instance of all humanity. That this, however, was not the intended goal of the American Revolution was clear to antebellum liberals, although they vigorously sought the ideology's broadest application. "While Revolutionary era liberals were concerned primarily with achieving democratic rights for white middle-class men, antebellum liberals hoped to extend those rights to women, children, Native Americans, African Americans, and immigrants."[11] Their antebellum hopes, however, would prove less than rewarding as the limits of freedom's boundaries were hardened, redrawn, and redefined to primarily accommodate America's newfound sense of white nationhood, to the exclusion of any serious long-term antislavery considerations. Though several of the founding figures expressed discomfort with the system of human bondage, few would attempt to condemn the system as a result of their willingness to view it as a property rights issue, not to mention the unfavorable consequences that such a decision would have created. Insofar as they were concerned, the U.S. Constitution protected the slaveholder's rights, thus allowing the significant expansion of slavery into nine new states between 1792 and 1845.[12]

While the enslaved expressed increased enthusiasm over the prospect of at last bringing their long night of suffering to an end, slaveholders expressed a growing need to counter their naive imaginings with a stern wake-up call. To allow them to persist in their futile freedom fantasy would only heighten the risk of unnecessary plantation uprisings and much feared revolts. There was a perceived need to inform them of their mistaken read of the social scene beyond the boundaries of plantation life. Haitian and American freedom did not translate into liberty for all in the broadest sense of the word. "All" certainly did not encompass and include them. Their hopes, therefore, were promptly stemmed by measures that would leave little doubt as to whether or not slavery would continue to exist and even flourish beyond a successful American revolution. Despite the shared anticipation, freedom would come for some, but as they increasingly discovered, independence was certainly not intended for all. If anything, the slave institution was deemed more valuable and necessary, in terms of its long-term economic benefits, in a post-Revolution America than before. Beyond the realization of the colonizers' independence, a nation was in need of being developed, making slavery a convenient and most profitable enterprise. Freedom and slavery would continue their long and awkward journey together, and they would do so in one of the more brutal forms known to human societies. To the dismay of their long-awaited freedom dream, the enslaved would experience their first of many backlash efforts designed to maintain the yoke of servitude and keep them "in their place." As Berlin explains,

> With the winds of revolution at their backs, slaves pressed to fulfill the expectations of the new era, if not with freedom, then at least with a greater measure of control over life and labor. Bracing themselves against the gale of change, slave owners labored to smother the slaves' rising expectations and, if possible, increase their control by extracting still greater draughts of labor.[13]

If freedom came, it would have to come by means of other avenues. For those fortunate enough to benefit from the war by serving in the military, purchasing their freedom through funds secured thereof or successfully escaping amid the turmoil, the road to full freedom beyond plantation life remained arduous and elusive to say the least. Few Americans, it would seem, were prepared to respond in kind to the upward adjustment of freed individuals as they migrated into northern populations in search of a "promised land." For the once enslaved, it was thought that the promised land represented any land north of the Mason-Dixon Line that would afford them a home and employment opportunities apart from the fear of subsequent enslavement. As David Reimers explains, "The increasing numbers of Negro Christians in the northern states, due to the emancipations of the revolutionary era, raised the problem of race relations within the churches. Patterns of segregation appeared, and with the passage of time, racial segregation became the main characteristic of Negro-White relations within Protestantism."[14] While "Negro Christians" were invited to participate in church and denominational life, particularly in the North, such interaction was rarely viewed as an opportunity to socialize as one's equal. Designated seating, the inability to participate at a core leadership level, and the lack of voting privileges served as constant reminders of their degraded second-class citizenship.[15] In time, those hopeful of a full and final freedom would discover that their desire to appropriate the American ideal might have been overly presumptuous and, in some instances, unmistakably naive. Vincent Harding underscores this growing reality:

> The Revolution had set the white Americans free to press on with their part in the breaking of African society and the raping of her children, just as white laborers in the southern colonies had earlier been granted greater freedom in exchange for their aid in repressing black struggles to achieve the same liberty. Therefore, in spite of the onset of a gradual movement toward the freeing of African slaves in the northern states and in spite of continued black uses of the revolution's rhetoric and ideology, many blacks realized that they

would have to look elsewhere for true revolutionary inspiration. The white American Revolution was not ours.[16]

Many looked to the church, only to discover that the sociopolitical and economic debate often moved in tandem with the church's theological thinking—particularly as the antislavery movement, a divergent movement that challenged political as well as religious reform, commenced in earnest. As members of the international community jockeyed for global prominence, the church expeditiously acquiesced and, in many instances, accommodated the sale and capture of human cargo in keeping with national interests. Reminiscent of this earlier era, King himself would come to lament the degree to which the churches and their leadership resisted the idea of assuming stands that moved counter to the whims and wishes of status quo thinking that affirmed the unjust treatment of others. If no other institution was suited to exercise moral conviction in response to their cruel and unusual suffering, if no other group would assume an advocate's stand, it was hoped that the church certainly would. Prior to the Civil War, however, the church at best remained ambivalent with respect to its position on the slave question. To be sure, as the nation approached the onset of civil war, slavery was discussed as *an issue* but certainly not as one that existed as a central policy question. The politics of the day, for the most part, conveniently conversed on the issue of slavery from life's margin, so as to give priority to the more urgent efforts bent toward the formation of the Republic above all else. The chief good was clearly associated with the idea of furthering the goals of colonial independence, and the church rarely challenged that perspective. In fact, silence on the issue occasionally moved in the direction of support for the institution of slavery. Early on, it would seem that the Protestant Church, though not without occasional exception, shared the ideological sentiments of its political and economic counterparts.

Reimers provides an insightful commentary on this uneasy relationship between slavery and Christianity during the colonial era. According to Reimers, the churches were not deeply concerned with the slavery issue, and while church leaders "urged that the slaves be made Christians, few said Christianity and slavery were incompatible."[17] While some slaveholders were apprehensive about the act of baptism and whether or not this would then alter the status of their enslaved, the churches and colonial laws coalesced to provide an assurance that baptism would not in turn mandate their freedom. The freedom that the enslaved would experience and would be encouraged to focus upon related solely to their liberation from spiritual bondage. Baptism simply announced and communicated their freedom from the shackles of sin and offered no hope of loosing the physical shackles of slavery. The only liberating hope was that of "going home to their Lord and be free." In more than a few quarters, the church gathered in support of slavery and the prevailing sociopolitical sanction. This was reflected in the general opinion of most churches by their initial decision to minimize the evangelization efforts of African life. Even in the instance of most Christian abolitionists, African freedom was rarely equated with African equality, and as a result theological constructs affirming divine intent with respect to racial separatism remained fairly rampant.[18] By the turn of the nineteenth century, while antislavery sentiment rose in the South, much of it due to the tendency toward colonizing the enslaved population. Not to dismiss the good intent of a few, the emphasis upon the Christianization of slaves was largely initiated, and gained significant support at the outset, with the hope of creating a climate conducive to willful subjection; after all, there was scriptural admonishment for slaves to "obey their masters." Hence the rationale for the evangelization of the enslaved population was to reinforce notions of servitude and submission. Despite the fierce resistance of some to the idea of chattel slavery, the stigma of an assigned racial inferiority as normative would continue to characterize the dynamics of race relations without and within the context of church life, as Reimers explains: "Thus, well before the Civil War, racial discrimination and segregation were part of Protestant Church life in both the North and South. The churches generally agreed that because Negroes had souls they were eligible for salvation, but this did not preclude discrimination and segregation within the religious community."[19]

In time, the slave issue would become a central ecclesial fact, roughly divided between the North and South by America's Mason-Dixon Line. Although thinking was anything but monolithic, the denominational rupture became geographically defined, with the question of slavery developing as one of the leading polarizing ideas in Protestant Church life. As Reimers suggested, "Although northern and southern white Protestants quarreled little over segregation before the Civil War, their divisions over slavery were acute, and the war and Reconstruction aggravated those divisions."[20] The divisions within Protestantism became more apparent as efforts to curb the much-dreaded slave rebellions and foster new ways of theologically understanding the slave-master relationship were under way. Beyond questions of baptism and marriage, denominations entertained the meaning of race, segregation, and, moreover, the extent to which the church should appropriately involve itself in the work of civil affairs.[21] In so doing, a host of Protestant agencies and societies came short of naming slavery as sin.[22] To view slavery as sin would, of course, necessitate some form of internal repentance and external rejection of the system as evil, which all too many were unwilling to do. Insofar as they were concerned, social systems were established by governments that were in turn established by God; therefore, many Protestant conventions simply opted for positions that

THE HISTORICAL CONTEXT   13

essentially left the issue up to the state and one's individual conscience. At best, slavery was viewed as an unfortunate social arrangement that would correct itself in time. At worst, it was seen as God's way of facilitating the progress of his chosen people. At bottom, these divisions, as Berlin indicates, diverted, delayed, and denied social progress that moved in the sure direction of the slave community's long-awaited liberation:

> Despite the myriad forces assaulting slavery, freedom progressed
> slowly and unevenly. The age of revolution witnessed the liberation of
> only a small fraction of slaves on mainland North America. In many
> places, the advance toward freedom could hardly be noticed, and in
> others the process worked in reverse, as slavery grew more rapidly
> than freedom during the late 18th and 19th centuries. Far more
> people lived in slavery at the end of the revolutionary age than at the
> beginning.[23]

Little, however, could diminish the antislavery proponent's capacity to view the institution of slavery through the lens of apparent human contradiction. If anyone was mistaken, they certainly did not consider themselves misguided in their cause to extend freedom's experience to that of the enslaved. Though limited in number, the abolitionists continued their rally for the eradication of slavery. For them, slavery was altogether unjustifiable, and any refusal to emancipate the enslaved was viewed as a gross inconsistency with the freedoms valued by those who sought liberty's full guarantee. Notwithstanding the obvious facts of economic expediency, slavery remained a moral deficiency in need of dissolution. The independence ideology fostered by the American Revolution was significant in terms of its adoption by the enslaved; it, however, was not the only underlying principle to inspire their freedom hopes. By far the more hopeful appeal for civil justice and the abolishment of slavery would come via the appropriation of theological reasoning. While socio-political arguments waned in the societal wings, attempts to forge and couple political reasoning with a meaningful religious rationale were under way. In the final analysis, the questions of liberty and equality were not simply political issues; the growing perception was that they had religious ramifications as well. Antislavery proponents insisted that they were ultimately accountable to God and God's intent for humanity. More than the secular rationale could admit, freedom had a moral quality that grew out of a theological worldview that sought to articulate what it meant to have been created in God's image. By and large, the church's antislavery stance was initially led by voices located within northern Quaker fellowships, which, as early as the mid–eighteenth century, signaled its opposition to the otherwise predominant pro-slavery social climate. By the 1770s, Quaker slave owners of the South commenced to free their slaves, some consenting to do so with the additional proviso to include some form of reparation.[24] King often acknowledged the early role of the Quakers and the ways in which they modeled meaningful ministry for the church by their willingness to translate their theology into meaningful social action. In defense of the keen sensitivities that positioned them alongside the abolitionary concern, King wrote, "Certainly no one can accuse many Quaker mystics of otherworldliness and lack of social concern. One needs only know of their stand against slavery, poverty and war."[25] Many antislavery advocates, in fact, expected that the church would lead in this moral crusade. Quaker activity, however, would remain the exception through the mid–eighteenth century, a period marked by revolution and swift societal transition.

In time, slaveholders would also receive pressure from evangelicals who were of the mind that God had in fact created all persons equal. As Ira Berlin notes, "Black men and women who joined and occasionally led the evangelical churches considered worldly freedom an obvious extension of their spiritual liberation, and many white congregants enthusiastically agreed."[26] Though Berlin's assessment of this congregational enthusiasm may seem overstated by some, the fact of an emerging theology concerned with the question of human equality and freedom, centered in this kind of spiritual reality, was certain. The social context predominantly defined by slavery fostered a theological reconsideration of the meaning of freedom and its relationship to the plight of the enslaved. Notwithstanding the political ramifications for a purer democracy, these laid hold on a theology of emancipation *for all*, one that highlighted humanity's shared origin and, hence, their shared future. Segregation, racism, and slavery, as concurrent social arrangements, though politically accommodated, flew in the face of their Kingdom of God concept. It ran counter to their notion of what otherwise might have been considered humanly possible. In their estimate, racial equality and a far greater degree of mutual regard were required by virtue of the fact that all were created in the image of God. This theological theme, dealing with the question of what it meant to have been created in the image of God, was embraced by some with hopes of appealing to the moral conscience of those who held, sold, and supported the immoral marketing of God's children. For them, this represented a supreme hope. Who, or so they reasoned, would ignore the affirmation of God's moral purposes? Despite the pro-slavery expansionist mood, Quaker, Congregational, Unitarian, and evangelical fellowships increasingly expressed their growing discontent with the system of slavery and called for its end.

These calls for the manumission of slaves were augmented by the emergence of organized abolitionism in the 1830s, primarily through the efforts of William Garrison's American Anti-Slavery Society and the socalled radical Christian sects. Though comparatively few in number, their collective voice was significant.[27] As McKanan explains, "Radical Christian liberals were a tiny minority of the United States culture between 1820 and 1860. In their activism and especially in their literature, they promoted a utopian vision of a society free of violence and coercion, organized entirely around its citizens' recognition of the divine image in one another."[28] The veracity of all human laws was in need of being adjusted according to this higher claim. Given this theological assertion of human life as distinctively created, freedom, of course, was the obvious conclusion. Contrary to popular thought, to enslave some as a means of enriching the enterprise of others was inconsistent with the theological affirmation of God's intent for humanity. It was this theological idea that rallied the social resistance against the forces of slavery so all those created in God's image might be included in "We the people." In this sense the language captured in the various sociopolitical creeds had reference to their own lives too. This message of God's image was later appropriated by King and reflected in his tendency to view civil rights activism as a redemptive movement of God in human history. More than a civil concern, the freedom cause for the enslaved gained sacred status. More than a human cause, the fight for their independence was fortified by the consent and approval of almighty God. God, not humanity, guided and governed their battle against tyranny and human oppression. As Martin Luther King Jr. would later argue, the image of God established the moral standard for understanding the humane and just treatment of all human life. As we shall see later in this chapter, King's affirmation of humanity created in the image of God was closely aligned with that of his abolitionist predecessors. His voice was a perpetuation of their call to freedom. Though few in number, the significance of their voices helped to shape the discourse and set the tone for antislavery sentiment.

Among the several notable voices connecting the idea of civil rights to that of humanity's creation in God's image, and in a manner reminiscent of King, was Henry Highland Garnet. Born a slave in New Market, Maryland, Garnet became a Presbyterian minister upon his escape to New York in 1824 and served several pulpits as pastor. A member of the American Anti-Slavery Society, Garnet crusaded for the cause of emancipation and later encouraged the emigration of U.S. blacks to Africa. For him, the theological idea conveyed through image of God language constituted humanity's indispensable drive and passion toward liberty. More than intellectual assent to legal argument, the image of God inspired a kind of restless interiority, a perpetual longing of the soul to rise to the level of holistic free existence. It was not sufficient that the soul was freed; the freed soul also longed for the freedom of mind and body. When denied, the withholding of true human freedom represented life's most serious and grievous crime against humanity and, moreover, their Creator. More than a human crime, a crime was committed against the one in whose image humanity was created. As witnessed in the writings of Garnet, a theological anthropology emerged that located and rooted an appeal for civil justice in the idea of being created in the image of God. It did so at a time when the slave enterprise also entertained forms of scientific validation to reinforce their justification.[29] In this sense, the idea of all life being created in the image of God could possibly be viewed as an argument developed to counter a rising pseudoscience attempting to weight the claims of pro-slavery advocates. In an 1843 address urging slaves to resist their enslavement, and in a tone and tenor that King would later assume, Garnet underscored the uncompromising relationship between freedom and human life as sacred:

> Slavery! How much misery is comprehended in that single word.
> What mind is there that does not shrink from its direful effects!
> Unless the image of God is obliterated from the soul, all men cherish
> the love of liberty. The nice discerning political economist does
> not regard the sacred right, more than the untutored African who
> roams in the wilds of Congo. Nor has the one more right to the full
> enjoyment of his freedom than the other. In every man's mind, the
> good seeds of liberty are planted, and he who brings his fellow down
> so low as to make him contented with a condition of slavery, commits
> the highest crime against God and man.[30]

A decade earlier, William Whipper, a spokesperson for the American Moral Reform Society, attempted to dispel the scientific myth of African inferiority by also underscoring and reiterating the slave's actual condition and nature. For Whipper, as for Garnet, human worth could not be simply measured in the terms of nineteenth-century race-based politics and its attending racial science. A much more thorough and ontologically correct account of humanity that recognized the innate worth of all human life and a more acceptable description of the enslaved, and hence their rightful place in human society, was needed. As Eddie Glaude rightly notes, in his 1837 address to the American people, Whipper "bluntly condemned those who viewed blacks as inferior and argued that all human beings were made in the image of God."[31] As Whipper further explained, "If there be those who doubt that we are made in the image of God and are endowed with those attributes which the Deity has given to man, we will exhibit [to] them our hands and side."[32] Slaves were not simply human beings in the scientific sense—although certain intellectuals attempted to call their very humanity into question on the grounds of their so-called newfound science—but were human beings entitled to certain unalienable rights, as a result of having been essentially created in the image of God.[33] Similar to King's view of humanity's interconnectedness, which shall be explicated in chapter 6, an element of the Eternal stirred within, thus establishing their tie to life's Author as well as to one another. Moreover, to have been created in the image of God prescribed the unmistakable manner in which harmonious social relations should be governed and regulated.

Frederick Douglass, a former slave and prominent figure among the abolitionists, became a voice King often resembled. Douglass, a former slave, fled to New York in 1838 and weeks later relocated to New Bedford, Massachusetts. Intrigued by the abolitionist writings of William Lloyd Garrison, Douglass subscribed to Garrison's weekly edition of the *Liberator*. In 1841 Douglass attended the Anti-Slavery Society gathering in Bristol. His opportunity to meet Garrison resulted in a feeling of mutual regard, and within days Douglass would be invited to speak at one of the society's meetings in Massachusetts. The address proved to be such a great success that Douglass was invited to serve as a lecturer for the society for the next three years. Interestingly, the two would later part company over significant differences in their thoughts on emancipation and how it should best be achieved. While Garrison assumed a position that denounced the church, affiliation with political parties, and even the Constitution itself, Douglass assumed a more reconciliatory stand. In opposition to Garrison's radicalism, Douglass affirmed the Constitution as a basis for arguing the case for the abolishment of slavery. As one of the leading spokespersons for the abolishment of slavery, Douglass argued, as did King, against the institution of human bondage on the grounds that it diminished and degraded God's purpose for human coexistence. He did so by providing a sacred analysis of the individual's human worth, a worth meriting just and civil social consideration within the context of America's freedom struggle. Moreover, Douglass argued against slavery in full recognition of their mutual created origin. More than mere chattel, slaves were to be viewed as the objects of God's irrefutable love and redemptive purpose, as were they. As Douglass emphatically stated in an 1850 address:

> The slave is a man, "the image of God," but "a little lower than the angels"; possessing a soul, eternal and indestructible, capable of endless happiness, immeasurable woe; a creature of hopes and fears, of affections and passions, of joys and sorrows; and he is endowed with those mysterious powers by which man soars above the things of time and sense, and grasps, with undying tenacity, the elevating and sublimely glorious idea of a God. It is *such* a being that is smitten and blasted. The first work of slavery is to mar and

deface those characteristics of its victims which distinguish *men* from *things* and persons from *property*. Its first aim is to destroy all sense of high moral and religious responsibility. It reduces man to a mere machine. It cuts him off from his Maker; it hides from him the laws of God and leaves him to grope his way from time to eternity in the dark, under arbitrary and despotic control of a frail, depraved, and sinful fellow man.[34]

For Douglass, an ordained minister of the African Methodist Episcopal Church, that form of institutional slavery, which was historically unrivaled in its kind and cruelty, was no more than an ill-conceived attempt to dismiss and distort that which God accomplished in creation. It was an overt and shameful attempt to shackle both body and soul, thereby perpetuating one of humanity's great and abominable evils. As King would later note, humanity's injustice against humanity was not simply a violation of physical being; it sought to dislodge and distort the spiritual identity of those being oppressed. But as Douglass and others would contend, not even the ravages of slavery could sufficiently mar the express image of the slaves' Creator or permanently impede their purpose and place within a humane and civil society by attempting to depict the enslaved as *other*. While acknowledging the importance of the Constitution as a political document that could speak to issues of emancipation and freedom of the enslaved, Douglass affirmed the theological idea of being created in the image of God. Contrary to his personal encounter with slavery and its degradation, the enslaved were creatures of God, created in God's likeness and image. Unlike the stereotypes and caricatures created by pro-slavery sentiment and their slaveholders, the enslaved shared sacred common ground with their taskmasters—not other, not a thing, not an object, but a fellow citizen of God's commonwealth. There was thus the need to reshape and redefine the prevailing manner in which the enslaved were described and hence viewed. James Cone reaffirms Douglass's argument from the previous century by reiterating the need for oppressed individuals to move beyond the debasing tendency to allow oneself to be labeled as an *it* or a *thing* by embracing an affirmation of self that was grounded in the theological conception of creation in the image of God. Cone writes:

> The biblical emphasis on the freedom of man also means that one cannot allow another to define his existence. If the Biblical *imago Dei* means anything, it certainly means that God has created man in such a way that man's own destiny is inseparable from his relation to the Creator. When man denies his freedom and the freedom of others, he denies God. To be "for God" by responding creatively to the *imago Dei* means that man cannot allow others to make him an It. It is this fact

that makes black rebellion human and religious. When black people affirm their freedom in God, they know that they cannot obey laws of oppression. By disobeying, they not only say yes to God but also to their own humanity and to the humanity of the white oppressor.[35]

Such arguments, of course, did not go unchallenged. While abolitionists such as Douglas and others insisted upon a theological anthropology that included the enslaved, counterarguments weighed in from theological, as well as political and judicial, quarters to firm up the institution's rationale. As antislavery advocates fought for the end of the slave era and a commencement of civil rights based on the equal opportunities afforded all persons created in the image of God, the judicial system weighed in with decisions that rarely concurred. In fact, with rare exception, the political, ecclesiastical, and judicial systems allied themselves in stubborn alliance against the provision of civil rights that would have assured the realization of first-class citizenship for the enslaved. Much of the argument was centered upon the nature of African life. This legal debate over the nature of African identity is acknowledged by Eugene Genovese as he writes, "Repeatedly, the courts struggled with and tripped over the slave's humanity."[36] Not a few courts, later conceding to the fact of their humanity, did so, at least in part, to have the legal leverage to try and charge slaves for their alleged crimes. Occasionally the court spoke in defense of the enslaved and their existence as fellow creatures created in the image of God. In a sympathetic effort to legally establish rights based on the slave's sense of human dignity in 1846, Judge Green of the Tennessee Supreme Court sought to distinguish the slave as human personality from that of property by characterizing the enslaved as being unmistakably created in God's image, an argument already made fairly popular by Douglass, Garnet, Francis Asbury, and Whipper, to name a few. Human rights, argued Green, should be extended by virtue of our common humanity:

> A slave is not in the condition of a horse. The slave . . . is made in the image of the Creator: He has mental capacities and an immortal principle in his nature that constitute him equal to his owner, but for the accidental position in which fortune has placed him. . . . The laws . . . cannot extinguish his high born nature nor deprive him of many rights which are inherent in man. The idea that chattel, as the states usually defined slaves, could have a high born nature, complete with rights inherent in man, went down hard with those who thought that even the law should obey the rules of logic.[37]

Many of the decisions, though well-intentioned, did not represent the mainstream thinking on the matter and as a result failed to have the kind of sweeping impact abolitionists hoped for. Notwithstanding the significance of the advocacy provided by judges such as Green and abolitionists such as Douglass, the prevailing thought continued to dominate the body politic. Little more than a decade following Green's hopeful appeal, with little regard to reasons of human rights premised upon judicial or religious rationale, many of the lower court arguments regarding the rights of persons of African heritage, slave or free, would be squarely settled with the 1857 setback of the Dred Scott decision. The decision essentially stripped Negroes of all semblance of rights, privileges, and protestation by systematically denying them the guarantees of constitutional citizenship. According to the verdict, blacks had no rights that whites in the North or South were obliged to respect.[38] In the decades preceding the Civil War, abolitionists, radical Christians, and antebellum liberals persisted in their hopeful exercise of moral suasion despite America's ambiguous and often waning interest in the freedom of slaves. Much of their effort, reminiscent of the optimism inspired by the Renaissance, would be considerably tempered, though not altogether abandoned, following the backlash enactment of the Fugitive Slave Law of 1850, the Dred Scott decision of 1857, and repercussions following the attempted John Brown insurrection of 1859. The hope of being able to abolish slavery through moral reasoning became less of a possibility as phobia-driven congregations continued to demonstrate their complicity with the courts. This trend was strengthened as the 1857 decision became codified through a series of backlash legal measures that were designed to slow and reverse opportunities for black achievement. If the longings for freedom were to be realized, they would not be satisfied by passionate reasoning alone. As McKanan points out, the freedom of the enslaved ultimately became a by-product of war, not moral suasion:

> Ultimately, however, sentimental power was not able to bring about
> a nonviolent revolution or a society free from coercion. The Civil
> War came instead. For many, the war experience gave the lie to
> radical liberal faith. The liberal goal of freedom for the slaves was
> achieved, but through military action rather than through the mutual
> recognition of the *imago Dei*.[39]

Against the hopes of creating a more humane society based on the acknowledgment of the divine origin of African humanity, the Civil War, as a militaristic measure to preserve the Union, *inadvertently* opened the door to their emancipation. Despite the unintended outcome, antislavery proponents interpreted the war through the lens of divine Providence. God was acting on behalf of God's suffering children and bringing deliverance on behalf of those created in his image. For them, their "new day" was ushered in as a gracious commencing of a healed nation and the expeditious transition of the freed into the American mainstream. After all, African American Union soldiers, though reluctantly enlisted, contributed to the Republic's favorable outcome. If for no other reason, they remained optimistic that mutual regard would come as a result of their demonstrable dedication to American nationhood and the exercise of God's sovereign will. Vincent Harding describes the advent of this anticipation when he writes, "Black men and women had been caught up in a radical expectation of fresh beginnings for America and themselves, believing that the Providence which broke the power of old slavery would also usher in a new kingdom."[40] Though the wait had been long and hard, perseverance and Providence had partnered to bring about the jubilant realization of their bright day. Even the more radical factions among the abolitionist movement agreed that fate and faith had commingled to end the long night of slavery. So assured that this vision of human goodwill would now prevail, insofar as the plight of the enslaved was concerned, William Lloyd Garrison hastily dismantled his Anti-Slavery Society, convinced that the war signaled a turn in the nation's domestic arrangement.

Beyond the war and the initial glimmer of hope, however, African Americans in both the North and the South were quickly reminded of the nation's central concern and the degree to which the full expansion of civil rights to the freed was not to be entertained in the wake of Lincoln's assassination. If the Lincoln era carried with it a kind of messianic hope for deliverance and the establishing of God's will "on earth as it is in heaven," his untimely death came as a sobering reminder of the national reality. Vincent Harding captures the prevailing sociopolitical mood during Vice President Andrew Johnson's succession to the presidency following Lincoln's death when he writes, "By summer's end, Johnson's direction was frighteningly clear, and in turn, newspapers were quoting his announcement that 'This is a country for white men, and by God, so long as I am President, it shall be a government for white men.'"[41] With the abrupt removal of Federal troops from the South and the unexpected enforcement of black codes and vagrancy laws, African American mobility was seriously curtailed, as pseudoslavery was all but reinstated with national sanction and reinforced by local groups of organized white militia. In 1868 Frederick Douglass supported the election of Ulysses S. Grant, who as president signed the Enforcement Act and Klan Act. The continued incongruity of black systemic oppression, however, led many black leaders to adopt accommodationist positions that promised *gradual* progress, or emigration as an alternative to the indefinite "Negro struggle" for American freedom. "The churches," as Reimers indicates, "did not often comment when the southern states passed a rash of Jim Crow laws after 1890. When they did comment, it was with approval."[42] As suspected, despite the Fourteenth and Fifteenth Amendments to the Constitution, Jim Crow laws would remain in force until the adoption of the Civil Rights Act of 1964, four years prior to King's assassination.

This, then, is the historical context that defines the freedom struggle that Martin Luther King Jr. entered into in the mid–twentieth century. Though moderately adjusted, it is the lingering social climate that he was birthed into and in time would seek to transform. It is perhaps of interest to note that King was aware of the counterarguments that were historically levied against the advocacy of African American social equality as he appropriated image of God language in his own day as the basis of his appeal for civil rights. His framework, as in the case of his predecessors, was developed with a clear understanding of the Constitution's three-fifths ruling and the theological sanction offered by the church as a means toward further rationalizing the appropriateness of slavery while categorically denying slaves their humanity.[43] On the occasion of his 1961 commencement address at Lincoln University in Pennsylvania, King drew upon the prevailing logic of this earlier era to illustrate that general stream of counterabolitionist thought: "He could say that all men are made in the image of God. This was a major premise. Then came his minor premise: God, as everybody knows, is not a Negro; therefore the Negro is not a man. And that was called logic."[44] In no uncertain terms, King incorporated the language of the activist tradition that preceded him to substantiate his argument for equal rights and facilitate his hope for reconciled race relations. The degree to which King similarly appropriated the abolitionist's image of God language was quite understandable given his proximity to the historical event, his affiliation with the church, and the manner in which the legacies of Jim Crow continued to impact and determine "Colored" life. Although institutional slavery and sharecropping had been all but eradicated, due in part to the Civil War and the inevitable tow of industrialism, vestiges of an earlier sociopolitical climate survived well into the year of King's 1954 installation as pastor of Dexter Avenue Baptist Church through a carefully mapped system of legalized segregation. Reimers comments on the prevalence and longevity of racism as a national and religious phenomenon:

> While the northern denominations were purging themselves
> of connections with slavery, they did not rid themselves of the
> practices of discrimination and segregation. These practices knew
> no geographical boundaries. The development of segregation within
> the religious community was well established by the time of the Civil
> War. It stayed to haunt mid-20th century white Protestantism.[45]

Notwithstanding the significance of the U.S. Constitution and Declaration of Independence as normative political guarantors of civil and social justice, King yet recognized the brightest basis and most crucial cornerstone for his civil rights appeal as residing in the church and its theological concept of God's creative work. While King's anthropological analysis was interdisciplinary and comprehensive in scope, it was understood that he ultimately lodged his appeal for civil rights in an interpretation of *imago Dei* that was grounded in the claims of scripture and his Personalist understanding of God and God's church. King's commitments to the church and its scriptural principles were expressed at a mass meeting in Montgomery in 1956: "We live in a Christian community in which brotherhood and neighborliness *should* prevail among all the people. We can only rely upon these principles to guide those in authority and other people of influence to see that the Christian way is the only way of reaching a satisfactory solution to the problem."[46] In his estimate, the theory of well-founded democratic social contracts had yet to be realized as a practical good, insofar as the fate of African Americans was concerned, and therefore remained ineffective conduits of justice apart from the intervention of a higher moral standard. The extent to which King grappled with the reality of the political documents' failed implementation is noted in his March on Washington address from 1963. His lament is reminiscent of the prophetic longings he studied as a seminary student and is consistent with the persistent pleas of the abolitionist predecessors. In it, he articulated the epitome of American history's haunting reality and the need to further advocate the rights of "God's children":

> Five score years ago, a great American, in whose symbolic shadow
> we stand today, signed the Emancipation Proclamation. This
> momentous decree came as a great beacon light of hope to millions
> of Negro slaves who had been seared in the flames of withering
> injustice. It came as a joyous daybreak to end the long night of their
> captivity. But 100 years later, the Negro is still sadly crippled by the
> manacles of segregation and the chains of discrimination; 100 years
> later, the Negro lives on a lonely island of poverty in the midst of a
> vast ocean of material prosperity; 100 years later, the Negro is still
> languished in the corners of American society and finds himself in
> exile in his own land.[47]

The adverse social climate depicted in King's most notable speech provided him with the raw experiential material from which he fashioned a relevant theology of social reform. His was a theological anthropology that emerged from a struggle to be, in a climate that inferred that he did not belong. The document stated that all were created with "certain unalienable rights," but his reality defied that bestowal of rights and certain citizen privileges. If the dignity, therefore, of American politics and its democratic ideals were to be redeemed, such a transformation would commence as a result of a moral critique from without. If the Republic was in the process of being perfected, as King also imagined, the ideal source from which the democratic concept was derived and directed toward had divine, not human, origins. This kind of theological thinking was evidenced in King's response to the legalized forms of systemic injustice and his adverse encounters with Jim Crow in Montgomery. As in much of the South, the Montgomery legal structure refused to extend all of the privileges of "first-class" citizenship to residents of African ancestry. The democratic ideal at the heart of American society, therefore, was in perennial need of a theological critique and moral corrective that were positioned external to the unjust policies and their illicit practice. Although a democracy "of the people, by the people and for the people" undeniably represented the most suitable form of just government, King often contrasted the "isness" of a less than desirable social policy with the "oughtness" toward which those created in the image of God could and should ideally be moved. The way things were did not reflect the way things could be. As such, the unjust social condition provided the catalyst and the material for his theological formations. King thought about God, himself, and his relationship to others and the world within this narrow context of persistent social denial often based upon race. In so doing, he placed himself in sync with the host of activists, abolitionists, and clergy who preceded him, and who also relied on a theology of God's image.

Although that stream of "struggle consciousness" continued by King found unique application as a result of his unique theological orientation and social context, his sense of the sacredness of life was readily appropriated as a shared construct. As in the case of the abolitionists who preceded him, King derived his sense of human worth and value from his understanding of what it meant to be a member of a human family divinely joined by a common origin and destiny. Apart from this sense of the sacred, the political discourse undergirding America's founding lacked the necessary moral substance to fully address the shortcomings of segregated society, not to mention all the social evils attached to that. Above and beyond any political discourse that would suggest that we were one nation under God, this seemed to be the most defining element in that proposed idea. According to King, if that political discourse was designed to serve the public square and the good of its general populace, a revisiting of what it meant to have been created in the image of God served as the political arena's ethical buttress and moral corrective. For him, any sociology was incomplete without a theology that could provide a metaphysical description of human existence. In keeping with the appeals put forth by his activist predecessors, all human life must be honored and protected because it is sacred, it is created by God, and thereby granted—by God—certain unalienable rights. In this sense, the image of God provided the question of civil rights with an ontological reason for reinforcing the meaning and experience of just political and judicial affairs. A consideration of life as sacred backed into a rich theological assumption about life's beginning. A conversation concerning rights and the political documents that prescribed them necessarily backed into a conversation about that which preceded sociopolitical reality, and ultimately defined how King understood human nature by establishing the theological relationship between moral and social experience. As C. Eric Lincoln writes:

> Civil rights presuppose human rights, of course, and human rights are derived not from human investment or human consensus, but from the very fact of being human. They are intrinsic to human identity. They are inherent and unalienable—perhaps because "man" bears the image of God or perhaps because Homo sapiens is, at this writing, the superlative expression of an unfolding universe.[48]

King affirmed the former as an anthropological fact and the latter as an eschatological hope. That humanity bore the image of God was an immutable anthropological and theological truth. That the universe was unfolding as a "superlative expression" of that reality was a manifestation of the end toward which God was directing history. The Declaration of Independence, therefore, gained currency in the movement's freedom struggle as a result of its interplay with and reliance upon the religious ideals set forth in an image of God framework. If King was duly impressed with the language of the Declaration of Independence, it was essentially because it affirmed the idea of humanity as created beings, thus bridging political process with sublime theological significance. More than rational beings equipped with the capacity of reason, humanity bore the image of God, thus making rationality possible. It was not enough to suggest with the naturalists that human life is distinguishable from animal life as a result of humanity's capacity to reason. Reason itself represented an aspect of what it meant to have been created in the image of God. Hence, reason and all that resulted from the exercise of its gift must back into an acknowledgment of life as a sacred bestowal. The relationship, therefore, between sacred personality and sacred documents was such that the existence of the document was inconceivable apart from the *Personality* by which it was inspired. In this way, the noble documents that eloquently framed the profound principles of a liberal pluralistic democracy were the product not simply of human intellect but of God's inspiring. At the bottom, the image of God permeated the whole of life as an expression of God's creative genius and intended goodness for all humanity. To, therefore, have a political document at hand that underscored this theological fact as a fundamental truth was of extraordinary value to King and the civil rights effort. In so doing, it underscored the idea that the human family was not simply the product of evolved matter; humans were made in the likeness and image of their Maker. The Declaration of Independence and U.S. Constitution in this sense were but expressions of sacred design, established as human safeguards against civil injustice. King explains: "There must be a recognition of the sacredness of human personality. Deeply rooted in our political and religious heritage is the conviction that every man is an heir to a legacy of dignity and worth. Our Hebraic-Christian tradition refers to this inherent dignity of man in the Biblical term the image of God."[49]

For King, as in the experiences of those who preceded him, a sense of the sacred was identified as an ideological imperative. Life, as sacred, could not be viewed as a mere ideological option; its high consideration was not a philosophical nicety that simply served as one of many ways to adorn the idea of what it meant to be human. Rather, an understanding of humanity created in the image of God was set forth as a theological necessity with sweeping and important practical implications. If the call to abolish slavery was an imperative, it was ultimately because of the ways in which it became an affront and an offense to God's created order. Human beings created in the image of God were not created to oppress and be oppressed in that manner. An understanding of humanity as divinely created called for a serious rediscovery and commitment to the idea of human civility in the broadest sense of the word. More than a feeling or even an idea, a sense of civility that is arrived at as a result of one's affirmation of individuals made in the image of God should transform the character of human relations. King insisted that our understanding of the other as created in the image of God should compel those who are resourceful to greater degrees of genuine philanthropy, not simply from a vantage of so-called enlightened self-interest, but because the other though less-advantaged represents an individual of inherent worth and dignity. Both prince and pauper are united by their common entrance into and journey through life. Beyond the assignment of title, rank, or position, both were individuals of worth because of their common essence. Hence, superficially assigned classifications of human superiority and inferiority that perpetuated poverty and oppression were viewed by King as tragic misreadings and misrepresentations of what it meant to have been created in the image of God. King explains:

> But the real reason that we must use our resources to outlaw poverty goes beyond material concerns to the quality of our mind and spirit. Deeply woven into the fiber of our religious tradition is the conviction

that men are made in the image of God and that they are souls of infinite metaphysical value. If we accept this as a profound moral fact, we cannot be content to see men hungry, to see them victimized with ill health, when we have the means to help them. In the final analysis, the rich must not ignore the poor because both rich and poor are tied together. They entered the same mysterious gateway of human birth, into the same adventure of mortal life.[50]

In an attempt, it would seem, to demystify the metaphysical element conveyed by the "image of God" term, King also referred to persons "who entered the same mysterious gateway of human birth" as "children of God." Given the diverse nature of his public venue and audience, King would often refer to individuals as "children of God" in a manner synonymous with the intent and meaning he assigned to his usage of "image of God" language. While *imago Dei* may have represented a term shrouded in theological mystery for some, "children of God" language remained a readily intelligible term for his broader listening and reading audiences, often represented by considerable diversity. For him, "children of God" language extended the notion of inclusivity without imposing the unnecessary risk of misinterpretation or noninterpretation. The human condition, more than the Darwinist claims of evolved matter suggested, was not primarily defined by a "survival of the fittest" theory but by the responsibility to celebrate and affirm the existence of self and others as a result of their common place within the human family. At bottom, we were of one flesh, of one lineage, and destined toward a shared human fate. Hence, "children of God" language was introduced as a way of enhancing and elaborating upon what it meant to have been created in the image of God. If image of God spoke to our common origin, "children of God" language spoke to the issue of our perpetual call to meaningful relations with self, God, and others. Moreover, the language conveyed the nature of God's loving relationship to an individual and the implications of that relationship for self and others. This idea was commonly conveyed in the once familiar language pertaining to the "Fatherhood of God and Brotherhood of man" conception. The language suggested that we are created in the image of God for the purpose of relationship with God, but more specifically, that the station of our existence invites us into relationship with our Creator and every aspect of the moral universe. Consistent with abolitionists from the preceding century, King often referred to humanity's sacred tie.[51] King referred to that universal condition of human interconnectedness in sermonic form:

Now let me say that the next thing we must be concerned about if we are to have peace on earth and goodwill toward men is the nonviolent affirmation of the sacredness of all human life. Every man is somebody because he is a child of God. And so when we say "thou shalt not kill," we're really saying that human life is too sacred to be taken on the battlefields of the world. Man is more than a tiny vagary of whirling electrons or a wisp of smoke from a limitless smoldering. Man is a child of God, made in His image, and therefore must be respected as such.[52]

In sync with the abolitionists who employed an image of God rationale in their struggle against the throes of slavery, King engaged similar language to defend his civil rights message and methodology. His generous anthropological view of all individuals as children of God is developed into another sermon entitled "Antidotes for Fear." "Man," he emphatically assured, "is not a wisp of smoke from a limitless smoldering, but a child of God created a 'little lower than the angels.'"[53] For King, everybody was somebody because everybody was a child of God made in the image of God. To suggest this position as generous given the historical circumstance and the personal context from which King conceived his anthropology, one cannot help but wonder how. How did King get to such an optimistic anthropology given his experience and awareness of the social climate? Having considered the degree to which image of God language became foundational in the development of King's ethical appeal for civil rights and the extent to which it paralleled that of his activist predecessors, the following chapter attempts to trace the influences that contributed to his theological outlook. More than faith formation, what circumstances, insights, and persons helped to facilitate a worldview that affirmed the possibilities for good in the lives of both friend and foe? While King appropriates language from a relevant and readily accessible social context, he does so with an acute awareness of those who significantly shaped his theological and doctrinal identity. In this respect, it is understood that King's theological preference is derived from his critical relationships with others. How the language of image of God was transmitted to King is the focus, therefore, of the following chapter.

2

The Host of Witnesses

As noted in the previous chapter, King represented a continuity of that antebellum liberal tradition in the sense that he viewed himself as promoting egalitarian ideas that were aligned with a historic freedom theme. Freedom appeals in the 1950s did not sound very different than the appeals of freedom made during the 1850s. He also understood that his view of *imago Dei* and humanity's optimistic capacity was appropriated in part from a political ideology that vigorously facilitated the freedom of the colonists while neglecting to address the freedom of the enslaved. One, therefore, cannot have a thorough explication of King's influences apart from hearing him and his host of witnesses against the broader historical social context that preceded him. To understand the various influences at work in the life of Martin Luther King Jr. is to understand his background within the legalized context of the firmly established system of Jim Crow, a mere fifty-two years removed from its initial founding. To understand King is to understand the conditions of his father's birth in Stockbridge, Georgia, thirty-four years from the close of the Civil War. At bottom, to understand how King interpreted human nature and the nature of God is to commence with a basic understanding that he was the *grandson* of former slaves.

To miss or ignore this harsh historical reality is to misinterpret King's theological complexity. While Luther and Jefferson recognized the significance of freedom's universal quality, each of them conceptualized the meaning of freedom in terms that made sense to their respective historical situations. King similarly cannot be understood apart from his context any more than Christianity can be understood apart from the Crucifixion. He did not live, study, and think about God, himself, and his world in a social void. The currents of freedom that flowed through the reformation were eventually filtered through the sands of his own social experience. King inherited a social situation, shaped and informed by a convoluted legacy that historically viewed freedom and slavery as fundamentally compatible projects. It is one thing to entertain an optimistic future as a social elite and another altogether to discover a theological pulse that offers a similar kind of optimism from an altogether different vantage point. Hence, one cannot fully appreciate King's optimistic interpretation of *imago Dei* apart from the influence imposed by this harsh social context and his reaction, both theologically and pragmatically, to the long shadow cast by the crucible of institutionalized slavery and its effects.

King's voice blended with those of his ancestors scarcely two generations removed. With social vestiges of the former era lingering, he joined the host of witnesses that preceded him in announcing their fundamental truth with respect to the human condition and in so doing linked his present with their past. The similarities were self-evident, for King also embraced a theology that defied the status quo by suggesting that all humanity was created in the image of God. Not just all European humanity, but all humanity, bond, free, male, female, of every color, creed, and culture. King's appropriation of their appeal, in the tone and tenor of their voice, cast him as an unmistakable product of his past, duly influenced and informed by the activism of his foreparents and ancestors. His rationale for the civil rights movement was framed by their passionate plea. As such, King's reclamation of image of God theology was, in part, historically inspired and contextually grounded. King essentially became who he was because of who they were. Their struggle for freedom, justice, and the acknowledgment of their full humanity was replicated in the life of young Martin King. To therefore suggest that King was shaped by his troubling social context and influenced by the host of eighteenth- and nineteenth-century abolitionist witnesses is well-founded.

In addition to this profound historical witness, which was discussed in the previous chapter, King was surrounded by a more immediate host of witnesses that served to shape, inform, and influence his sense of what it meant to be human(e). This chapter shall therefore consider the degree to which King was influenced by his church, home, community and academe, and the extent to which each of them contributed to his theological and epistemological outlook. Fortunately, scholarship has provided a fairly good account of King's childhood influences, so that there is no need to repeat the kind of formative overview provided by historians such as Taylor Branch. Rather, this chapter is specifically interested in determining the extent to which his childhood influences shaped his theological anthropology. How did the home environment impact his understanding of what it meant to be a human being given the overt forms of racism that he observed and personally had to contend with? How did the church speak to the issue of social injustice in ways that influenced his thoughts about what it meant to be a human being who "does justly, loves mercy, and walks humbly with God"? What did the nature and character of his community convey in terms of how he understood the dynamic regarding human community? To what degree did the academe inform and influence his belief in human capacity?

In the final analysis, this chapter is primarily interested in analyzing the relationship between King's influences and the impact they had upon the shaping of his ideas about what it meant to have been created in God's image. While thinking from within a specific social milieu that was attached to a significant struggle history, King was largely guided by the faith inspired by his family, mentors, and fellow colleagues. As we shall see in the three following chapters, King consequently developed a theological anthropology consistent with this early orientation. Conversations about slavery and its twentieth-century ramifications for freedom occupied a place within the family circle. The stirrings of social activism reminiscent of some early black churches characterized the freedom longings of Daddy King's Ebenezer Church pulpit. The segregated living and public facilities were constant reminders of an imposed badge of inferiority that clearly divided communities along the race line. In time, the academic communities provided King with the opportunity to critique and develop his own theological response to the social questions at hand. Each of the following venues exerted tremendous influence during King's formative years as he contemplated the implied meaning of his theological anthropology against the backdrop of his personal experiences. The task, therefore, of this chapter is to identify the early influences that facilitated the development of his theological conclusions.

The Home

The "eloquent testimony of two Americas" and the core values associated with black culture located within, and at times set against, American culture were transmitted to succeeding generations by means of oral transmission, cultural mores, traditional values, and the later contribution of various literary forms. In no uncertain terms, the witness of King's home during his formative years set the tone for how he would eventually understand human nature and, hence, humanity's complex relation between God and others in the realm of civil rights. David Garrow is correct in pointing out that "few, if any commentators, have fully appreciated the underlying link that existed between the predispositions King drew from his youth and the ideas that he was drawn to as a young man."[1] These life lessons, sustained by the community and its black church, were conveyed to young Martin by his parents and the indelible ideological imprint created by the King household. By the early twentieth century, King's primary conveyors and catechizers of black culture were undoubtedly his parents. Although the various other influences were major factors in his development, King's home made the greatest impression on his assessment of human beings and their relationship to God and one another. Through their witness, historical, theological, and sociological meaning intersected for the purpose of providing King with a cross-sectional perspective of God and God's dealings in human history. Incidentally, they also intersected to provide him with a snapshot of humanity and humanity's historical dealings with one another.

As a testament to his parents' nurture, the sometimes unfriendly climate of his social surroundings did not overshadow or suppress his inclination toward an optimistic view of the world. Although King would occasionally drift into the waters of resentment, he rarely anchored his thoughts about the world there. The home served to buffer him from this human tendency to view humanity as heartless, self-centered tyrants that were governed solely by an "eye for an eye and a tooth for a tooth" life philosophy. Instead, his good-natured home environment served to orient him to an appreciation of a good-natured universe. King therefore acknowledged his home as the primary source of his anthropological optimism: "It is quite easy for me to think of the universe as basically friendly, mainly because of my uplifting hereditary and environmental circumstances. It is quite easy for me to lean more toward optimism than pessimism about human nature mainly because of my childhood experiences."[2] An appreciation of King's willingness to accept this more optimistic view of human nature as a result of his parental influences and the home his parents attempted to establish is critical to our understanding of his basic theological approach. As we shall see in chapters 3 through 5, King developed an extremely generous theological anthropology given the real circumstances of his social context and the suffering it produced. That he would have such a high estimate of human capacity is less surprising given the consistent affirmation provided by his parents with respect to the significance of the social gospel, the struggle for human dignity, and the assertion of a life that should essentially be governed by an ethic of love and forgiveness. If King embraced a holistic conception of the gospel, that included the desire and need to address sociopolitical concerns, it was largely due to the hopeful witness of his father's pursuit of social justice and his mother's reconciliatory spirit—lessons learned from those who formed his immediate family circle.

King's introduction to social justice and the idea of civic religion occurred via the home. The ministerial model provided by King's father, then pastor of the prominent Ebenezer Baptist Church, uniquely conveyed aspects of this hopeful struggle. Daddy King's ability to combine traditional evangelistic preaching with activist leadership in economic and political affairs is well attested to.[3] In reflecting upon his personal call to the ministry, King would say of his father: "My admiration of him was a great moving factor; he set forth a noble example that I didn't mind following."[4] His father's example, even prior to his introduction to Walter Rauschenbusch's social gospel, provided the initial paradigm through which the concerns of pastoral compassion and political advocacy were engaged as noncontradictory acts of faith. Decades prior to the Montgomery bus boycott, King's activist father refused to commute on a segregated bus system, fought for parity in teacher salaries, and desegregated courthouse elevators in Atlanta's "tension packed atmosphere."[5] To have a model that translated theological principles of love, power, and justice into social efforts designed to confront and overcome injustice seemed to King a "noble example." While others associated with church life may have been of the opinion that it was somehow an act of "meddling" to mix religion with politics, King found in his father a fine theoretical and practical foundation upon which to further develop his social gospel. In the final analysis, Rauschenbusch simply provided a "theological basis for the social concern that had already grown up" in him as a result of the "early experiences" that validated the serving of humanity as an expression of one's service to God.[6]

King's formative years were equally influenced by the shaping of his self-hood and the development of his high regard for human dignity. The anthropological optimism, unmistakably located as a chief characteristic in King's appeal for civil rights, points back to his earliest childhood encounter with race matters. Rejected at age six by a white playmate at the behest of his former friend's father, King recalled the consolation of his mother's attempt to interpret the event by rehearsing the historical reality of slavery, its conclusion with the Civil War, and the subsequent forms of discrimination that Jim Crow assumed in an attempt to create and sustain a legalized system of racial segregation. "Then," as King recalled, "she said the words that almost every Negro hears before he can yet understand the injustice that makes them necessary: 'You are as good as anyone.'"[7] This sense of "belonging" was also dramatically conveyed by the open display of outrage that was often accompanied by his father's unapologetic refusal to comply with the demands of a segregated system. Departing a shoe store following his father's refusal to be served in the "colored only" section, King recalled his father's reluctance to conform to that status of social inferiority with an affirmation of self that said, "I don't care how long I have to live with this system, I will never accept it."[8] It was not, therefore, surprising that an adolescent King would develop a similar assessment of self and the social system that threatened to demean and denigrate it. "I could never adjust," said King, "to separate waiting rooms, separate eating places, separate rest rooms, partly because the separate was always unequal, and partly because the very idea of separation did something to my sense of dignity and self-respect."[9] Initially, with his parents as intermediaries of an accumulated black culture, King received a transmitted sense of "Somebodyness" long before his formal academic introduction to the theological significance of Martin Buber's "I/thou" relationship.

In addition to explicating the meaning of social gospel and the struggle for human dignity, King's parents, as conveyors of the black struggle tradition, communicated the affirmation of a life essentially governed by an ethic of love. Beyond his embrace of a gospel that addressed itself to humanity's social condition as a result of humanity's inherent worth and dignity, King was grounded at an early age in a theological assumption that emphasized the centrality of love in the exercise of all human relations. In addition to nurturing his sense of optimism about the universe, the King household, as such, represented the social microcosm through which King's initial views of his relationship with God and others would be shaped. In an autobiographical essay written at Crozer Theological Seminary, King revealed, "It is quite easy for me to think of a God of love mainly because I grew up in a family where love was central and where loving relationships were ever present."[10] Ultimately, his love ethic would be challenged and severely tested in the oftentimes hostile social environment that existed beyond the cultural refuge offered by home, the black church, and its extended community. As a child growing up in the segregated South, King would have ample opportunities to explore the challenges associated with the idea of "loving your enemy." Intimately aware of the rampant acts of violence that continued to threaten and adversely impact black life, King came "perilously close to resenting all White people."[11] That he did not was due to his parents' unswerving admonishment to model the love ethic experienced within the home beyond the immediacy of his family circle. If need be, love was to be extended despite the conditions he deemed "oppressive and barbarous."[12] "My parents would always tell me," King later recalled, "that I should not hate the White man, but that it was my duty as a Christian to love him."[13] More than a theological nicety, love was a practical social necessity.

This convergence of historical, theological, and sociological awareness that set the influential themes of social activism, human dignity, and love against the contextual background of institutionalized slavery was made evident in an address King, at the age of fifteen, prepared for his high school's oratorical contest on April 13, 1944. Written five months prior to his enrollment at Morehouse, his subsequent seminary studies at Crozer, and the culmination of his graduate work at Boston University, the essay reflects the formative influences, both ideological and experiential, that would eventually become the principle characteristic of his theological construct in the years that followed. His address, entitled "The Negro and the Constitution," displayed an attentiveness to the paradoxical coexistence of slavery and democracy. As such, King provided insight into how the vestiges of this duality continued in his contemporary day, the degree to which he viewed this as a Christian contradiction, and his yet hopeful anticipation that these deep social differences could be resolved and reconciled. Although King would further explicate these basic conceptions during his academic years, it is evident that his optimistic regard for the human capacity to reconcile the racially driven divide *initially* emerged much to the credit of those who shaped and informed his journey through adolescence, those who constituted his home. In his oratorical address, King declared:

> America gave its full pledge of freedom 75 years ago. Slavery has been a strange paradox in a nation founded on the principles that all men are created free and equal. Finally after tumult and war, the nation in 1865 took a new stand—freedom for all people. The new order was backed by amendments to the national Constitution, making it the fundamental law that thenceforth there should be no discrimination anywhere in the "land of the free" on account of race, color, or previous condition of servitude. . . . Black America still wears chains. The finest Negro is at the mercy of the meanest white man. . . . So with their right hand they raise to high places the great who have dark skins, and with their left they slap us down to keep us in "our places." Yes, America you have stripped me of my garments, you have robbed me of my precious endowments. We cannot be truly Christian people so long as we flaunt the central teachings of Jesus: brotherly love and the Golden Rule. . . . Today, 13 million black sons and daughters of our forefathers continue to fight for the translation of the 13th, 14th, and 15th amendments from writing on the printed page to an actuality. . . . My heart throbs anew in the hope that was inspired by the example of Lincoln, imbued with the spirit of Christ, that they will cast down the last barrier to perfect freedom. And I, with my brother of blackest hue possessing at last my rightful heritage and holding my head erect, may stand beside the Saxon—a Negro—and yet a man![14]

The Black Church

Interpreters such as James Cone and David Garrow are *partially* correct in underscoring the significance of the black church and the Bible as that which was most formative in King's theological development.[15] While rightly associating King's liberation emphasis with that generally of the black church, less effort is made to acknowledge the distinguishing characteristics of King's richly textured theology and the extent to which his positions, though aligned with some of the resistive tendencies discovered in earlier periods, also placed him at odds with the twentieth-century black church and its general epistemological view. At some level, there must be a reckoning that King "came unto his own," and his own, particularly in the later years of his life, "received him not." This tendency, therefore, to oversimplify King's identification with the "black church" and the Bible, notwithstanding the considerable support he initially received in Montgomery and his unquestionable reliance upon scripture, tends to overlook the careful ways in which the young scholar nuanced his understanding of the Bible, the subsequent manner in which the National Baptist Convention distanced him, the lamented absence of black clergy support, most notably expressed in his 1963 letter written from the Birmingham jail, and the black church's diversity and historical complexity.[16] Gayraud Wilmore explains, "It must be conceded that the black church in its national institutional form—almost as much as the White church—was more of a sympathetic spectator than a responsible participant in the events that marked the progress of the movement."[17] More than theology, more than the institutionalized presence of the black church, the black church's *tradition of struggle* facilitated and influenced King's capacity to mediate the social contradictions created by slavery while providing a way of *being* in America.

This tradition of struggle, born of the early black church's evolved experience, conveyed the essence of how to survive in a "strange land" marked by its strange conception of freedom. The struggle tradition conveyed the general will of the early black church irrespective of any outward evidence of resistance that may, or may not, have been a distinguishing quality of the institutionalized fellowship. In the end, African Americans in both the North and the South, with their various and sundry ideological approaches, collectively longed to be free in the fullest sense of the term. The enslaved, who were initially evangelized in significant numbers during the 1740s, sensed early that their Creator did not condone the myopic enterprise of human bondage and shunned sociopolitical philosophies and theological constructs that proved incompatible with their freedom aspirations. As noted by Albert Raboteau, "Nor did slaves share the exaggerated optimism of white Americans about human ability."[18] Essentially, the church adopted and created themes, most attuned to its black struggle, and mediated them in a manner that best assured their liberation outlook. Eddie Glaude alludes to this tendency to contextualize theology when he writes, "Even though the use of ideals of democracy within the political articulations of African Americans recasts American ideals, the presence of violence, suffering, and death in the lives of blacks distinguishes, generally speaking, their use of the ideals from America itself."[19]

This distinction was particularly true with respect to the manner in which the early black church divested itself of liberal schemes of human progression that failed to acknowledge the universal character of divine liberation. Instead, it chose to place their hope in the transcendent activity of God's benign power on behalf of all human life. God, not human beings, was located in the center of their hope and joy. If the enslaved were hopeful, if they rejoiced in the prospect of their own impending exodus, it was not due to some inevitable human tendency toward a more benevolent human situation. Their hope was laid squarely upon a complex theological conception of *God* as liberator. Raboteau writes, "Trapped in a system from which there seemed little, if any possibility of deliverance by human actions, they emphasized trusting in the Lord instead of trusting in man."[20] It should be noted that their "trust in the Lord" did not simply follow the spiritualized version presented them by most missionaries, who complained of the slaves mixing of "Christian beliefs with the traditional practices of their African homelands."[21] The idea of trust was not limited to that which was essential for the saving of one's soul; their notion of trust implied much more than freedom from sin. For them, freedom entailed much more than the pious conception of becoming freed from one's former lifestyle. Rather, their conception was holistic and insisted upon the liberation of the individual in his entirety. As Raboteau further explains: "Inevitably the slaves' Christianity contradicted that of their masters. For the slaves knew that no matter how sincerely religious slaveowners might be, their Christianity was compatible with slavery, and the slaves' was not. The division went deep; it extended to the fundamental interpretation of the Bible."[22]

The early black church had an epistemological approach to the Bible that was fundamentally different. In addition to its critique of America's "natural rights" philosophy, the religion of white America was critiqued, appropriated, and translated into an instrument of struggle and liberation. As Vincent Harding suggests, "The scriptures, the theology, the doctrine, the very places of worship were repeatedly transmuted in the alchemy of the black movement."[23] In an attempt to make sense of its pathos and human suffering, the early black church creatively fashioned a suitable theology of liberation. It was a theology of freedom amid the hopelessness of human ruin and social tragedy, a theology best suited to answer the deep-seated questions of who God was and how God operated on behalf of the oppressed in human history. One of the more difficult propositions of these early believers was to discover a way to reconcile their belief in a loving God with the unlovely circumstances of their unbearable human existence. What kind of theology makes sense of the forced bondage of millions of African lives—fathers, mothers, and children? How would they interpret their God's silence in the time of their unmerited suffering? One of the predominant themes in the biblical exposition appropriated by the black church was that of the Old Testament account of Exodus. Though intricately enmeshed in puritan conceptions of American destiny and its notions of divine Providence, the black church embraced the narrative and interpreted it in accordance with their unique social context. As such, its distinctive interpretive approach bespeaks the degree to which the Black church refused to labor under the illusion that "We the people" was somehow inclusive of them and its freedom concerns. Raboteau acknowledges as much when he writes:

> From the earliest days of colonization, white Christians had
> represented their journey across the Atlantic to America as the
> exodus of a New Israel from the bondage of Egypt into the Promised
> Land of milk and honey. For black Christians, the imagery was
> reversed: the Middle Passage had brought them to Egypt land,
> where they suffered bondage under a new Pharaoh. White
> Christians saw themselves as the New Israel; slaves identified
> themselves as the Old. This is, as Vincent Harding remarked, one
> of the abiding and tragic ironies of our history: the nation's claim to
> be the New Israel was contradicted by the Old Israel still enslaved in
> her midst.[24]

In fact, the early black church's identification with the Exodus event was so thorough that it significantly influenced its New Testament conception of Christ, so that even Jesus became interpreted through the lens of Old Testament emancipation motifs. Jesus not only was interested in saving humanity from their sin but also was committed to liberating them from the sinful imposition of slavery and the cause of its unmerited suffering. While identifying with Moses as God's instrument of emancipation, the black church also readily identified with the image of Jesus as "suffering servant." Negro spirituals attesting to the intimacy of this association declared, "Nobody knows the trouble I see," nobody, that is, but Jesus (not even Moses). For the black church, his knowledge was not simply a fact of his omniscience; it was a by-product of Christ's personal encounter with the slings and arrows of outrageous injustice that ultimately granted this unmistakable insight into the depth of human suffering. If Moses reflected the slaves' freedom aspirations, Christ's passion mirrored their tragic experience of humanity's cruelty against humanity. The black church's gospel, therefore, emphasized their Savior's willingness to empathize with their sufferings and, moreover, his sovereign ability to effectuate their social deliverance. As such, Jesus, though viewed through the lens of the Exodus event, was primarily celebrated as that one who was both *willing*, as a result of his intimate identification with every dimension of their suffering, and *able*, as a result of his sovereign power, to bring them forth from bondage. Raboteau provides such an insight as he conveys the observation of a Union army chaplain:

> A white Union Army chaplain working among freedmen in Decatur, Alabama, commented disapprovingly on the slaves' fascination with Exodus: There is no part of the Bible with which they are so familiar as the story of the deliverance of Israel. Moses is their ideal of all that is high and noble and perfect, in man. I think they have been accustomed to regard Christ not so much in the light of a spiritual Deliverer, but as that of a second Moses who would eventually lead them out of their prison-house of bondage.[25]

Essentially, the black church structure, particularly during the brief years of Reconstruction, formed what E. Franklin Frazier often referred to as the "nation within a nation" as it interpreted, informed, and implemented strategies of social uplift. The message and mission were synonymous, and both sought to negotiate and navigate an oppressed people through the nation's double consciousness that the actualization of deliverance and freedom for America's citizens of color might also be realized. In time, the black church, though multifarious in expression and denominational affiliation, became the community's most definitive cultural dynamic as a result of its common social infliction. As Raboteau explains, "In all denominations, the Black churches formed the institutional core for the development of free black communities. Moreover, they gave black Christians the opportunity to articulate publicly their own vision of Christianity, which stood in eloquent testimony to the existence of two Americas."[26]

The black church, as producers and caretakers of a rich theological tradition that "stood in eloquent testimony" of "two Americas," appropriated the antebellum liberal message from this stream of consciousness and revised it to accommodate the particularities of its liberation hopes. Though radically altered to align with their "black sacred cosmos" and the specifics of their egregious historical experience, King understood that an ancient impulse guided the early black church's recasting of the raw material provided by the Declaration of Independence, the Exodus event, and the gospel into a theological expression unique to their freedom struggle. As such, it could be said that King embraced the God of his ancestors' "weary years and silent tears." He identified with those who embraced the liberating God of the early black church; yet, unlike his more skeptical predecessors, he also embraced aspects of the antebellum liberal's hopeful optimism in humanity's capacity to successively move toward *imago Dei*'s moral imperative.

In so doing, King reached back beyond the decades of the church's skepticism regarding human capacity and invested a significant amount of hope in human possibilities. While alluding to promised land language as a metaphor, because of its compatibility with eschatological imagery (of which more shall be said in chapters 6 and 7), King did not choose to center his message in the demise of Pharaoh and the rise of a new nation. He was not interested in extrapolating and expanding this theme of sociopolitical displacement. His was a theological optimism in the capacity for Pharaoh's social conversion and the subsequent creation of an integrated community. Neither did he choose to adopt a Christology with a view toward seeing Jesus as a kind of second Moses. Rather, he acknowledged Jesus as humanity's liberator of the oppressed as well as the oppressor and, in stride with liberal conception, tended to place the greater emphasis on the reconciliatory themes of Christ's love ethic—a theological position that placed him at odds not only with white segregationists but also with the radical growing edge within the black community during the late 1960s. His ability to persist despite increased opposition was in large part due to a belief that social progress was ultimately orchestrated by and for God's good intent and that humanity created in the image of God possessed the ability to comply, a view not readily embraced by the church.

More than a literary commentary, therefore, in the form of a black theology, the black experience in general and the church in particular communicated a manner of existence. King's worldview, to be sure, was the product of literary exposure, but at a far deeper level, it was the product of an experience that was much more visceral. His experience was one of both learned and intuitively appropriated truisms, such that he appropriated a liberal theological conception of humanity that had been filtered and nuanced through the prism of his specific historical lens, primarily interpreted by the black experience in America and conveyed through its customs, values, and culture. Beyond his exposure to literature, the experience of being African and American transmitted a pragmatic yet fluid intuition of the church's struggle tradition, thereby facilitating King's capacity to negotiate the existence of having to be *in* while not essentially *of* the American mainstream. If his cognitive life lessons comprised the body of literary data through which a conscious awareness of the world about him was developed, his subconscious orientation remained intuitively informed and influenced by the mores of the black church.

In the final analysis, King was intuitively influenced by a worldview that was transcribed by life's contradicting and duplicitous realities, and the ever-hopeful thought of reconciling life "as is" with life as it "ought to be." King articulated how these distinct streams of deeper consciousness provided him with the capacity to cope with the harsh and oftentimes humiliating circumstances of a segregated South. In an interview following the success of the Montgomery bus boycott, King was asked how it finally felt to sit at the front of the bus. His response was that his mind was never seated at the back of a bus; it was always seated at the front. In 1956, his body simply caught up with his mind. His response was indicative of the deeper influential currents at work in his life. His mind-set was the product of constitutional rights, but moreover, it was the by-product of lessons observed, lessons that were orally and intuitively transmitted through his home and the institutionalized embodiment of the black struggle that was epitomized by the early black church.

The Community

As King matured and developed intellectually, he encountered a number of voices in the larger community that also served to dramatically influence and inform his theological anthropology. To overlook them would be a significant oversight of this chapter and this work. While many King biographies recognize the formative influences provided by his immediate family circle, the church, and the academic communities he subsequently benefited from during his studies at Morehouse, Crozer, and Boston, few acknowledge the significance of the several black writers, scholars, and theologians who undoubtedly inspired and contributed to his thinking as well. In addition to the direct impact of his home, the black church, and the community of fellow scholars which he engaged in academe, King's theological outlook was also indelibly shaped and directed by the ponderings of his intellectual mentors.

Although King was not afforded the opportunity to sit under their immediate tutelage, with the exception of Benjamin Elijah Mays, he was aware of and influenced by their respective records as authors and activists. This cadre of national scholars, renowned for their writings on race issues in America and abroad, influenced King. A few of the more notable role models who intrigued the mind of King through their writings and work included Samuel Dewitt Proctor, Benjamin Elijah Mays, Mordecai Wyatt Johnson and Howard Thurman, Adam Clayton Powell Jr., and W. E. B. DuBois. Though King makes little mention of them in his student papers, his tremendous appreciation and high regard for this circle of black genius are evidenced as he assumed the senior pastoral leadership of his first and only pulpit. As the newly appointed pastor of the Dexter Avenue Baptist Church, King made it a point to invite the individuals who mentored him from afar to Montgomery as guest speakers. His intent, of course, was to expose and introduce his congregation and community to some of the brightest thinkers of his day.

The first spring lecturer of record was none other than Samuel Dewitt Proctor, then vice president of Virginia Union University in Richmond, Virginia. In a letter of invitation written in October 1954, shortly after his installation as pastor, King discussed his intent for the proposed annual church lecture series:

> I am seeking to make this an annual event at which time I will
> attempt to bring some of our best minds to Dexter Avenue Baptist
> Church, to discuss some of the major doctrines and issues of the
> Christian faith. . . . I am sure that with the right speaker, it can be
> worked into one of the most significant events of the church year. I
> know of no one who is more qualified to initiate this series than you.[27]

On April 27 to 29, 1955 Proctor presented a lecture titled "The Relevance of the New Testament to the Contemporary Situation." As King generated this letter, it is certain that he recalled the several conversations and meetings that were previously enjoyed with this Virginia Union, Crozer, and Yale graduate, the earliest of which occurred at Crozer during the period of King's studies there. Proctor was sufficiently qualified indeed!

More than credentials and experience, however, King shared Proctor's theological framework. His theological outlook, as in the case of King's, began as a homespun conception. From the knee of his grandmother, though she was birthed into slavery, Proctor first received the notion that "we are created in the image of God, with the same human equipment as the Queen of England, the same intellectual potential of all others, evenly distributed on the same normal curve. Differences in outcomes derive from differences in opportunities."[28] It was a theology that buttressed concepts of worthiness and human dignity and that guarded his soul from absorbing any notion of inferiority. This basic theological claim also implied that those who could afford blacks the opportunity to progress in fact would do so. As Proctor observed, "In my limited life's experience I had already seen that not all white people were programmed for bigotry. Even in the South, where racism was a way of life, they were capable of change."[29] God would assure that change would come, he believed, as long as human beings assumed their part. As a fellow Baptist minister, Proctor believed that the doing of "their part" of course included a nonviolent appeal to the mind and conscience of the conveyors of injustice, a role that should necessarily be assumed by the church, which he believed to be "a social service agency as well as a vital religious center."[30]

King also benefited greatly from the theological mentoring and activist model provided by Benjamin Elijah Mays. Mays was born in South Carolina toward the close of the nineteenth century of parents who were formerly enslaved. His mother could neither read nor write, and his father's writing skills were seriously limited. Mays was four at the time of the violent Phoenix riot and twelve during the eruption of the Atlanta riots that were organized to facilitate the lynching, beating, rape, and intimidation of blacks. Although an heir of gross racial discrimination and social disenfranchisement, Benjamin Mays rose to become dean of Howard University's School of Divinity and a distinguished professor and president of the prestigious Morehouse College. King often referred back to Mays as one of those impressively towering models that merged activism, theology, and intellectuality in ways that helped him reconsider his own call to the ministry during his formative years at Morehouse. As in the case of Proctor, Mays received his initial theological orientation at home. Long before the so-called radical awakening of black pride in the sixties, his mother instilled the seeds of theological anthropology that insisted, "You are as good as anybody." For Mays, the black church provided the social space for the stabilizing of black sanity and the development of blacks' sense of Somebodyness, which served a role that was as significant as its spiritual mandate.

The conducting of his joint studies with Joseph W. Nicholson and the Institute of Social and Religious Research on the significance of the black church at the turn of the twentieth century soundly confirmed this fact. Notwithstanding his transcendent hope in God and the role of the church in fostering the freedom of the oppressed, Mays maintained a basic pessimism regarding human nature and its capacity for good. In contrast to Socratic assumptions that attached civility and morality to education, Mays countered with claims that education alone rarely improved an individual's inclination to do "the good." While humans are birthed with the inherent ability to choose good and evil, Mays argued that one's knowledge of the good and right action did not necessarily produce that behavior as an end result. For Mays, hope for human civility did not ultimately rest in the role of education but in the fact that humanity created in the image of God could never be divorced from the internal compulsion to conform to that higher moral law. Although unjust laws of the land were instituted to sanction and protect separatist ideologies that erroneously stratified race, Mays held that the fact of humanity's divine origin would continue to beckon each generation to a place of moral and social decency. To that end he tirelessly labored as a scholar, minister, theologian, and activist.

It is imperative that Mordecai Wyatt Johnson be included among this lit-any of black scholars who provided a deep and lasting impression on King's emerging theology. Johnson's influence found application during a critical period in King's studies at Crozer. Johnson, then president of Howard Uni-versity, engaged the graduate student on the occasion of his scheduled visit as guest lecturer at the Fellowship House in the nearby city of Philadelphia. The year was 1950, four years prior to King's installation as pastor of Dexter Ave-nue Baptist Church, and Johnson's address for that evening was developed in response to observations gleaned from his recent return from India. Following Johnson's "profound and electrifying" message on the relationship between Gandhi's methods of nonviolence and the ongoing pursuit of black freedom in America, King expanded his personal library with the purchase of a half dozen publications dealing with Gandhi's life and methodology. King said of the experience that evening, "As I delved deeper into the philosophy of Gan-dhi my skepticism concerning the power of love gradually diminished, and I came to see for the first time its potency in the area of social reform."[31] Prior to hearing Johnson, King was on the theological verge of embracing Niebuhr's neo-orthodox analysis of love and its ethical application. From that perspec-tive it seemed naive to think that social groups could benefit from a love ethic originally expressed to give meaning to the quality of relationship between two individuals. Johnson's lecture, however, afforded King a period to rethink and seriously evaluate the helpfulness of this methodology prior to implementing it five years later during the Montgomery bus boycott.

Anthropologically, Johnson believed that human destiny was proceeding in a direction that was in sync with the God who created a universe that was both good and orderly. His faith, therefore, maintained that community could be discovered as a historical reality. Of this Johnson said, "If the Negro studies the human will, human motive, human organization, the philosophy of social life, in order to discover how he may become free, with the consent of the other elements of the American population, he is sure to discover something about the human will, something about human motives and human organiza-tion that may be to the advantage of mankind."[32] In many ways, King followed Johnson's critique of Booker T. Washington's industrial educational model in preference of the fruits of higher education. Justice and complete freedom, Johnson thought, could come as a result of developing the intellect. To the extent that the disenfranchised increased in their understanding of anthropol-ogy, history, sociology, economics, biology, and social philosophy, they could then intelligently critique and correct their otherwise complex social dilemma.

Joining the cadre of imminent scholars and theologians who most influ-enced King was Howard Thurman. It was said that King rarely traveled without his copy of Thurman's book *Jesus and the Disinherited*. Howard Thurman, a Morehouse, Colgate-Rochester graduate, was instructed by Benjamin Mays during his studies at Morehouse. Thurman was thought by Mays to be one of the most talented, gifted, and brilliant students to occupy his classroom. Consistent with Mays's expectations, Thurman became one the most renowned theological thinkers of the twentieth century. Perhaps the most prominent aspect of Thurman's theological anthropology that found application in that of King's was his concept of humanity as both interrelated and interdependent. This conception, referred to by Thurman as the "unity of life," concluded that humanity's fundamental drive is toward that of community. Although humanity has been created to choose either chaos or community, the desire is to rediscover that original state of being by approximating and re-creating the conditions that make for community. While Thurman acknowledged the reality of evil, oppression, and social dysfunction, he also believed, as did King, in the potential unfolding of a social order that would become whole and integrated. This principle of unity and order observed in life could overcome, or at least minimize, the effects of human disunity and isolation. Beyond the actual, humanity has within it a creative urge to realize "the more perfect union," to live in what King and others called beloved community. Believing that the destiny of humankind was good, Thurman embraced a theology that emphasized the so-called growing edge of hope, an optimism that dared believe in the national and global ability to reconcile and integrate its social differences.

Adam Clayton Powell provided King with a contemporary model that promoted a theology of social and political activism. Powell, having completed his studies in theology and education at Colgate and Columbia, pursued a life of advocacy in the pulpit and politics. As successor to his father's Abyssinian Baptist Church pulpit located in Harlem, New York, and as congressman of the same district, Powell forged a platform that allowed the two worlds of politics and pulpit to inform one another. For Powell, there was no contradiction in preaching messages of salvation on Sunday and then flying to Washington, D.C., on Monday morning to leverage civil rights for the community he was called to serve and represent. The two roles essentially were synonymous. As in the case of his African ancestors who were presented the gospel during the eighteenth and nineteenth centuries, salvation represented more than the alteration of one's soul. for Powell, salvation provided a holistic theology of hope. Even as Thurman recognized the interrelatedness of human society, Powell recognized the need for a theology that integrated and took into account the whole human need, mind, body and soul. As such, the church could never be reduced to a mere "Sunday-go-to-meeting" institution that separated spiritual reality from sociopolitical reality. His parental influences and the perpetual injustices that challenged his New York congregation and community prompted Powell's unapologetic response. Salvation, then, facilitated internal transformation of one's soul, but it also addressed the systems that restricted the freedom of mind and body. So emphatic was Powell that he insisted that any true Christian, having experienced a spiritual conversion, should also be compelled to convert and transform the social landscapes of injustice into havens of justice and social equality. With regard to community, Powell envisioned the building of what he called the "Great Black Society." Disinterested in images of a heavenly afterlife, Powell insisted on the need to establish a promised land that the descendants of an enslaved population could appropriate in the "here and now" instead of the "sweet bye and bye." Powell embraced the slogan calling for "Black power" and viewed the empowerment of blacks as the avenue by which dignity, equality, and civility would be realized.

Much of King's theological anthropology was also indebted to the influential scholarship and social activism provided by W. E. B. DuBois, a graduate of Fisk and Harvard. Born toward the close of the nineteenth century, DuBois assumed the roles of scholar and activist, theoretician and practitioner of human rights, author and organizer. Although DuBois authored twenty-one publications and more than one hundred essays during the course of his lifetime, his most critical literary contribution was "The Souls of Black Folk." Consistent with the views of Mordecai Johnson, DuBois criticized Booker T. Washington's promotion of industrial education and was personally impassioned with a desire to maximize his own intellectual capacity. His study, research, teaching, and writing in the area of black social life in America noted him as a pioneer of sociological studies. Perhaps Dubois's most troubling question involved his inquiry concerning the relationship between God's justice and black suffering. As opposed to raising religious questions from a strict biblical or theological view, DuBois relied on psychological, sociological, philosophical, and historical perspectives to inform his religious conclusions. This, of course, intrigued King, who also had an appreciation for the ways in which extrabiblical literature served to facilitate the interpretation of scripture. In reflecting upon the troubling facts surrounding the Atlanta Riot of 1906, DuBois entered into a philosophical and theological dialogue with God in the form of a poem entitled "A Litany of Atlanta." He does so in an attempt to reconcile the brutality of that event with the nature, love, and power of God. How and why would an engaged God permit the perpetuation of unmerited and unbridled human suffering? DuBois observed that if God did not intervene, deliverance would scarcely come from any other quarter of human society. Every other facet of life seemed to conspire against the safety and survival of black life. How, therefore, would American residents of African descent successfully become both black and American in a nation that seemingly disallowed the possibility of both?

The Academe

Beyond the years of his childhood, although only fifteen at the time of his entry to Morehouse, King would spend the next eleven years processing, critiquing, revising, and sharpening his theological conception of human nature and its God-given capacity to acknowledge and reflect the image of its Creator. As such, the academic environment provided King with the opportunity to identify and further evaluate the historic *sources* of black cultural optimism witnessed in the dynamic of home, church, and community life. What is the social gospel, and how does it relate to broader questions of freedom and social justice? What constitutes being human(e), and how does this condition speak to the implications of human dignity? What are the requirements and possibilities offered with respect to the exercise of God's love in human relations? Essentially, King carried forward the litany of concerns and hopes expressed in his high school oratorical address for further scholarly analysis and hopeful resolution. In so doing, he deepened his understanding of the relationship between his challenged present and painful past and further developed a theological rationale for an optimistic future. While his initial introduction to the enduring influences "nurtured in the womb of the Black church" occurred within the context of his Atlanta home, church, and community, the academe revealed the degree to which each of these institutions derived their themes from the numerous liberal sources that predated and inspired the American Revolution. King writes:

> Ever since the days of the Renaissance, men have continually
> subpoenaed ideas and theories to appear before the judgment seat
> of scientific method. . . . Liberalism and fundamentalism grew
> out of these changing conditions. Whenever man finds himself
> amid a changing society, his thinking goes one of two directions:
> either he attempts to adjust his thinking to the changing conditions
> or he attempts to hold on to old dogmatic ideas amid the new.
> Fundamentalism chose the latter while liberalism chose the former.[33]

Unknowingly, in stride with this liberal tendency at the age of thirteen, King chose to "adjust his thinking to the changing conditions" early on by attempting to adjust his Sunday school teacher's fundamental exposition of the Resurrection to the growing demands of his inquisitive mind. With the data derived from his childhood experiences, the influences of the academe afforded him the tools and the intellectual environment in which to continue a course of inquiry that seemed to come quite naturally. In accordance with his desire to comprehend human nature, as will be demonstrated in the following chapters, King attempted to synthesize intersecting truisms into a coherent whole so as to make sense of the historical tragedy of slavery and charter a hopeful path toward fuller freedom. As a result, he indiscriminately critiqued both liberal and fundamental concepts, thereby engaging a journey that facilitated the development of his "theological basis" for a *meaningful* social gospel conception, without having to altogether forsake the foundation previously laid by his home, church, and community. Quoting Theodore Gerald Sores's essay "Three Typical Beliefs," King concurred with the intent of the liberal process and its goals. This passage provides the best summary of King's overall perception of theological studies and its purpose:

> The liberal does not discard old beliefs neither does he discard
> the Bible. On the contrary, he seeks the truth that is in them. With
> supreme reverence he joyously cherishes the religious heritage of the
> past. Only he feels free to bring it to all critical examination of the
> modern historical method. Thus he attempts to make the spiritual
> discoveries of the Christian traditions available for modern use.[34]

As a student of the modern historical method, King was introduced to and guided by a specific kind of epistemological influence. Though nurtured by the social pragmatism conveyed by the "black experience in America" in general and the black church in particular, it is within the academe that his thinking about God, humanity, and social issues is most thoroughly examined and systematically developed. Having begun with the data derived from his childhood experience, it is of little surprise that King was attracted to a synthesized anthropology that can be dated back to the fifth century and that he embraced methodologies supremely suited to his quest for social justice and racial reconciliation. In some sense, King simply connected the essence of his childhood traditions with their earlier theological and political sources. While the influential impact of several modern theologians, mentors, and professors has been thoroughly documented by numerous authors, each of these academic influences conveys and constitutes evolved aspects of a single liberal tradition at work that includes and yet precedes the development of the modern historical method. As in the case of the black church and the Bible, "the social and political philosophy of Dr. King," as Samuel DuBois Cook writes, "was built on the solid rock of the existential character of the American liberal, humanistic, idealistic, and democratic tradition, with its capacity for growth, renewal, and extension to the world of higher possibilities and more inclusive realities."[35] Within this larger context of liberal theological and sociopolitical thought, King embraced Personalism and the tenets of a social gospel as the chief methodological means whereby the particulars of his day would be addressed, thus making the "spiritual discoveries of the Christian traditions available for modern use."[36]

As King would discover, the influences of the academe, though obviously broadened beyond the scope of his former church school experience, were not considered altogether dissimilar from those of his childhood inasmuch as they were derived from a common ideological core. In time, King would develop the dialectical skill required to critique and harmonize the compatible themes located within the various traditions in a manner offering the most optimistic theological assessment of God and human nature, notwithstanding the realism of historic tragedy. Though King was initially repulsed by fundamental rigidity and overt emotionalism, his formal theological studies would help him overcome many of the apparent inconsistencies discovered in a literal interpretation of scripture while maintaining an appreciation for the undergirding principles of his faith and its polity. As a Boston University student, King wrote, "At present I still feel the effects of the noble moral and ethical ideals that I grew up under. They have been real and precious to me, and even in moments of theological doubt, I could never turn away from them."[37]

The Overlapping Influences

While King undoubtedly shaped theology, theology conversely shaped him. Beyond the cadre of personal witnesses, past and present, King was also the beneficiary of a collective school of theological thought that was prevalent by the mid–twentieth century. In fact, there is a sense in which this certain school of thought influenced those who in turn would influence King's worldview. Hence, one could say that King was guided by and responded to a stream of evolved philosophic and theological thought that proceeded from the early days of Christendom. As King emerged onto the social scene, certain anthropological assumptions were being debated by biologists, sociologists, psychologists, and theologians on the heels of the Enlightenment and two world wars. King was exposed to the dynamic of a cold war era engaged in a host of conversations about the meanings attached to human existence and human destiny. The home, church, community, and certainly the academe were all privy to the latest trends of thinking and the scholarship being provided by the respective disciplines of thought. Admittedly, the church maintained a course inclined toward doctrinal orthodoxy, but even here the undertow of mainstream thought created some observable ideological overlaps. This broad panoramic view is occasionally minimized as scholars attempt to categorize and itemize the particular influences and sources involved in the development of King's theological construct. David Garrow's three-volume set is perhaps one of the more comprehensive nonbiographical examples of this sort of cataloging of King's thought to date. Compiling a wide range of significant voices and insights with respect to King and his several formative influences, Garrow writes:

> Many commentaries have argued that one or another predominant
> influence was ignored or slighted by other commentators, and,
> unfortunately, much of the literature can be characterized as a
> multi-party tug of war, with different scholars seeking to claim King
> for Walter Rauschenbusch's social gospel, for Boston University's
> Personalism, for Mohandas K. Gandhi's satyagrahic nonviolence, or
> for Reinhold Niebuhr's Christian realism.[38]

To this litany Garrow adds two additional traditions, the Christ narrative and the black church. Colleagues closest to King argue that the most influential figure in King's life was not Reinhold Niebuhr, Paul Tillich, Dietrich Bonhoeffer, or Gandhi, but the "barefoot Galilean named Jesus." In the final analysis, however, each of these descriptions, with the exception of certain elements within the black church, merely represented facets of a greater whole. The black church, family, community, and King's academic preparation, while distinctive in terms of emphasis and view, each formed the warp and woof of a larger ideological fabric dating back many thousands of years. That is to say that their thinking about the world and the humans who occupy it was based, in part, upon the prevailing consensus of thought. To some degree even King's Christology was viewed through the lens of modern thinking. Long before King entered Morehouse College, Crozer Theological Seminary, and Boston University, societies and civilizations had contemplated the meaning of being human. Theologians, philosophers, and naturalists alike formulated their respective propositions regarding the essence of human life on behalf of their institutions and societies. There is a sense, therefore, in which Garrow's contributors must simply represent individual expressions, subpoints of thought, as it were, that follow a larger general heading that can be traced to the fifth century, with influences rooted in even earlier philosophic conceptions of humanity. Dan McKanan discusses the development of liberal theology and its relationship to the idea of *imago Dei*:

> Liberal theology revolved around the doctrine of the *imago Dei*.
> This, of course, was no innovation of the 19th century. It placed the
> reformers in a long, if somewhat discontinuous, tradition.

In Genesis, God creates humanity "in our image, after our likeness" (1:26). In the context of the Hellenistic world, this teaching fit nicely with the Platonic doctrines that each human soul is a seed or spark of divinity, and that likeness is the basis of love. Christian Platonists taught that the essential kinship between God and the soul allowed humans to grow steadily in likeness to God, ultimately achieving full divinization. Various schools of esoteric and mystical Christianity have preserved this view through the centuries.[39]

In this sense, King's theological approach to *imago Dei* and civil rights could be said to have been influenced by each of the aforementioned traditions cited by Garrow and his contributors, with each of the traditions having their influences previously derived from a stream of philosophic and Christian thought dating back to earlier centuries, such as those popularized at the outset of the Renaissance that also emphasized humanity's freedom and capacity to choose. As detailed in chapter 4, this thread of thought, introduced in the first half of the fifth century, emphasized humanity's possibility, the extent to which human fallibility challenged this reality, and the need, therefore, to acknowledge and cooperate with God's good intent for creation.[40] Within this vein of thought, humanity, though certainly less than perfect, had nevertheless been endowed with the capacity to imagine, responsibly participate in, and hence transcend many of life's vicissitudes with the aid and assistance of a loving God. This innovative frame of reference, typified by its optimistic hope for human nature and its destiny, initially sought emancipation from ecclesiastical hierarchy and anthropological pessimism by integrating the most compatible notions of human freedom afforded within the respective classical and biblical traditions. With the birth of this alternate assessment of the human condition and the subsequent evolution of reform theology, a fledgling theology of liberation emerged as society's voice of qualified human independence (free, that is, within certain moral limits). While numerous attempts to minimize this generous account of human nature were under way via the efforts of Patristic writers such as Augustine and the subsequent efforts of reformers, such as Luther and Calvin, versions of Catholicism's comparatively high anthropology continued to present themselves in the writings of the semi-Pelagian, sectarian Protestant, and nuanced secular positions that would develop and prevail during the later era of the Renaissance and beyond.[41] Niebuhr writes: "The Renaissance is interested in freeing human life, and more particularly, the quest for knowledge, from the inordinate social, political and religious restraints and controls. It is, therefore, the direct source of the struggle for freedom in human society, which has characterized the Modern age."[42]

This suggestion that humanity could progressively move toward a more perfect end permeated Renaissance thinking (particularly among the social elites) with a newfound anticipation for the furtherance of that liberating experience. Freed from the antiquated restraints imposed by religio-political norms, societies forged ahead with all the more determination to experience greater levels of intellectual and social expression. For those engaged in the pioneering of their brave new world, a new day had dawned. There was a sense in which the human spirit was catapulted from the so-called Dark Ages, with its parochial worldview, into the brighter days of modernity. Much of this thinking, of course, was precipitated by the rapid rise and expansion of human innovation. The astounding rate of human progress over that abbreviated time span marked by the Renaissance seemed to confirm the best of their humanistic hopes, thus setting the stage for later accounts of social Darwinism. After all, if there was substantial evidence to support the selective survival and adaptation of species observed in the natural order, perhaps, they thought, humanity is involved in a similar evolutionary social process. All these served as indicators that human beings were standing at the threshold of a new golden era. If nothing else, their celebration of social advancement could be attributed to their unprecedented scientific and economic advances. As Niebuhr further explains, the swift realization of social development in the arts and sciences represented an undeniable confirmation of this inevitable human tow:

> Since the dawn of modern history, the advance of science, the phenomenal increase of wealth and comfort which the applied sciences have made possible, the revolutionary changes in government and industry, the discovery and settlement of new continents, the expansion of commerce to the point where it encircles the globe, all these developments were conducive to the support of the spirit of historical optimism.[43]

This "spirit of historical optimism" emerged first in assertions that resulted in the divorce from the less than optimistic assessments of human nature, in theses that breached ties with the restrictive forces of ecclesiastical rule, in declarations that liberated voiceless masses from oppressive monarchies characterized by overtures of religious and social intolerance, and finally, and most notably insofar as King's development was concerned, in the abolitionist efforts that came forward in opposition to the unparalleled ravages of institutionalized slavery. Hence, in thinking about King's formative years and the several influences that nurtured and guided his development, one cannot afford to overlook this long history of freedom seeking and the overlapping manner in which it has manifested itself at various junctures in human history. Be it the spontaneous

outgrowth of the Protestant Reformation or the abolitionists' cry for the manumission of the enslaved, the underlying imperative was the same, *full* freedom.
A continuity of thought overarched and permeated each of the venues of influence considered. Though the Reformation and hopes for emancipation were
attached to the unique circumstances of their respective time, with their distinct
political agendas and social aspirations, the theme remained fairly consistent
from period to period. The essential spirit of liberty, once brought to bear, found
new manifestations and expressions. McKanan underscores the manner in
which egalitarian ideas were appropriated from these various sources:

> Many antebellum liberals saw the movements for peace, abolition
> of slavery, and temperance as a harvest of egalitarian seeds sown by
> Martin Luther's gospel revolt and Thomas Jefferson's Declaration of
> Independence. They did not see themselves as promoting new ideas.
> Indeed, for them the principles of freedom and equality were rooted
> in human nature and had simply been recognized by such prophetic
> figures as Jesus, Luther, and Jefferson.[44]

Many of these undergirding principles would prove to serve King well as
he transitioned from his years of theological preparation with a genuine determination to *practice* theology. In so doing, King remained consistent with his
concept of the liberal process. In his view, "The liberal starts with experience
and constantly returns to experience to test his findings."[45] As a product of the
southern black church, King at first was inclined to return to the familiar venue
of his childhood experience with hopes of introducing the church to his refined
theological basis. His rationale for this kind of return with his recent bride,
Corretta, is succinctly stated in his account of the Montgomery bus boycott
entitled *Stride toward Freedom*: "Since racial discrimination was most intense
in the South, we felt that some of the Negroes who had received a portion
of their training in other sections of the country should return to share their
broader contacts and educational experience in its solution."[46] With this kind
of synthetic imagination at work, it is not at all surprising that they would be
inclined to proceed from the academe and return to the South with an obligatory "desire to do something about the problems that [they] had felt so keenly
as youngsters."[47]

Inspired by the presumption that God was humanity's leading liberation
proponent, King's nuanced appropriation of image of God language implied
that humanity was ontologically deserving of civil treatment by virtue of their
shared divine origin. He further reasoned that all possessed the innate ability (reason) to recognize and to realize this universal truth. Individuals maintained the moral will and ability to choose to do the just thing inasmuch as they

(will and ability) existed within the scope of human volition. Stephen Oates explains, "As a student of Personalism, King was certain that man could cast out evil from the world—by confronting his own sinfulness and opening himself to the Father's incandescent love and goodwill."[48] The dialectical method that most shaped King's theological thinking during the Boston years continued well beyond the academe as he assumed his role as pastor of a local Montgomery congregation, Dexter Avenue Baptist Church, where the national civil rights movement originated. This careful avoidance of extremes is clearly evident in King's 1955 address to the Montgomery community on the occasion of his first of several speeches as the newly elected president of the Montgomery Improvement Association. King states:

> We must avoid extreme optimism—the notion that we have come
> a long way and have nothing to do but await the inevitable. We
> must also avoid extreme pessimism—the notion that we have
> come nowhere and can do nothing to alter our lives. We must say
> realistically that we have come a long way, but still have a long way
> to go. We must realize that change does not roll in on wheels of
> inevitability, but comes through struggle.[49]

His exhortation, aimed toward galvanizing efforts for the Montgomery bus boycott, was indicative of his acquired academic skill and reminiscent of abolitionist voices that, on occasion, also reminded their nineteenth-century audiences of the unavoidable relationship between progress and struggle. For Frederick Douglass, as with King, there could be no real social progress apart from social struggle. As in the case of antislavery activists, King also insisted that the theological fact of having been "created in the image of God" served as the basis of his civil rights appeal. In so doing, the usage of image of God language may be viewed as an appropriation of this earlier activist tradition although, for King, it would become theologically nuanced to speak more clearly to the complexities associated with the negotiation of social conditions nearly a century removed. For King, as for those who preceded him, this theological datum also established the benchmark by which all other laws were to be critiqued and governed. Notwithstanding the significance of legislation, the pursuit of civil rights was morally justifiable on the grounds that they were essentially and inalienably God-granted. Oppressed human beings were, therefore, fully warranted in their persistent appeal for civil rights, and their assurance of a greater degree of civility was indeed achievable. It was this growing realization of the terms by which this egalitarian conception was in fact achievable that distinguished King's conception of human nature and its capacity from that of his predecessors.

For King, the *solution* commenced with his 1954 acceptance of an invitation to serve as pastor of the Dexter Avenue Baptist Church in Montgomery, Alabama. He ambitiously suggested the same in his Annual Recommendation to the Church in 1955: "Since the gospel is a social gospel as well as a personal gospel seeking to save the whole man, a Social and Political Action Committee shall be established for the purpose of keeping the congregation intelligently informed concerning the social, political, and economic situation."[50] King, however, "returns to experience" with an awareness of the church's gradual shift toward delegating the responsibility of direct action over to civic associations such as the National Association for the Advancement of Colored People (NAACP), Congress of Racial Equality (CORE), and the Urban League since the turn of the century, organizations readily embraced because of their identification with the institutional core established by the goals and aspirations of the black church. By the mid–twentieth century, most churches, it seemed, were neither willing nor prepared to embark on a massive faith-based social justice endeavor. The sanguine influences of home and academe, however, coupled to reinforce King's conviction that humanity could indeed experience dramatic change through the exercise of nonviolent direct action, and that the church could, in fact, be its chief advocate. In addition to viewing the image of God as the basis for his civil rights appeal, King also considered this defining characteristic of human nature as the means by which social transformation was made possible as humanity chose to cooperate with God's natural law. Though circumscribed by the fact of human finitude, it was a conception that held forth a most hopeful prospect for authentic reconciliation, the realization of a sustained form of justice, and, hence, the hope for beloved community (of which more shall be said in chapter 4).

Hence, King may be understood as standing within a lengthy tradition of individuals who chose to interpret human nature in more generous and hopeful theological terms, whereas the black church, particularly during the earlier centuries, chose not to. His was a liberal alchemy of black church theodicy and sectarian anthropodicy. As Robert Franklin writes, "King was one of those remarkable thinkers who comfortably combined liberal philosophy, theology, biblical evangelical faith, insights from the human sciences, and his own black cultural tradition."[51] Therefore, as King enters the Dexter pulpit, we cannot simply categorize and prioritize the significance of one influence over another. Each of them contributes to the overall significance in light of their common ideological assumptions that point back to the inherent goodness of God and hence of humanity created in God's good image. It is this larger tradition, one could reason, that eventually informed the black church's social views, abolitionism's hope, Thoreau's civil disobedience, Rauschenbusch's social gospel,

Gandhi's nonviolence, Brightman's Personalism, and even the manner in which King essentially viewed the Christ narrative and its social implications.

Of particular interest is how these overlapping streams of liberal consciousness discover cogency at each new level of King's theological awareness and development, and how these various institutions—home, church, academe, and civil associations—facilitate the transmission of this specific manner in which God and humanity are viewed by him. It is understood that King's worldview was initially shaped by the buffered influences of home, church, and community—the institutions that served to shield him from the ambiguities of a nation still deeply divided over the question of race. As King, however, is matured by his demanding leadership role, the influential contributions of the various institutions tend to overlap and dialogically inform each other as he seeks to adjust his liberal theological assumptions to accommodate the evolving challenges presented by an extremely fluid civil rights agenda. As he transitions from the nurturing of community to the academe, King engaged the task of theological inquiry as a way of developing his personal assessment of the human condition and its possibilities for social transformation. In the brief years that followed, he remained informed and influenced by grassroots leadership and the fluidity of his tense social situation. Hence, his core theological understanding of what it meant to have been created in the image of God overlapped with and remained dialogically informed by the day to day dynamic established by the movement and its participants. The enduring quality of King's cumulative experience guided this theological trajectory throughout his remaining years.

Notwithstanding the reality of evil in the world, King's numerous life experiences and influences informed the manner in which he appropriated *imago Dei* language and the high estimate he assigned to human capacity. He therefore proceeded with an assurance, certainly following the bus boycott success, that injustice is surmountable and social relations may be altered in pursuit of a "more perfect union." Chapter 4 will further explicate the implications of King's *imago Dei* conception by considering the degree to which this inclusive vision of American sociopolitical ideals translated into his conception of beloved community as the logical end to his social justice concern.

A close read of King's anthropology reveals the extent to which he engaged, critiqued, and shaped theology, adjusting and mediating his positions in a manner that offered the clearest vision of humanity's capacity to address and amend their adverse social reality. As King lifts the theological theme of *imago Dei* in the twentieth century, he aligns himself with analogous discourses dating back to the fifth century by affirming, or perhaps reaffirming, as the case may have been, humanity's ability to negotiate and choose to pursue either evil or good ends. Despite the sixteenth-century caps? Reformers' claims of utter depravity and King's acknowledgment of human imperfection as historical reality, he adheres to a belief in the inherent, though fragile, goodness and dignity of human nature, created in the image of and enabled by God. It is this acknowledgment of human possibility that, in the end, formed the basis of his appeal for civil rights and invigorated his dedication to the civil rights agenda, despite the escalation of fierce sociopolitical and white church resistance.

PART II

Theological Meditation

3

King as Critical Thinker

Martin Luther King Jr. was a theologian. King's life journey was governed and guided by his theological orientation. While science and psychology became the normative approach by which some of his colleagues interpreted their world, King's was primarily informed and viewed through a theological lens. King operated out of a sacred worldview or, as C. Eric Lincoln appropriately coined it, a "black sacred cosmos." Life was created with sacred intent and therefore took on sacred meanings. Above and beyond descriptions of humanity as rational, although King certainly espoused as much, humanity represented spiritual being. Human beings and the world they occupied were created by a personal God to live in loving relationship with their Creator, each other, and their environment. More than a response based purely on reason, humanity was challenged to exercise their moral prerogative to serve God and others by virtue of their common sacred origin. Human beings and the world they occupied were expressions of Creative Genius. Far from an evolved primate, humanity was created in the image of God. As King understood, and certainly discovered to a far greater degree, image of God represented a chief theological treatise in that it provided the most profound record of humanity's distinctiveness and their relation to God and others.

The scriptures taught that humankind was created in God's image and after God's likeness, but how should that be interpreted? What meaning should be assigned to that ancient textual reference?

From the earliest days of the church fathers, individuals such as Irenaeus, Tertullian, Origen, and Clement of Alexandria attempted to make sense of what it meant to have been created in the image of God. Was the language of image and likeness intended to call the reader's attention to two different aspects of human existence? For some the image was thought to be reflected in humanity's intellectual and natural abilities, while likeness reflected their moral and supernatural capacity. Or as commonly held, was the choice of image and likeness simply the use of two different words to convey the one wonderful reality, that which distinguished humanity from the rest of creation? While all agreed that the image of God called attention to humanity's spiritual nature, it was considerably more difficult to decide what to think about our physical form. Could bodily traits give expression to God's image? Some affirmed that it could, but others rejected the idea of God in physical terms as heretical. Beyond the era of the church fathers, this doctrine of the church continued to assume a primary place in conversations about human nature, the existence of evil, and the progression of human society. The doctrinal exposition of image of God was appropriated, nuanced, and explained in answer to these anthropological questions and the challenges they presented.

In keeping with the need to conceive of a position that came in answer to the modern quest, King similarly engaged the discussion of what it meant to have been created in the image of God. With the force of historical conviction behind him, King took on the challenge of imagining, and in some respects reimagining the theological concept for his day. Although his role in the trenches as a civil rights activist tended to veil his enthusiasm and commitment to scholarship, King was a critical theological thinker who seriously engaged the thoughts of others. This is to say, the student of theology did not simply read the theologians and select a given position from the various schools of thought presented to him during his years of academic study. Rather, he approached the literary task with a critical eye and mapped out a specific course. He did not gravitate toward fundamental interpretations of the scripture simply because he grew up in a church and in a household that embraced these approaches to biblical interpretation. Neither did he agree with every whim and wind of liberal doctrine engaged as a student of the academe. Instead, King demonstrated a high degree of scholarly care as he critiqued both schools of thought, determined to charter his own theological path. In order to develop a theological outlook that spoke to his contemporary situation, King scrutinized the doctrine and dogma of others. As we seek to contrast and compare King's thoughts on human nature with those of the classic theological and philosophic thinkers, we are, and not surprisingly so, immediately introduced to his progressiveness. In some sense, it could be said that the inquisitiveness that led King to reconcile his Sunday school lessons with the curriculum conveyed during the years of his public education was continued throughout his years as a university student. In an essay on personal religious development written for George W. Davis while a student at Crozer Seminary, King recalled having critiqued the Sunday School lessons taught at his home church as early as age thirteen:

> I guess I accepted Biblical studies uncritically until I was about
> 12 years old. But this uncritical attitude could not last long, for it
> was contrary to the very nature of my being. I had always been the
> questioning and precocious type. At the age of 13, I shocked my
> Sunday School class by denying the bodily resurrection of Jesus.
> From the age 13 on, doubts began to spring forth more unrelentingly.
> At the age of 15, I entered college, and more and more I could see a
> gap between what I had learned in Sunday School and what I was
> learning in college. The conflict continued until I studied a course in
> Bible in which I came to see that behind the legends and myths of
> the Book were many profound truths which one could not escape.[1]

To the surprise of few, it was evident early on that King would enter the intellectual environment intent upon locating new answers to age-old problems, specifically related to his inquiry into human nature and its capacity for good. The old problems of racism, classism, and militarism were in need of new answers and new theological understandings that would lead to new conclusions and new social arrangements. As noted in the previous chapter, King's childhood influences conveyed the idea of a "friendly universe" despite the harsh social realities that seemed to counter that outlook. It was not unusual, therefore, that King would have considerable suspicion about doctrinal positions that rejected a notion of human nature as potentially good, irrespective of how that would place him at odds with the prevailing claims of fundamentalist positions affirming a historical Fall and humanity's resulting depravity. Consistent with the intuitiveness he exhibited as a youngster, King challenged the theological assumptions proposed by fundamental thinkers, many of which were readily accepted by many of his contemporaries. He exercised equal concern in his scholarly critique of the extreme liberal views that understated humanity's fallibility and God's goodness.

Having considered the historical context and many of the prevailing influences, in this chapter I provide illustrations of King's commitment to theological thinking and the degree to which he exercised considerable discretion in arriving at a position that would define his theological anthropology. The manner in which he came to imagine human existence informed his preaching and practice from the pulpit to the public square. It is critical, therefore, that a far greater appreciation for King's theological thinking be established. To date, King's theological contribution has not been taken very seriously and in fact has taken a backseat to his more obvious efforts as a civil rights advocate, as might be expected. In part this may be attributed to the sparse selection of scholarship in this area. Scholars prior to the early 1990s were not afforded the benefit of accessing King's papers as they have now been chronicled by Clayborne Carson and his colleagues. Additionally, while King wrote and spoke extensively about the movement during the years of his public career, he never published a systematic theology. As such, he was rarely viewed in the same light as that of his academic contemporaries. He did not have the kind of academic platform that would give credence to serious theological conclusions as in the case of a Niebuhr or Tillich. This, however, is certainly not to suggest that King was not a theological thinker with something of great significance to contribute to his existing body of theological thought. As a result of his day-to-day commitment to the work of Southern Christian Leadership Conference (SCLC), King was not afforded the luxury of being able to develop and think through his anthropology in a more systematic fashion, as in case of his mentors. He nonetheless came to affirm a significant theological conclusion. His attentiveness to theological detail led him to believe that no one school of thought, liberal or fundamental, maintained a monopoly on truth. Prior to exploring King's critique of liberalism's weaknesses, let us consider the manner in which he critiqued the various orthodox assumptions developed by thinkers during the patristic and Reformation eras.

King's Orthodox Critique

While King would eventually develop a greater appreciation for the fact of human fallibility, he vigorously disputed the fundamental doctrine of "utter depravity." The notion of utter depravity suggested that human beings were altogether ruined by the introduction of sin to the Garden of Eden resulting in the biblical record of "the Fall." Though humans were originally created good, sin thoroughly tainted, distorted, and destroyed all that was good and godly. This tragedy rendered humanity helpless and hopeless apart from the intervention of God's reconciliation as an act of unmerited grace. Apart from this act of grace, humanity could only choose to do that which was sinful and self-serving. King was very clear in voicing his discomfort with fundamental formulations such as these, which left little or no room for constructive human capacity. His departure from the positions provided by some of the more orthodox thinkers of antiquity, as well as the biblical literalism of his youth, is apparent in his critical analysis of that which he considered a less-than-generous assessment of the human condition. In his estimate, those created in the image of God could not have been rendered as impotent and corrupt as reformationists and reactionists to the Renaissance tradition claimed. "The reformation," according to King, "wrongly affirmed that the image of God had been *completely* erased from man which led to the 'lopsided' concept of the total depravity of man."[2] This critical concern with doctrines and theology that seemed lopsided or one-sided guided much of his personal reflection as he examined the classical theological meanings attached to image of God.

Among the earliest conveyors of an orthodox theological anthropology that King would read during his student years was Augustine. Born in the African township of Tagaste, baptized in Milan by Ambrose in 387, and returned to Africa to become the bishop of Hippo (now Annaba, Algeria) in 396, Augustine (354–430 A.D.) became a leading voice in the formation of Christian doctrine. Of Augustine, Reinhold Niebuhr said, "When some of Augustine's earlier lapses into neo-Platonism are discounted, it must be recognized that no Christian theologian has ever arrived at a more convincing statement of the relevance and distance between the human and divine than he. All subsequent statements of the essential character of the image of God in man are indebted to him, particularly if they manage to escape the shallows of a too simple rationalism."[3] Some fourteen centuries prior to the American abolitionists' popularization of *imago Dei* language as an antislavery argument, Augustine and other theologians of the patristic period sought to examine and set forth a doctrinal framework with which to describe, discuss, and defend the teachings of their Christian faith.[4] As Niebuhr noted and as King understood, Augustine's theological anthropology was among the most novel and notable.

For Augustine, analogous to Plotinus and most Neoplatonists of his period, the image of God was located within one's intellect, one's rational capacity, one's mind, a thought that King also affirmed. However, unlike Plotinus, Augustine dismissed teachings espousing that human beings were created out of polluted, previously formed substance with a diabolical allure to nonbeing. Augustine rather affirmed the essential goodness of humanity and the inhabited world by proposing a view of creation that viewed God as having created ex nihilo, that is to say, "out of nothing."[5] This theological premise, though not without its own set of perplexing implications and challenges, provided the normative theological framework for Augustine's understanding of the soul as image of God. In addition to affirming Augustine's theological assessment of human reason, King also agreed with this Augustinian contention that human beings, and the material world they occupied, were created *good*. It was, therefore, neither the material world nor physical bodies but humanity's interiority that was in need of being rescued from the damaging effects of Adam's sin, a view clearly not shared by all of Augustine's contemporaries. The plunge from paradise and the resulting biological and juridical transmission of guilt transferred as the actual consequence of inherited sin were remedied by the soul's capacity for renewal by God's grace.

Although Augustine's anthropological view came short of the sixteenth-century reformers' more thorough denouncement of human goodness, allowing for significant overlap, it was still far too wed to notions of utter depravity for King to embrace in its totality. One of the major difficulties King had with Augustine's theological construct was that he premised the doctrine of utter depravity upon the Fall as a historical event. Unlike Augustine, King did not affirm the idea of a historic Fall that resulted in the biological transmission of depravity from Adam to succeeding generations. Insofar as King was concerned, a framework based upon a historical account of biblical literalism created too many inconsistencies with an array of truths discovered in other disciplines of study. Although he was nurtured in a Christian environment that, for the most part, held to biblical views that were considered historically infallible, King found it increasingly difficult to reconcile many of these ideas with the new forms of biblical interpretation that were based on other historical and scientific facts. As a graduate student he applied this new approach to biblical interpretation to his studies of creation, humanity, the Fall, sin, and redemption, to name a few. King's departure from Augustine on this question of historical event was expressed in his critique of Karl Barth's attempt to revive the doctrine of humanity's depravity following the First World War. In an paper prepared for Davis's class entitled "Christian Theology for Today," King wrote:

> Their basic argument is that man was once made in the image of God, but this image and likeness of God were totally effaced by the fall, leaving not a trace behind. . . . This view of the fall of man held by Dr. Barth and others seems to me quite inadequate. It seems more reasonable to hold that the fall of man is psychological rather than historical. In other words, I would be inclined to accept, along with others, an individual fall rather than a racial fall.[6]

Included among the "others" that King had in mind was the public theologian Reinhold Niebuhr, who was one of several individuals noted in his day for their neo-orthodox approach to biblical interpretation known as Christian Realism. In a paper presented to the Dialectical Society just months prior to leaving Boston to accept his invitation to serve as the senior pastor of Montgomery's

Dexter Avenue Baptist Church, King alluded to his approval of Niebuhr's explication of original sin and the Fall. As King explained:

> The fall is a mythological[7] expression for what is psychologically true
> in each person. The fall, says Niebuhr, is an outward conflict between
> the "is" and the "ought" of life, between the ideal possibilities to
> which freedom encourages man and the drive of egoism, which
> reason sharpens then assuages. . . . By now we see that, for Niebuhr,
> original sin and the fall are not literal events in history; they are
> rather symbolic or mythological categories to explain the universality
> of sin.[8]

His identification with this and similar assessments of human nature significantly distanced King from Augustine and the prevailing fundamental
approaches to biblical interpretation. At bottom, it was this theologically adjusted
interpretation of original sin and the Fall that placed King in a position to dis-
pute Augustine's conclusions regarding human depravity. King writes:

> Concerning the origin of sin the Bible teaches many things. It must
> be stated at the outset that the Bible teaches no doctrine of original
> sin. It is true that Paul comes pretty near the doctrine in Roman 5:12
> in affirming that sin came into the world through Adam, but he
> never states how and why. In a word, the doctrine of original sin as it
> was later formulated by Augustine is not found in the Bible.[9]

If the patristic period, with its systematization of a Christian anthropology, commenced the hope of *some* promise in *imago Dei*'s limited capacity
to acknowledge and actuate that which is good and just, the Reformation
with its pivotal figure, Martin Luther (1483–1546), developed a departure
from these comparably more sanguine Augustinian positions. The doctrinal
thesis that undergirded Augustine's idea of human beings as depraved was
revisited and deepened by Luther. While Luther acknowledged the idea of
the original creation as good along with Augustine, his theological description of the human condition emphasized the human will's bondage to sin.
Central to Luther's critique of Catholicism's practice of indulgences was
his conception of humanity as utterly depraved and dependent upon divine
intervention, thereby rendering humanity wholly incapable of altering their
condition through any human efforts or means. This basic thinking ran the
gamut of Luther's theological framework, thus dramatically influencing his
anthropological analysis of what it meant to have been made in the image
of God. Humanity was utterly wretched and therefore understandably incapable of desiring to do that which is good. As such, Luther's reformed focus

emphasized humanity's radical departure from any and all original descriptions of creation as good.

Whereas Augustine pointed to the creation narrative to substantiate humanity's goodness and likeness to God, Luther argued the complete loss of God's image and pointed to the shift in this original state of being. Luther establishes this premise by contrasting Adam's condition before the Fall with that of his son's and all subsequent births. Following the tragic event, Luther explains, "Moses says that Adam begat Seth after his own image. He himself was made in the image of God. However, he did not retain this image but fell into sin. Therefore Seth was not created in God's likeness, but in that of his (sinful) father."[10] According to Luther, from Seth forward, it was no longer the originally conceived image of a "holy Parent" that best described and depicted the human condition but the assumed fallen image of his "paternal father" Adam. Humanity in its post-Adamic state suffered the loss of God's image in its entirety, thus becoming heir to the unavoidable successive transmission of Adam's sin, guilt, and consequence. This development in Luther's theological anthropology marks a serious parting in the ways that King and Luther understood the human condition and its capacity for redemption and transformation. Whereas King and his activist predecessors appealed to society for the realization of a more just society on the grounds that all were created in the image of God, Luther insisted that the image of God was eradicated by the Fall.

As a result, any and all of Luther's conversations about the image of God were in need of being restricted to that period prior to the catastrophic historical Fall of humanity. Hence, for Luther, all descriptions of humanity as essentially good needed to point back to a period of "innocence" that existed in paradise prior to the Fall. Considerations of humanity as essentially good could not serve as current descriptions or indicators of the human capacity. As such, Luther's Reformationist view of *imago Dei* was emphatic and sweeping in scope. Unlike Augustine, even reason, according to Luther, was altogether darkened, the physical body was altogether corrupt, and one's will, as opposed to having the capacity to exercise memory and move in the direction of that which was good and godly, remained fallen apart from grace. Human reason was unwilling and, moreover, altogether incapable of making choices that were essentially good and reasonable. Although King would point to reason, intellect, and will as reflecting aspects of God's image and likeness, for Luther, all resemblances of God's image became unrecognizably skewed and irreparably damaged. Clearly, Luther's primary concern was to be found in the fact that any affirmation of the asserted goodness of humanity would invariably overstate their capacity for good and understate the need for grace and faith as the sole instruments of human regeneration, thereby deepening the illusion of human self-sufficiency. In the end, Luther was clearly suspect and critical of any and all attempts, including Augustine's, to salvage any of humanity's original qualities as current human possibilities. He remained consistent in his repudiation of views that suggested otherwise. As such Luther writes:

> Most (ancient) teachers follow Augustine, teaching that the divine
> image consisted in the powers of the soul, such as memory, intellect,
> and will. That is to say, the intellect was enlightened by faith, while
> the memory was strengthened by hope and perseverance, and
> the will was adorned by love. . . . To this was added the argument
> concerning man's free will, which (allegedly) has its origin in the
> divine image. . . . But I am afraid that since we have lost the divine
> image by our sin, or fall, we shall never be able to fully understand it
> (what it was). We indeed have a memory, intellect, and will, but (it is)
> altogether leprous and unclean.[11]

This kind of theological anthropology, of course, became extremely problematic for King, whose theological rationale needed to convey the promise and hope for constructive social change in a nation yet divided by race and class. Obviously, a "lopsided" theological construct that rendered human beings incapable of moving beyond the deprecating tendency to objectify and oppress the disadvantaged was quite troubling. For Luther, however, the taint of human depravity was so prevailing, so entrenched, that the hope of a reconciled life, apart from the church, could never be realized in this transient existence. This by implication provided no hope for a reconciled society apart from the experience of grace. Apart from the church and its salvation, society could not know, or even desire to know, the highest good for itself and others.[12] Human transformation of any constructive nature was exclusively determined and discovered by faith through one's encounter with biblical truth and its Christ. Within Luther's framework there could be no theology of the human condition that entertained a minimization of the severity and finality of sin and its consequences. Luther therefore wrote, "So they (the scholastics) say that all persons, though having lost their original righteousness, still retain their natural (spiritual) powers (and are still) as man was when first created. Of this error, which minimizes original sin, we must beware as of poison."[13] In no uncertain terms, sin, as Luther explained, must be viewed as utterly deplorable and thoroughly devastating, a view deemed extreme by Martin Luther King Jr. Thus in reading Martin Luther, as a student at Crozer and Boston University, King carefully critiqued the degree to which the Reformer dismissed all hope for human transformation and as a result proceeded with theological conclusions that represented a less "lopsided" view of human nature. His critique of the Reformed tradition is conveyed in his analysis of the twentieth-century reformer Karl Barth:

> Here the [Barthian] view is posited that man was completely good, made in the image of God. This complete goodness, however, was lost in the fall when man misused his freedom. Not only was his goodness lost but the once present image of God was also totally effaced, leaving him totally helpless in his desire for salvation. Any such generalization about man is preposterous unless it be merely an inaccurate way of stating the fact that man sins on every level of moral and spiritual achievement.[14]

King was equally critical of the theological conclusions developed by the reformer John Calvin (1509–1564). Having never met Luther, but being familiar with his writings, John Calvin developed a considerably nuanced theological view from that of his contemporary, much of which was readily apparent in his description of humanity as created in the image of God. The most appreciable contrast was to be found in how Calvin imagined the image of God as a *retained* aspect of the human being. While absolutely tarnished with self-evident deformities "so that no part is free from the infection," the image of God, not simply the image of a fallen Adam, remains. This delineation from Luther's position was subscribed as a result of Calvin's insistence that the "tainted image" was yet resident and retained as an original, though altered, aspect of the human condition. The image of God survived the fall, though imperfect and deformed. As Calvin explained, "There is no doubt that Adam, when he fell from his dignity, was by this defection alienated from God. Wherefore, although we allow that the Divine image was not utterly annihilated and effaced in him, yet it was so corrupted that whatever remains is but horrible deformity."[15] This is an important move in Calvin's thought inasmuch as it opened the door to a consideration of human possibilities that seemed altogether unlikely in a stricter Lutheran framework. At the very least, Calvin, as did Augustine, affirmed an estimate of unregenerate humanity in terms that were less extreme.

Whereas Luther held to a stricter reformed anthropological view suggesting that "the image of God cannot be known nor understood," Calvin exhibited a theological tendency to consider a perspective that placed significant emphasis upon the hopeful albeit severely wounded human condition. Although fallen and tainted, the image of God was not altogether lost; it survived the Fall and was retained as a precious human possession. In a strangely wonderful mix, humanity was both depraved (by virtue of the Fall) and dignified (by virtue of Divinity's faintest reflection). For Calvin, the flame, having lost its ardent original glow, retained embers and sparks of Divinity amid the smoldering ashes of depravity, reminiscent of that "which was" prior to the Fall in ways that Luther dared not imagine. Calvin writes, "Let us conclude, therefore, that it is evident in all mankind, that reason is a peculiar property of our nature, which distinguishes us from brute animals, as sense constitutes the difference between them and things inanimate."[16] Although Luther denounced the value of reason, and any other aspect of unregenerate human existence for that matter, Calvin's understanding of the image of God allowed for a much more generous affirmation. Although King does not find it necessary to make this kind of distinction between the two reformers because of the ways in which both of their positions remained significantly distanced from his own, Calvin does open the door to theological ideas that King furthers. On this question of what in fact was retained beyond the Fall, Calvin marked his departure from Luther by approaching a theological framework that was much more in sync with Augustine's fourth-century writings.

Calvin's reliance on Augustine, particularly with regard to his understanding of the human will, is made evident in his third chapter of *Institutes* as he explains, "From these passages the reader clearly perceives that I am teaching no novel doctrine, but what was long ago advanced by Augustine, with the consent of pious men, which for nearly a thousand years after was confined to the cloisters of monks."[17] It is not at all surprising, therefore, that Calvin, unlike Luther, would have a far greater appreciation for humanity's natural capacity. For Calvin, a vestige of God's image survived the Fall. Whereas Luther's framework depicted a thoroughly depraved and hence utterly hopeless and useless life devoid of God's image, Calvin affirmed the survival of the image of God and, as a result, affirmed an anthropological view that acknowledged the human capacity as potentially engaged in that which was good and socially beneficial. King, however, had to determine whether or not Calvin's more generous position was actually generous enough for the theological framework out of which he operated. Did Calvin go far enough in his consideration of humanity as beings who were essentially capable of choosing that which is morally good? In the end, the subtle distinctions that existed between Luther and Calvin would not suffice. King's twentieth-century inquiry regarding human nature and its capacity for social change would position him well beyond that of Calvin's as well. While the reformers' fundamental emphasis later assisted King with his need to develop a more balanced theological anthropology, their views regarding human nature remained too unapologetically distanced and too inclined toward utter depravity to be of much help in formulating his general framework. King writes:

> Both [Luther and Calvin] affirm that man was originally righteous,
> but through some strange and striking accident he became

hopelessly sinful. Yet it has become increasingly difficult to imagine any such original state of perfection of man as Luther and Calvin continually presupposed. It is not within the scope of this paper to enter into any argument concerning evolution. However it is perfectly evident that its major contentions would refute such a view. We are compelled, therefore, to reject the idea of a catastrophic fall and regard man's moral condition from another point of view. Man's fall is not due to some falling away from an original righteousness, but to a failure to rise to a higher level of his present existence.[18]

This assignment of utter depravity was deemed problematic by King because it adversely implicated the human condition in its entirety: mind, body, and soul. If human nature was as limited as the Reformers pessimistically claimed (although Augustine and Calvin were certainly more generous than acknowledged in King's critique of them), could it be that a loving God consigned the oppressed of the world to their tragic fate, despite their inability to choose, reason, or will that which was good? This appeared to be a theological assumption presented by the doctrine of utter depravity, and the troubling implications were far too numerous for King's broad outlook to have found acceptable. Insofar as King was concerned, humanity was created good and, notwithstanding the reality of evil, maintained a degree of that goodness via the image of God and the capacity to reason. Unlike Luther, the gift of reason and the possibilities regarding humanity's progress, given their rational capacity, signaled a hopeful note for King. As in the instance of an Augustinian conception, the merging of classical and Christian concepts of human being resulted in the idea that reason, more than any other characteristic, defined what it meant to be created in and reflect the likeness of God.

It was unthinkable that individuals created in the image of God would not exercise their God-given faculty of reason to contemplate the reality of God and their intended relation with others also created in God's image. Unlike the schools of conservative thought that narrowed truth to principles located in the Bible, King believed that the exercise of reason could assist with the task of discovering that which is true by allowing multiple sources to inform a given inquiry. For example, a "thinking mind" could not arrive at a true understanding of what it meant to be human apart from an appreciation of the ways in which theological, historical, and scientific truisms served to rationally inform one another. While the Bible provided the ground and basis for such a conversation, King encouraged a rich discourse with hopes of discovering the meaningful intersections. In thinking about the validity of the "rational in religion," King understood, as stated in his critique of William E. Hocking, "that truth, including religious, is based on the assumption that the mind is valid and that the cosmos is rational."[19] This was crucial to King and the development of his theological anthropology. The mind, though imperfect in its capacity, could never be so depraved as to altogether abandon its thoughts of God, inclinations toward good, or the viability of serving humanity's best interests. As King writes, "Thus, reason, when sincerely and honestly used, is one of the supreme roads that leads man into the presence of God."[20] Reason represented that indispensable aspect of human existence by which truth could be perceived and applied. The capacity to discern the degree to which science and theology were mutually informative was essentially determined by reason's ability to identify and mediate truth wherever it might have been discovered. Any proposal, therefore, that held to a conception of humanity minus the availability of reason was viewed by King as one that should be considered unreliable and wholly inconceivable:

> I cannot follow the Barthian interpretation of reason. This Barthian attempt to undermine the rationale in religion is one of the perils of our time. As Dr. Brightman says, unless religion allows man to retain some degree of self-respect and of intelligence, it is doomed. A God about whom we dare not think is a God a thinking mind cannot worship.[21]

King's discomfort with the orthodox/reformed tradition grew out of his sense that it negated humanity's obligation to act responsibly. To suggest that humanity cannot do good was to create a self-fulfilling prophecy that somehow justified humanity's inhumanity against itself. It was to suggest that society could not rise above the self-defeating cycles of racism, classism, and militarism. At bottom, it was to suggest that the dream for the creation of a pluralistic democracy, characterized by high degrees of mutual regard, was no more than a misnomer. For King, the Protestant reformers' respective doctrines of utter depravity discounted too quickly the kind of human possibilities he imagined and ignored the proposition for human responsibility all too severely. To eradicate reason was to eradicate choice, and to eradicate choice was to eradicate the obligation to do good, which in turn eliminated hope for the kind of dramatic social transformation that King ultimately envisioned. For King, a thinking mind must possess the ability to think about God, self, and others, and that capacity to think must in turn be demonstrated by one's capacity to choose a moral good based on the conviction of one's reasonable thoughts. Whatever else might be said about humans and their imperfections, human beings must above all retain the ability to choose and act accordingly. To eliminate the human elements of reason and choice as agents of potential moral good was to see the image of God as a symbol of what once was without assigning the moral substance to imagine or implement what could be. For King, little could have been more troubling or theologically defeatist. In the final analysis, any conception of human depravity that undermined humanity's freedom to choose that which represented the moral good failed to satisfy King's theological sense of what being made in the image of God entailed. His view regarding human capacity is shared in an assignment prepared for Harold DeWolf's Old Testament course at Boston University:

> Here it is implied that goodness is a foreign thing to human nature. In fact men don't even know how to do good. They are only skilled in doing evil. We may question such a conclusion. Does man ever become so corrupt and wicked that he can have no conception of the good? I think not. It seems to be that no matter how low an individual sinks in sin, there is still a spark of good within him.[22]

King, of course, understood that his critique was not without historical precedence. In many ways he simply assumed the privilege of a modern-day reformer by asserting his theological questions and claims in the tradition of the orthodox and Reformation thinkers who preceded him. Far from a monolith of opinion sanctioned through an ecclesial hierarchy, the fifteenth-century Reformers, though unanimous in their desire to reassert the fundamental premise of humanity's utter depravity and dependence upon grace as the only means of human restoration, varied in their conclusions and implications regarding the image of God. As King examined the ways in which patristic and reform thinkers framed what it meant to be made in the image of God, he too felt obligated to exercise the need to critically reflect upon, clarify, and describe what it meant to be human within the context of this image of God framework.

While the sobering doctrinal positions offered by the reformers were found acceptable to many earlier thinkers, King was too compelled by the weight of current scientific theory and its apparent incompatibility with literal biblical interpretations to consider the viability of theological positions that ignored its newfound truths.[23] In lieu of the kind of Biblicism that supported a historical approach to the Genesis narrative, King allowed for in-depth conversations between various intersecting disciplines of thought. Insofar as he was concerned, psychology and science offered essential and indispensable truths that could assist in leading one to a more thorough theological understanding of human nature. This after all represented the responsible role of the theologian/scholar, namely, to acknowledge his theological limitations and progressively adjust his theological outlook to bring greater light and truth to bear. Biblical positions and theological orientations had to shift when it was discovered that the world was not flat and that the universe was not trileveled. This kind of syncretic approach to biblical interpretation, however, required the kind of critical and probing literary analysis that King brought to the text. As Richard Lischer explains:

> Given the theological climate in which King was trained, his own analytical step back from the text frequently led him to the authority of psychology. By mid–20th century, psychology had become the secular successor of pietism and had established itself as an objective science of human behavior. The laws of psychology were premised upon an idealized essence of humanity that can be known apart from the authority of biblical revelation. This is the credo of liberalism, and insofar as King was a participant in that theological subculture, it is discernible in many of his sermons.[24]

In the final analysis, fundamentalism failed to provide King with the kind of intellectual fluidity that was critical to his theological development. Fundamentalism essentially held to concepts of human failure that disallowed any real reliance on secular sources. Insofar as reformers were concerned, the sciences, even in their finest form, represented conclusions that were attained through skewed and distorted intellectual faculty. Any and all reliable truth was discernible only by the Holy Spirit and confirmed only by the scriptures as a result of "darkened human understanding." References to thinking deemed "enlightened" remained questionable as a result of their extrabiblical origins. Whereas proponents of reformed theology held fast to these ideas of human unreliability, theological liberalism explored and entertained evidences of God's truth across discipline lines. Unlike the rigid dogma followed by fundamental interpreters, liberalism, *as a mode of thought and interpretation*, offered King the intellectual environment in which he could freely explore and examine the complex relationships between theology and the social world in which he lived. His analytical step back from the text was encouraged and expected, and King enthusiastically assumed the exegetical task. But that is not to say that he did so uncritically. As we shall see in the following section, King exercised the same discretion with liberal ideas that he did in the case of those fundamental concepts that did not square with the discoveries of his modern day.

King's Liberal Critique

Having explored King's critique of orthodox and reformed theology, let us now consider the manner in which he critiqued the various liberal theological anthropologies developed by thinkers during the eras of the Enlightenment and Renaissance. King was equally critical of the prevailing optimism with which liberalism espoused their utopian views of society and the inevitable progress of humankind. Whereas the Reformation moved theology to an area that, for King, represented a fundamentalist extreme, the Renaissance created a school of thought that embraced theological conceptions too far in the direction of liberal extremism. In his estimate, both views were equally lopsided and hence misleading when critically assessed. Perhaps the most dramatic demonstration of King's commitment to scholarly criticism is to be discovered in this somewhat less anticipated critique of these evolved Enlightenment concepts of human nature and its potential. His discomfort with the doctrine of utter depravity was considerably more understandable, inasmuch as it placed the insuperable burden of sin and its devastating consequences at the very center of human nature. Doctrines of utter depravity hopelessly restricted humanity's capacity to improve its contradicted social condition. If a degree of human possibility was held forth in humanity's capacity for self-transcendence, this reality was tempered and even severely limited by humanity's fallibility. Although King would later develop a more profound appreciation for human fallibility, even his acknowledgment of evil in the world could not be unconditionally equated with the reformers' idea of utter depravity and complete human impotence. As such, King's unequivocal break with the fatalistic aspects of Reformation theology and his identification with liberalism, which posed the highest prospect of human transformation, seemed theologically and pragmatically compatible.

And, yet, a careful read of King's scholarship indicates that while he may have gravitated toward liberal ideas and their methodologies of interpretation, he expressed a similar displeasure with the ideological weaknesses apparent in Renaissance thought that he did with regard to his critique of Reformation extremes. The liberal "theological subculture" of which Lischer speaks, and to which King applied his critique, had its roots firmly planted within the soils of the Renaissance period, which began in Italy during the late thirteenth century, spreading throughout Europe into the early seventeenth century, of which King was also wary. While the Reformation attempted to free Christian thought from the classical tendency to overstate human capabilities, Renaissance thinkers commenced and continued the development of a humanist construct that sought to liberate their enlightened thinking from the Reformation's understatement of human possibility. The Renaissance, however, while appropriating aspects of Catholic and Protestant individual pietism, dismissed the notion of a grace offered in answer to human depravity and identified yet another source as their locus of personal human perfection. As Niebuhr explained, "The idea of the 'inner light' and the 'hidden seed' always suggests that the divine element in life may be found at the deepest level of consciousness or the highest level of the mind."[25] In lieu of strict reliance on an external transcendent change agent, the Renaissance tradition identified the source for human transformation as existing internally, thereby dismissing the need for supernatural enabling from without. Instead of a Fall, the so-called lag in humanity was attributed to the unrefined and unrepressed passions of human nature, thus precluding the idea of original sin. Hence, not the theological construct of grace but the notion of rationality and reason discovered within the classical construct became the primary vehicle whereby the human condition was restored and perfected. Rationality provided the impetus for human change and progression. As in the case of the church, human life could be elevated; the Renaissance simply offered an alternative means of realizing that transformation.

Similarly, Renaissance thinkers embraced a historical outlook that viewed human fulfillment in philosophical terms that paralleled the eschatological hope held forth by the church and its earliest theologians.[26] Within the framework of the eschatological presuppositions provided by the early church, it was assumed that human history was moving toward the culmination of time, or the *eschaton*, as it was commonly called, which held forth the glorious hope of history's final redemption and the creation of a new "heaven and earth." King often concluded many of his sermons and speeches with biblical references to this kind of redemptive end toward which human history was triumphantly marching. Despite the many difficulties presented as obstacles to that bright day, King conveyed and communicated his vision of the "promised land" for which the committed must and toward which the convinced must continue to press. This hopeful march toward human fulfillment as historical reality was readily adopted by Renaissance thinkers, minus the distinctively Christian conceptions of grace and final judgment. Niebuhr writes, "It neither needs nor expects either an infusion of power for the fulfillment of individual life or the operation of 'providence' in the fulfillment of history. The 'laws' of nature and the 'laws' of reason are its surrogates for providence. They give meaning to the whole of history, for they guarantee its growth."[27] Ultimately, the Renaissance, with its revival of Neoplatonism, demonstrated the immensity of its influence by its capacity to survive and, in some respects, triumph over the accomplishments of the Reformation. These inescapable optimisms so characteristic of the Renaissance were conveyed to King via the rise of sectarian Protestantism and its nuanced beliefs regarding individual human perfection and the more eschatological attempt to understand the perfection of human history. While both views were considered biblically based, Protestant sects also filtered their theological approaches to personal piety and human history through the philosophical lens of Renaissance and Enlightenment thinking.

Pietism, a seventeenth-century movement originating within the ranks of the Lutheran church, with its pragmatic hope of bridging orthodoxy with orthopraxis, that is, a hope in joining the sound interpretation of doctrine with the sound practice of doctrine, scarcely anticipated the impact that Renaissance thinking would prove to have on its undertaking.[28] Unlike proponents of the Reformation who rejected the notion of human perfectionism, followers of the Pietist movement affirmed a biblical interpretation of human perfection and its process. For them human perfection was more than a statement of being; it required the evidence of a morally transformed life. More than simply conveying mere symbols of perfection through the forms of liturgy, creed, and art, Pietists believed that the reception of God's grace should produce an appreciable evidence of human perfection within the lives of its adherents and their respective church communities. In keeping with the apostolic teachings of James and his first-century doctrine, "faith without works" was dead. Interestingly, the Pietists' development of this belief displayed the shortsighted tendencies inherent in that of their own. Often their harsh critique of others was exercised without fully recognizing the theological oversights within their own conception of human optimism. Similar to the anthropological optimisms so overwhelmingly characteristic of the Renaissance, the tendency within their own circle of zealous Pietistic sects was to define the image of God as that element of divine essence that provided the capacity to liberate individuals from the so-called lag created by the Fall. In so doing, followers of Pietism, unlike Augustine or the Reformers, deified the meaning of *imago Dei*, thus moving it beyond orthodox descriptions of image as mere "likeness." Within sectarian Pietism, to possess the image of God was to have a human nature that was indwelt with and empowered by Godself. As such, human beings did not simply possess a distorted reflection of God's likeness as an imprint of God's character; they were like God. Niebuhr explains: "The root of the error of sectarian perfectionism is to be found in a conception logically and historically related to those held by secular perfectionists. The 'hidden seed' and the 'inner light' is an immanent Christ, which corresponds to the immanent logos of the mainstream of Renaissance thought."[29]

Akin to this optimistic view regarding Christian perfectionism, Protestant sectarianism also developed a biblical eschatology that shared the optimism in terms of humanity's capacity to be perfected as a historical social reality by projecting its societal implications into the future. In the spirit of the Renaissance, radical Anabaptist sects envisioned and indeed anticipated that the kingdom of God would confront and defeat the corrupt kingdoms of this world, thus liberating the righteous from the oppressive rule of monarchal tyranny. The eschatological beliefs embraced by seventeenth-century Protestant sectarians were of particular interest to King inasmuch as they provided the foundations upon which he could later develop theological frameworks that looked beyond issues of personal piety by focusing on the sociopolitical overtones of God's earthly kingdom. As a student at Morehouse, King was introduced to Walter Rauschenbusch's social gospel, which was one of several theories influenced by this sectarian school of liberal theological thought. Rauschenbusch's introduction in his work *A Theology for the Social Gospel* is theologically unapologetic and emphatic: "We have a social gospel." He does not, nor does he seemingly allow others to, question the certitude of his religious conviction, one that most certainly would have been viewed by secularists as an "outside the church there is no salvation" conception. For Rauschenbusch, failure on the part of the church to address the sociological dimension of sin had given the "kingdom of evil" an opportunity to exercise social sin against the powerless masses. For him, injustice and social oppression could have been averted had the church announced and given attention to sin as a social fact. In this, Rauschenbusch held that the church, as Kingdom of God, represented "the social factor in salvation bringing social forces to bear on evil." Short of the introduction and intervention of the social gospel, the institutional church existed under an indictment marked by miserable failure and their tragic partnership with society's unrestrained perpetuation of evil.

For individuals such as Rauschenbusch, biblical eschatology spoke to the dynamic of human history in general, and the church's hope in the perfect society (not simply the perfect person) in particular. Overt forms of social corruption challenged the rethinking of his conception of sin and necessitated the development of a socialized theology that called for radical social reform initiatives via the efforts of the church and the agency of its redemptive influence. Sin, as socially transmitted "selfishness," could only be addressed and reformed by the employment of a socialized gospel, of which the church represented society's chief redemptive agent. Inspired by the gospel sentiment that "God's will be done on earth as it is in heaven," the eschatological sects set out to usher in this hopeful age, and at times by any means necessary.[30] For Rauschenbusch, no alternative process, methodology, or institution was available, beyond church, as a viable social corrective. Rauschenbusch gave expression to this conviction when he wrote, "The social gospel is the *only* influence which can renew the idea of the Kingdom of Evil in modern minds, because it alone has an adequate sense of solidarity and a sufficient grasp of the historical and social realities of sin."[31] It was incumbent, therefore, upon the church to act decisively on behalf of fallen society in addressing its *sinful* condition by offering its gospel of grace as the means of securing society's salvation. This would result in a significant recession of greed and an enhanced degree of benevolence, philanthropy, and social goodwill, thereby hastening the transformation of this world's kingdoms into the Kingdom of God and his Christ. The Cromwellian sect, as Niebuhr explained, expressed their hopes not simply for a transformed individual but for a transformed commonwealth:

> The insistence of sectarian Christianity that the kingdom of God is relevant to all historical social problems and that brotherhood is a possibility of history is certainly a part of the Christian gospel. The debate between the Reformation sects and the Reformation itself joins the issue between the Renaissance and the Reformation within the heart of Biblical Christianity. The sects prove how thoroughly Christian the impulse is to fulfill the will of God and to realize the possibilities of man in history.[32]

Although much of the recent scholarship in this area intimately aligns King with the liberal thought commonly associated with the developments of nineteenth-century conceptions that grew out of this Renaissance and Protestant sectarian thinking, a closer read of King, particularly during his senior seminary and graduate years at Boston University, reveals that the theologically savvy student and soon-to-be civil rights leader may not have been as naively attuned to the optimisms of the previous centuries as assumed. By all accounts, he does not, in fact, offer his uncritical consent either to claims of neo-orthodoxy, as we have seen, or to certain presumed liberal hopes, as supposed. King's evolving position, though once affirming of liberalism's unbridled optimism, shifts. King initially believed that Christian liberalism provided answers to new problems of cultural and social stagnation, unlike its theological adversary, fundamentalism, which sought to "preserve the old faith in a changing milieu."[33] As he continued his studies, though, King found his initial attraction to liberal theology "going through a state of transition," as Clayborne Carson explained.[34] Whereas his predominant concern initially led him to resist the extremities with which fundamentalists narrowed the anthropological discourse, his critique of liberalism would interestingly lead him to once again rely, though only in part, upon the sources of his earlier refutation. Neo-orthodoxy provided the much needed corrective to the equally improbable aspects of theological liberalism and the pacifist doctrines that once prevailed. During his student years at Crozer, King explained:

> I realize that the sinfulness of man is often overemphasized by some neo-orthodox theologians, but at least we must admit that the many ills in the world are due to plain sin. The tendency on the part of some liberal theologians to see sin as a mere "lag of nature" which

will be progressively eliminated as man climbs the evolutionary
ladder seems to me quite perilous.[35]

While thoroughly committed to the sciences, King the theologian objected
to liberalism's minimization of evil and the idea of inevitable human progression, apart from divine cooperation. A once-adamant adherent of the belief that
society was on an *inevitable* march toward human perfection and the "upward
(evolutionary) movement of man,"[36] King would now find it necessary to exercise the freedom discovered within the liberal methodology to rethink and
revise his liberal leanings. Although King obviously did not disagree altogether
with the idea of a "lag," nor with the general conception of human progression
as an unfolding historic reality, he did come to oppose the idea that humanity could gradually improve itself of its *own* accord and innate goodness. King
acknowledged his appreciation for a balanced assessment of human nature
when he wrote, "It seems to me that one of the great services of neo-orthodoxy,
notwithstanding the extremes, is its revolt against all forms of humanistic perfectionism. They call us back to a deeper faith in God. Is not this the need of the
hour? Has not modern man placed too much faith in himself and too little faith
in God?"[37] From Augustine to Barth, the redeeming value of their contribution to orthodox theology was to be found in their unapologetic description of
human beings as fragile and fallible. The failure of liberalism, at this point, was
in its neglect, due to the adoption of a "rugged individualism," to fully appreciate the idea of *imago Dei* as a cooperative enterprise between God and humanity. To ignore this glaring element in their description of human existence was
to leap into the abyss of unbridled idealism and unfortunate naïveté. To affirm
humanity's capacity to redeem history apart from its theological source and
ground of being was for King as troubling as denying its capacity to do so at all.
King explains:

> I have studied Barth quite sympathetically; but I am as far as ever
> from being Barthian. What I wish to commend to you is that there is
> a great corrective and great challenge in this theology of crisis. It calls
> us back to the depths of the Christian faith. . . . They do proclaim that
> apart from God our human efforts turn to ashes and our sunrises
> into darkest night. Much of this is good, may we not accept it?[38]

As in the case of the theological corrective he applied to neo-orthodoxy,
King's discomfort with liberalism's alluring appeal also had a pragmatic premise. The biblical rationale offered by reformed thinkers provided the theoretical
grounds upon which his pacifist beliefs warranted challenge, but it was his
personal confrontations with social evil that provided the practical basis for

questioning the idea of evolved human perfectionism. In this regard, King's great awakening to the disappointments of liberalism's empty promises was initially developed from the database of his own personal experiences. Each experience that ran counter to the claims of supposed human benevolence served as a reminder of that which was amiss in human nature. His once naive optimism, initially shaken as a youth, would continue to encounter additional episodes of "human efforts turned to ashes." The sum total of these real-life encounters reinforced his suspicions and caused him to seriously rethink and challenge the practicality of liberal extremism.[39] Oppressed communities could not afford to believe that all was well in the world when all was clearly not well in their world. A glowing conception of human nature minus evil could not be uncritically endorsed; the reality of human tragedy was all too apparent from the perspective of his lived experiences. Although King was raised in a social structure deemed middle class, when it came to grand conceptions of *human inevitability* the old adage of an idea being "too good to be true" rang true. The so-called friendly universe was not without its unfriendly reminders that all was not well with the human condition and that apart from the intervention of a friendly God and good-willed individuals, society would not voluntarily progress.

This growing personal conviction was also confirmed by King's review of history's bloody record and the sobering counterfootnote on humanity's tendency toward evil. The observance of the world's tragic headlines served to further his conviction that an alternate theological verdict was necessary. Liberal ideas that ignored, downplayed, or explained away humanity's downside as inconsequential had to be revisited given the alarming scope of global injustice. The promise of an evolved human goodwill had not in and of itself put an end to slavery; it required the assist of a bloody Civil War. In King's own generation, human goodwill had not in and of itself demonstrated a serious commitment to dismantling Jim Crow in America, nor had it presented a convincing case for abolishing human oppression and exploitation in South Africa or elsewhere in the world. As Stephen Oates explains, "The more King examined history, the more he wondered whether he could be a pacifist."[40] How could one fully affirm pacifism and not be considered complicit with the oppressive forces that give expression to evil in the world? How, thought King, could one seriously entertain the liberal idea of human progression and overlook the need for human activism and the intervention of divine agency? Insofar as King was concerned, the human drama underscored the sentiment of both Frederick Douglass and his foreparents, who were of the mind that struggle is always the required element for constructive social change. While giving his nod to the sentiment of liberal thought, King understood as well as any that human progress is rarely if ever inevitable. His tempered conviction is conveyed in a paper composed for a systematic theology course at Crozer:

> Somehow we must rethink many of our so-called liberal theological concepts. Take the doctrine of man. There is a strong tendency in liberal Protestantism toward sentimentality about man. Man who has come so far in wisdom and decency may be expected to go much further as his methods of attaining and applying knowledge are improved. This conviction was put into a phrase by an outstanding humanist: "the supreme value and self perfectibility of man." Although such ethical religion is humane and its vision a lofty one, it has obvious shortcomings. This particular sort of optimism has been discredited by the brutal logic of events. Instead of assured progress in wisdom and decency man faces the ever present possibility of swift relapse not merely to animalism but to such calculated cruelty as no other animal can practice.[41]

The brutality with which humanity sought to negotiate human existence was, at bottom, a manifestation of the fact that there was something inherently amiss with humanity. A lag and yet more than a lag, this "brutal logic of events" as reflected in human history was explicable only, according to neo-orthodox belief, through an admission of sin and its effects. King readily concurred. In this process of theological critique so characteristic of his quest for truth, no ideology was above or beyond the need for critical revision or rejection. At the detection of its perceived theological deficiencies and with no alternative position at hand, King forsook significant aspects of the liberal conception that previously appeared most promising. The glaring data could not be ignored; the idea and immanent potency of evil had to be addressed. Allen Boesak reiterates this decisive move by aptly describing the elements most crucial to King's theological shift within the content of his liberal conception. Certainly the social gospel, with its concern for social justice, with its emphasis on the here and now, on love and brotherhood, would appeal to King. But, as King himself discovered, it was indeed too optimistic. After reading other theologians, especially Reinhold Niebuhr's *Moral Man and Immoral Society*, King would begin to question this doctrine of humanity. The tragedies of history, he would learn to see, were all too real.[42] Although Augustine, Luther, Calvin, and Barth, to name a few, aided in influencing and shaping King's theological shift, ultimately it was Niebuhr's Christian Realism, as measured against the facts of history, that King found most informative and persuasive. The expressions of evil, in addition to discrediting the inexplicable aspects of liberal optimism, brought renewed credibility to the insights provided by Niebuhr's more moderate description of the human condition. As King adjusted his position, he did so not unaware of Niebuhr's personal drift from his once devout adherence to a pacifist position. "It was," Niebuhr asserted, "an absurd and wicked faith which held that sinful man could perfect himself and his world. In claiming that he could, liberalism was a naïve victim of the 19th century 'cult of inevitable progress,' which blinded it to man's inherent evil."[43]

The inconsistent facts of history simply could not be explained away as atypical compromises of the utopian ideals espoused by Enlightenment thought, nor could they simply be dismissed with a Darwinian explanation of social evolution based on the "survival of the fittest." The theological center out of which King operated moved toward an opinion that could not ignore liberalism's flaw. Humanity's inhumanity against itself was far too glaring. Nature's harsh survival realities could not displace the premise of God's intervening work by some natural process that would inevitably evolve and preserve the noblest of human qualities. Although King's appreciation for the sciences and their place in understanding human nature is clearly evidenced, he remained critical of this Renaissance trend toward understanding human social progress as an assured possibility apart from God and humanity's direct intervention. His objection to this cadre of liberal beliefs was to be found in the fact that its underlying objective, unlike that discovered in most Christian concepts, was primarily to highlight humanity's self-sufficient autonomy. Equally troubling were the arguments for gradualism that seemed to lean on the liberal conception. As we shall discuss further in the following chapters, King developed a growing concern with respect to those who argued that he should reconsider his civil rights position because it did not allow for the gradual progression toward the "kinder, gentler nation" envisioned by adherents of the Enlightenment. Their appeal to King was, "Just give the social arrangement time, and things will eventually work themselves out." This, however, represented a view that failed to take the issues of sin and humanity's fallenness into account. As a result of this basic philosophical flaw, extreme forms of social liberalism failed to provide King with the balanced view of human nature that he so desperately sought.

Summary

This writer's contention is that King mapped out a specific theological course and brought to it the distinctiveness of his theological concern and emphasis, an idea that has been keenly debated particularly within academic circles. While his preaching ability and charismatic leadership style are readily acknowledged and celebrated, all too few are willing to share in a discourse on King's theological adeptness with equal regard and fervor. This is most unfortunate given the extent to which King went to understand the relationship between good theology and its good practice. Insofar as King was concerned, theology could not be entertained for its own sake but rather must be rigorously engaged for the sake of understanding and demonstrating the ways in which we are called upon to love God and neighbor. Abstract theology was in need of being tested and grounded in the real world of complexities and contradictions, and King grounded theology as few did prior to his arrival and since his departure. Regrettably, his contribution to this field of study has scarcely been tapped for at least two reasons. The first has to do with claims of plagiarism, and the second with King's inability to undertake the writing of a formal theological project. As a result of Clayborne Carson's careful attention to the King Papers project, an observation emerged during the early 1990s regarding King's inclination toward inserting the words of other writers into his student essays without providing the appropriate citations. This tendency combined with the absence of King's development of a theological treatise has led to a minimization and discounting of King as a credible theologian.

Considerations of King and his theological thinking were dampened by the announcement of his tendency to "borrow" the language of others without crediting the originality of the idea to the author. While it was permissible and even complimentary for preachers of his day to appropriate the content of other significant preachers, the same practice was obviously not expected to carry over into scholastics, although many did and continue to do so. This is not to excuse or make light of King's practice but simply to contend that King's illicit use notwithstanding, there is yet sufficient grounds to support his contribution to theological formation. Although it is less evident in his writings subsequent to his studies, King did provide a preview to his theological leanings in many of the essays prepared during his student years. The works do not reflect the mature musings of theologians who have dedicated a lifetime of study, research, and reflection to a given subject, but they certainly do capture the inquisitiveness, discipline, and conviction of one who took the task of theological thinking quite seriously. His student essays, though not without occasional fault, reflect the thoughtfulness of a committed mind. Carson said of King's writings, "The significance of King's academic papers lies not in their cogency or originality, therefore, but in their reliability as expressions of his theological preferences." There is an unmistakable direction in the progression of King's anthropology, and as such his essays are indeed reliable indicators of his theological convictions. As Carson further explains, "The Boston essays trace the course of King's theological development, revealing how he constructed a theological identity by carefully selecting insights from various perspectives that were consistent with his own." I would add that King's theological identity was not simply one of redundant repetitions, a kind of embellishing of another's intellectual investment. Instead, as seen earlier in this chapter, King nuanced, reconsidered, and even rejected several well-founded positions to arrive at an anthropology that reflected a thoughtful intersection of contemporary truths. When Professor S. Paul Schilling, a reader of King's doctoral dissertation, was informed of King's failure to properly cite the works of others, he responded by stating, "I stand by the comment in my Second Readers report: 'The comparisons and evaluations are fair-minded, balanced, and cogent. The author shows sound comprehension and critical capacity.'" Notwithstanding Carson's findings, King's theological positioning was of utmost significance to his later involvements with the civil rights movement and to our continued need to understand the important relationship between theology learned and theology lived.

There is little doubt that King enjoyed integrating theological ideas into his sermons and may have, particularly in his earlier years as a student, seen himself as a preacher who appropriated ideas "rather than as an academic producing such scholarship." And yet one can scarcely imagine the kind of work he could have produced given the opportunity to do so. Although King accepted a pastorate, it is almost certain that he would have assumed an academic career at some juncture in his professional journey. It must be remembered that as King prepared to enter Boston University's doctoral program in 1951, fewer than 10 percent of all African American Baptist preachers were seminary trained, and only a few dozen held earned doctorates. His good friend and much-admired mentor Samuel Dewitt Proctor, then president of Virginia Union University, offered King the position of dean of the School of Theology. Many recognized his ability, and still others, including Henry H. Mitchell, encouraged King to systematize his theology and offered to assist in that regard. How do we understand theology, theological formation, and those who might rightly be termed theologians? In the most formal sense, while King's foreparents were not considered theologically inclined, they produced a canon of Negro spirituals from the raw material of their experience that captured the essence of their theological positioning. The spirituals continue to communicate their theology about God, self, others, the world they occupied, and life beyond. Hence, this viewing of King as a thinker demonstrates the extent to which he critically examined theology and formulated a position unique to his experience.

4

King among the Theologians

Where among the classic theological thinkers did King position himself? This chapter details where King stood theologically and identifies the theologians who stood in closest proximity to him. That King exercised care in mapping out his theological preference is clear. As shown in the previous chapter, King was a critical theological thinker. His student essays and later public writings reflect the work of one who demonstrated an appreciation for and understanding of the many ways in which human nature was historically argued. He studied the church fathers, engaged Augustine, reviewed the Reformers, examined the claims of the Renaissance, contemplated the meaning of the modern movement, and finally formed opinions that were based on his personal influences, scholarship, and research. King formulated a theological anthropology and developed his understanding of what it meant to have been a human being created in the image of God. Other theologians were guided by their sense of the theological convictions that spoke to their eras, and King, having committed his academic years to the study of theology as the major of choice, allowed himself to do no less. Individuals such as Carson and Lischer are of course correct in observing the manner in which King employed his newfound concepts homiletically as he prepared his sermons, but more than participating in a mere exercise of "wordsmithing" and "pulpit pontificating," King engaged the study of theology as an area of keen personal interest. In fact, more than a rising theologian, King should be viewed as a theologian in his own right with theological insights worthy of our serious consideration and engagement.

Though my interest here is not to argue what constitutes authentic theological thinking or even who has the "right" to be considered an authentic theologian, perhaps it might be helpful for me to suggest that meaningful theological contributions can be attributed to frameworks as formal as that of Niebuhr's and to those as folksy as the Negro spirituals. Both provide a meaningful lens through which individuals, learned and lay alike, have discovered profound insights with respect to how we might think about and coexist with God, the world God created, and its inhabitants. Although he was not afforded the longevity of years in which he could formalize his theological thoughts in way ways that Niebuhr and others did, King's approach to theology and its application is of great significance. In him we discover the discipline of one who not only thought and wrote theology, but lived and implemented his theological theory in ways that few have accomplished before him, and none have attempted since. Increasingly, scholars are longing to understand how we best live the theology we profess to be true in our modern day. In fact, as this book is being written, a host of academic institutions from the University of Virginia to Harvard are engaged in projects that seek to understand and bridge the theory of theological thinking with the grassroots practice of the local pulpit/parish. In my estimate, King introduced one of the clearest expressions of that model for us more than fifty years ago, and while he is undoubtedly remembered for the oratory and leadership traits attached to that model, the theological rationale that grounded his conviction for both must not be minimized or overlooked.

One should never forget that King was governed and guided by a personal sense of theological conviction. Theological ideas of what it meant to be created in the image of God directed his passionate march as a drum major for justice. It was not simply the principled language of any sociopolitical document that provided the ground for his thinking, but the Bible and the theological understandings that King attached to sacred text. It must be remembered that theology, not sociology, was the normative ideological center out of which King operated, although his faithful reliance on forms of sociology, science, and psychology is well documented. At bottom, King was a theologian with a heart and head attuned to the need to imagine, articulate, and live theological truth. Hence, while it may come as a surprise to some, King, the theologian, developed a theological anthropology. That is, he held to a clearly defined theological position of what constituted our having been created in the image of God. King gravitated toward and developed a specific kind of anthropological outlook. That is to say, King came to his undergraduate, seminary, and graduate studies with a sense of what the human potential looked like. His sense of human nature as a created condition, not simply as an evolved existence, took on distinctive characteristics. King did not merely parrot the theology of his professors; he appropriated and prepared his own position in keeping with the rough conceptions formulated during his youth, and as such framed a theology that could be considered his own. As in the case of most students, King had a circle of professor/mentors who inspired and reinforced certain theological leanings, but the inclination to adopt and move in these ideological directions was preconditioned. The primary concerns of this chapter, therefore, are to define King's theological anthropology and to compare and contrast that position with other similar views found within the broad matrix of theological thought that deals specifically with the nature of human being.

It is one thing to come to some conclusions about what King critiqued and therefore did not embrace, and another altogether to understand what he did finally come to affirm as an approximation of what it meant to have been created in the image of God. If, as we observed in the previous chapter, King's critique of fundamental and liberal extremes as "lopsided" led him to reject positions posited at either end of the theological spectrum, where then was he positioned? If human nature was neither all bad nor all good, how did King understand the complex median in which the two human possibilities merged? As noted in chapter 3, King's critical analysis of excessive theological concepts led him to conclude that any one-sided position conveyed only partial truths in their attempts to describe human nature. In his view, the idea of "utter human depravity" represented a one-sided position. The liberal idea of human progress as an inevitable hope divorced of any divine intervention also represented a one-sided position. In some instances it could be said that these partial truths inevitably amounted to narrow distortions that either limited or exaggerated their respective conceptions of human nature and its capacity. King, however, believed that a truer estimate of humanity made in the image of God existed in a blend of the two concepts. As opposed to embracing an either-or approach to what it meant to be human, King assumed that a more accurate read could be discovered in a synthesis of fundamental and liberal anthropologies. His anthropology was developed as a synthesis of two diametrically opposed positions. His critical analysis of certain fundamental and liberal ideas directed him to embrace a more eclectic approach to thinking through his theology. It was the adoption of this approach, as an interpretive methodology, that greatly enhanced King's ability to mediate the theological extremes found in both schools of interpretation. As we shall consider King's anthropology, we shall discover the degree to which he labored to arrive at a compatible medium between the opposing opinions. That medium, that which King affirmed and believed to be a truer assessment of human being, is what we are interested in clarifying and presenting.

The next task of this chapter is to locate King's theological anthropology within the wide range of positions that parallel the way he came to think about humanity created in the image of God. This exercise should not be read as an attempt to lend credibility to King's anthropology; King's work is quite capable of standing on the merit of its own conclusions and does not require such reinforcement. King is no more in need of theological "coat-tailing" than is Barth or Tillich. Rather, this attempt to place King in conversation with kindred classic voices is to simply illustrate the degree to which his conception is consistent, and perhaps even compatible, with other historical theological voices of the past. The purpose of this chapter, therefore, is to simply provide us with an opportunity to view King within the spectrum of other theological beliefs that similarly addressed human nature and its concerns. We have seen who King would not align himself with and why; this chapter identifies other positions he would have found appealing and also helps us to understand why. Positions that announced the human condition as utterly depraved and therefore utterly incapable of reconciliation were refused, as were positions that applauded human achievement apart from an acknowledgment of God. This work, however, is not simply interested in presenting King's negation of theological ideas but also in stating his affirmation of certain kinds of theological anthropologies. Therefore, in addition to clarifying King's position, the other intent of this chapter is to hear King thinking, writing, and practicing theology in the company of his classical theological colleagues. As such, it recognizes that King stood in the company of others and in some ways envisioned new theological terrain as a result of the elevated platforms of scholarship and insight provided by his contemporaries.

As we first begin to consider the specific parameters and boundaries of his theological anthropology, it will be helpful to once again remember King's unavoidable need to reflect on what it meant to be created in the image of God from within a specific social context circumscribed by the urgent concerns of civil rights. Although King enjoyed the intellectual and social side of university life along with his peers, the real social concerns back home were never far removed from his thinking. While appreciative of the opportunity to study and forge new friendships, King never forgot what was at stake, nor could he forget the sense of assumed obligation laid upon the fortunate to "give back" to the community. As one, therefore, who was aware of and concerned by the social dilemmas of his day, King remained acutely interested in understanding "the complexity of human existence" and the human propensity toward realizing that which was morally compelling. Central to King's theological musings was the recurring question of humanity's ability to adjust and in some respects "maladjust" to humanity's inhumanity. As King examined the doctrinal development of image of God thought, he did so with this specific kind of inquiry in mind. Are all human beings still sufficiently influenced by the image of God so as to overcome the pressures of an unjust status quo and move toward greater degrees of social parity? More particularly, could America move beyond the remaining vestiges of racial oppression and the practice of systemic racial segregation by taking decisive steps toward the more sublime realization of "life, liberty and the pursuit of happiness" for *all* of God's children? This basic preoccupation regarding the status of human nature and its capacity for good, though not pronounced, was certainly present in King's mind as he mediated and merged various literature forms from the Western canon.

As a result of his careful theological critique, King concluded that an otherwise ambivalent society could in fact dismiss historically unjust laws in favor of a new social arrangement deemed more conducive to the egalitarian principles preserved in the nation's sociopolitical documents. Although King shunned liberal positions that overstated humanity's ability to master the future, oblivious to evil as an obstacle and God as humanity's chief aide, he was of the mind that human beings possessed sufficient control over their decisions to be held morally accountable for them. Whereas the Reformers essentially understated human freedom and narrowed the scope of human possibilities, King championed a theological position that upheld humanity's ability to participate in the determining of their future. Although sin and evil were acknowledged as distinct realities, King concluded that the human will was not held captive by these forces, as argued by Luther. His was a theological anthropology affirming that humanity retained sufficient moral resolve to choose to do the right thing in the interest of those who represented the "least amongst them." In so doing, King arrived at a position in which the idea of responsible human existence and even the possibility for meaningful coexistence were enthusiastically affirmed. For King, the achievement of civil rights on the scale that he had imagined could only be realized as a result of humanity's capability and willingness to discern and choose the good. In the final analysis, a theologically sound anthropology could not point to conclusions of humanity as utterly depraved or as utterly good; a truer estimate for King could be discovered only by joining the truths discovered within both theological concepts. King outlines this basic conclusion for a course in Christian theology taught by George Davis:

> Man has within himself the power of choosing his supreme end. Animals follow their nature; man has the power of acting upon his own nature almost as if from without, of guiding it within certain limits, of modifying it by the choice and prosecution of life's ends.

Man entertains ideals, and ideals become his inspiration. Man
can be true or false to his nature. He can be a hero or a fool. Both
possibilities, the noble and the base alike, indicate man's greatness.[1]

This view, purporting humanity's ability to choose to cooperate with God's
design for the created order, remained consistent with King's overall assessment of human nature and its capacity. King believed that human beings possessed the power to guide their nature within the certain limits imposed by
sin. Human beings could choose to be true or false to their nature, which,
for King, pointed to the genius with which humanity was created, a genius
that distinguished it from basic animal life. It is here that King decidedly parts
company with Patristic, Reformation, and later neo-orthodox thinkers who
refused to acquiesce to any of the more generous conceptions of their day. To
the extent that King understood moral transformation as a mutual enterprise
between God and humanity, he clearly diverged, at least on this point, with
many of the orthodox thinkers who preceded him. In their estimate, humanity
forfeited the ability to choose that which was good as a result of the grave choice
made to disobey God in the Garden of Eden. The only choices that remained
were those that decided between the various degrees of evil, since humanity
did not even possess the notion or desire to choose that which was morally
good. Whereas King ascribed to a position that included "both possibilities,"
fundamental conceptions insisted that humanity remained false to its nature,
and fools in its thinking and action, whereas liberal ideals held to the human
condition as altogether true, heroic, and noble. Both extreme positions were
considered less than helpful and even theologically irresponsible insofar as
King was concerned.

In sharp contrast to fundamental conceptions, King believed that human
beings could not be held fully accountable for their actions and/or behavior
without the freedom and ability to choose. To suggest that individuals could
not entertain that which was good and to imply that they were inherently bent
toward evil alone was to handicap human possibility and scapegoat human failure. For King, neither could have been farther from reality. Human possibility
was not handicapped. Human possibility may have been challenged by the fact
that humanity held the reins that governed the choices made, and by the fact that
the choices made could run counter to their best interests. But humanity could
never be considered so handicapped as to ultimately stifle the hopes for human
development. The right to choose the good was always considered a reserved
right, a plausible alternative to wrong. Wrong and evil could never be the only
human options. Human beings created in the image of God reflected the wonder of their Creator and distinguished themselves from the rest of the animal

kingdom by the power they were able to exercise via the making of a conscientious choice. As opposed to being driven by the passion of fallen nature, humanity could assume the path paved by the better angels of their nature. To affirm this level of human accountability was to say that human beings could no longer blame their base nature or any other force external to them for their actions and behavior. In his oft-quoted poem by James Russell Lowell, King reminded his audiences that while "truth may appear to be on the scaffold while wrong is on the throne, yet it is the truth that shall sway the future." Human beings could chart a course that represented the betterment of human societies. Moving from an either-or approach to anthropology, King insisted that a description of humanity is best characterized by a both-and alternative to describing what is at work in the human experience.

Having a sense now of where King grounded his personal anthropological convictions, the question yet remaining for this chapter is that of where he stood in relation to other like-minded theologians. The image of God doctrine, as we have seen, spans a significant history. Theologian and philosopher alike have toiled over its meaning and in some cases have produced volumes of literature for the sake of posterity. Many represent the classical voice on human nature without which we would miss how we arrived at a specific place in our thinking in time. Whether in the final analysis we agree with them or not, their historical influence is felt, duly noted, and must therefore be dealt with. As such they help to define the mainstream of thought and in some ways even supply the tributaries that seek to establish their unique course of flow. In this respect thought(s), theological and otherwise, must be viewed in relation to previous and subsequent thinking about a subject. King's significant imagination regarding the human condition and its possibility, therefore, must be seen in connection with those other significant theologians who preceded and followed him. It is good to know King's theological anthropology, to understand how he understood human existence, it is good to know why he came to the conclusions that he did, it is good to see the implications he attached to such a view, and it is equally beneficial to know his position in relation to others so as to see his within the context of that historical panorama. If one listened to King carefully, one could detect the several social currents that flowed through his thinking. Certainly persons such as Frederick Douglass, Henry David Thoreau, and Mohandas Gandhi come to mind. To discover a similar theological framework, however, one could travel well beyond the nineteenth century. Theological anthropologies similar to that of King's existed as early as the fifth century A.D. Interestingly, from Augustine forward, King's mid-twentieth-century assessment of human nature would come closest to that of one he rarely, if ever, made mention of, John Cassian. The similarities are indeed striking.

Considered the chief pioneer of semi-Pelagianism, Abbot John Cassian (360–435 A.D.) of the monastery of Saint Victor at Marseilles, forced Augustine to deepen his Pelagian critique. While disagreeing with Pelagius's belief in the absolute freedom of the will, Cassian (a pupil of Chrysostom) embraced a belief system that allowed for the limited exercise of one's free will by merging elements of Augustine's thought with those of Pelagius. The distinctions between these two systems of thought prior to Cassian's synergy were significant. Whereas Augustine espoused a view substantiating the inability of the human will to embrace or desire good, Pelagius taught that the human will in its post-Fall condition was free, possessing the same capacity for good as evidenced in that of Adam's nature. Apart from this uninhibited freedom to exercise personal judgment and behavior, how could one be held accountable? How could one assume personal responsibility for choices bent toward evil when, in fact, the individual had been stripped of the volition and/or ability to do that which is good? As Niebuhr explained, "The essential characteristic of Pelagianism is its insistence that actual sins cannot be regarded as sinful or as involving guilt if they do not proceed from a will which is essentially free."[2] One could be guilty only if there were no option to choose that which would free one from the penalty and consequences of sin. Augustine viewed human nature as fallen and severely limited and thus unable to choose, while Pelagius attributed humanity with the ability to exercise the human potential which approached that of Adam. Cassian, however, found it difficult to embrace either school independent of the other. For him, as in the case of King, who would emerge fifteen centuries later to synthesize fundamental and liberal systems, the two positions informed one another. As stand-alone belief systems, those of both Pelagius and Augustine seemed extreme and one-sided. Informed by each other, they seemingly overcame many of the weaknesses evident in both.

Critical of both Augustine and Pelagius, Cassian synthesized the two opposing positions to arrive at a single conception that incorporated the overlapping elements of each. As such, Cassian, who disagreed with Augustine and Pelagius, due to their respective "one-sided" generalizations concerning human nature, formulated a view that supported humanity's freedom to cooperate with God in the process of social transformation. King would obviously follow a similar path as he sought to reconcile reformed and liberal ideas centuries later. Whereas Augustine obscured human will and Pelagius essentially declared divine assistance as obsolete, Cassian's mediated position affirmed humanity's capacity to initiate the move toward God and "the good" by choosing to do so. For Cassian, human will was neither absolutely obscured as to render humanity wholly dependent upon divine intervention, nor absolutely free as to render divine assistance unnecessary. Rather, humanity cooperated with

God in the transformation process. Human beings, made in the image of God, were not altogether powerless. While divine grace remained indispensable and necessary for salvation, it did not necessarily precede the freedom exercised by the will. The will could choose to initiate the move toward God and that which is good, with God acting in response to further enable the decision. A sickness, to be sure, had been inherited through Adam. Cassian, as did King, agreed with this basic Augustinian premise. Depraved humanity, however, possessed the moral capacity to recognize that it was living beneath the terms of the good life intended in creation and could choose, through the agency of human will, to move in the direction of its former state with God's gracious assist. If "utter depravity" suggested utter impossibility, Cassian and King gravitated toward a position of humans as less than perfect that did not apply the same kind of restrictions.

In so doing, both Cassian and King critiqued positions deemed dubious, while formulating and shaping new theological convictions. For them, neither Pelagius nor Augustine, the Reformer's nor the Renaissance thinker's view of *imago Dei* provided a satisfactory framework in and of themselves. Resolution would come only through a synthesizing of the two. This mediated position affirming an Augustinian teaching of assisting grace while incorporating the Pelagian teaching of human self-determination toward good is the nearest approximation to that of King's theological anthropology. In keeping with Cassian's explication of image of God thought, King held to a view that celebrated the idea of *cooperative grace*. As in the case of Cassian, he embraced a theological anthropology that emphasized humanity's freedom of will, and thus their ability to spontaneously desire and to choose God and the good offered as God's will for the individual and his social order. The ability to choose coupled with God's assist and empowerment to realize the good were reflections of God's grace. In this sense humanity possessed the capacity to cooperate with God's intention for creation. This was to say that humanity was neither impotent, in the sense that all constructive capacity was destroyed, nor omnipotent, in the sense that progress could be made independent of God. Rather, in a mysterious mixture of the two, humanity was able to choose to cooperate with God who by grace created them in God's image. Cassian and King arrived at this position by synthesizing aspects of liberal and orthodox theological assumptions about human nature. In both cases the opposing positions were considered "lopsided" and incomplete. For them, humanity could choose to progress, but each believed that the realization of the will to progress ultimately depended upon God's divine ordering of human affairs. Progress was never fully realized as a human inevitability without God's involvement. If human beings adjusted upwardly into kinder, gentler beings, it was to the extent that they chose to cooperate with God. Humanity might commence the journey, but they certainly could not complete it alone. In this sense, human progress was ultimately seen as being interdependent upon God, who graciously facilitated their God-granted capacity to act in accordance with their true and noble nature. This theological anthropology, which pointed to a free-willed humanity capable of choosing to cooperate with God, provided King with the *basis* and the *means* by which humanity might improve their individual and social arrangements. King writes:

> Man is no helpless invalid left in the valley of total depravity until God pulls him out. Man is rather an upstanding human being whose vision has been impaired by the cataracts of sin and whose soul has been weakened by the virus of pride, but there is sufficient vision left for his eyes to be lifted unto the hills, and there remains enough of God's image in him to turn his weak and sin-battered life toward the Great Physician.[3]

Although, as King described, the vision was impaired and the soul was weakened, God's image proved to be an adequate reservoir of sight and strength to redirect individuals toward the "Great Physician" and Healer of every soul. Human beings possessed the ability to charter a path and, as such, to determine a brighter future. While sight was impaired, it was not nonexistent and could be corrected; and while the virus of pride produced a serious sociospiritual ailment, it could be inoculated and cured by the redirecting influences of God's image. In this regard, God's image was not simply an abstract symbol of sacred human life created by God. It was not just another way of creating a theological category that would theoretically distinguish humans from all other creature forms. God's image, that element made available to every born traveler upon birth, actually provided the individual with the power and ability to steer his life in the direction of God and that which was morally good. Whereas Luther altogether dismissed the existence of God's image as a human characteristic, and Calvin admitted though severely limited its function, King acknowledged its reality and function to alter human decision and human destiny. Human life may be sin-battered, but even the sin-battered condition may be overcome as human beings realize their true nature and commence their move back toward God. Although Christian in his faith perspective, King believed that all human beings irrespective of creed or culture possessed this innate ability to rediscover their sacred origin and once again desire to know and live up to the moral implications attached to such a discovery. The image of God was both substantive and significant in this sense. More than a sacred icon of the past or some hopeful symbol of future aspiration, the image of God in humanity provided the real internal impetus and force for social change. Human lives, human societies, and even the world could experience an altered course in history provided there was sufficient individual and collective awareness of their interrelatedness to God and one another. Short of being a helpless invalid in the valley of depravity, human beings could imagine themselves beyond the quagmire of utter hopelessness because of the ability to choose. As King explained:

> The tendency in liberal theology has been to affirm that man is free
> and then to deny that his conscious purposes are predestined by God.
> This seems to me a more logical mode of thought. We must believe
> that man has the power of choosing his supreme end. He can choose
> the low road or the high road. He can be true or false to his nature.[4]

At bottom, King's optimism regarding the possibilities for social progress was grounded in his affirmative theological conclusions about the human capacity created in the image of God. More than the Naturalists' rational capacity, human beings possessed a spiritual capacity, discernible at far deeper levels of human experience. Humanity possessed a "soul force" that potentially empowered and galvanized society's urgings toward constructive social transformation. Basic to King's understanding was the idea that humanity, originally created in the image of God, not only possessed the image beyond the Fall, but that this preserved image also maintained the capability to remain true to its divine nature. Hence, the essence of human nature was not, at best, characterized by descriptions of utter depravity, although sin and evil could never be discounted. Rather, it was best understood in relation to the inward bestowal of God's likeness at creation and humanity's resulting freedom to choose in ways that were consistent with the divine image and God's gracious desire for the created order. Humanity was not as helpless as Luther concluded, thought King, because human beings have retained the ability to choose between good and evil. Our choices, according to King and Cassian, were not limited to the realm of evil; humanity could choose to live beyond their condition, they could choose the high road. To choose the high road reflected a choice to live in accordance with the so-called moral law of the universe, a life guided by principles of moral regard for self, others, God, and the world that God created for humanity's enjoyment and enrichment. Hence, the wonder of being created in the image of God assumed the freedom to make choices in ways that allowed human life to become governed by a series of personal choices. In this sense humanity could freely exercise their will in accord with their conscience. Short of this ability to choose, the sentence of guilt would be ascribed to the actions of one who of his own volition could not choose to do otherwise. Only those with the capacity to choose God and the good could assume accountability for their condition and full responsibility for their behavior.

Contrary to sixteenth-century Reformation conceptions of persons destined by God to a particular end, King embraced a theological orientation that sought to liberate humanity from this otherwise predetermined fate. To conclude that individuals were birthed into a foreordained pathos, which somehow resulted in a castelike future that was inflexibly sealed, was ideologically untenable for King and altogether inconsistent with his Personalist view of God.[5] Humanity was not predestined to travel either road, but in keeping with the principles of free choice could decide at a given time to travel one or the other. Otis Turner summarizes King's thought in this regard when he writes, "Man has the ability to choose the high roads of justice or the low roads of injustice. And while he may be conditioned to respond instinctively, he is not *determined* by instinct. It is man's ability to choose that makes him free."[6] This was an extremely important distinction for King theologically. To not be free in this sense was to suggest that individuals committed heinous crimes because they had to. It was to suggest that racism and segregation and even lynchings were an unavoidable by-product of what it meant to be human. In some sense it was to reconcile human existence to perpetual acts of brutality in ways that made this kind of behavior normative and even expected. For King, nothing could have represented a greater departure from the theological truth of what it meant to have been created in the image of God. Human beings could respond instinctively, but they were not destined by instinct. As opposed to being blindly driven by instinct, humanity was created and born with the ability to respond, reevaluate, and return to a path marked by high and noble ambition. As such, King's anthropology was guided by a theology that refused to concede to the idea that God had somehow already determined an individual's behavior and destined his collective fate. To adopt such a theological concept was to forfeit hope. To embrace the doctrine of predetermination was to unleash a self-fulfilling prophecy of doom. To say that some were subjected to reigns of tyranny and gross injustice by divine design was to discourage faith in a brighter future forged by a faithful God. None of these theological options suited King.

According to King, as in the case of Cassian, human beings were created free, and as such, they must ultimately assume ownership of their choices. Humanity possessed the internal ability, the innate power to choose good or evil, justice or injustice, and was thereby rendered capable of and accountable for it's choices. Tragic historical events were manifestations of human choices moving in the wrong direction. They represented the activity of ill-intentioned human beings choosing to violate the lives of other human beings via the vices of human exploitation, oppression, and genocide. They thus created moments in human history that reflected humanity at its worst. And yet King viewed these actions of outrageous injustice as one of many expressions of the human experience. These and other historical global travesties likened unto them did not tell the whole of it. For King, there was more to be said about the human story. Since humanity could choose, the story of the human drama need not always read like a sad saga of linked tragedies. Human beings could exercise their God-given influence to change. As King contemplated these profound possibilities, he concluded that a disturbing social past did not necessarily dictate or predetermine the human predicament. The fact that the freedom of the enslaved necessitated a civil war did not establish precedence for future advances toward freedom. As noted in an essay written for James Pritchard's class on the Old Testament, King insisted that religion is "democratized" as a result of humanity's freedom to choose, thus liberating his anthropology from the idea of individuals having been predestined to a specific "lot in life." He writes, "Liberating religion from all externals, at the same time the New Covenant strengthened and democratized it by placing responsibilities squarely on the shoulder of the individual, and purified and deepened it by making it a matter of conscience."[7] Thus humanity's capacity for responsible existence and increased possibility was essentially determined from within.

This mediated anthropology presented by John Cassian in the fifth century, of humanity as free-willed agents who may choose to cooperate with God, was furthered some seven centuries later by Aquinas. Aquinas's was a name, unlike John Cassian's, that King would evoke often. Thomas Aquinas (1225–1274 A.D.) was born at Rocca Secca, midway between Naples and Rome, Italy, during a period defined by Europe's so-called emergence from the Dark Ages, an era noted for its strict adherence to an ecclesial worldview that often suppressed the place of reason and logic. By the age of fourteen, Aquinas relocated to the first state university in the Western world, where he would become acquainted with the discipline of the natural sciences, logic, and the Greek philosopher Aristotle, the one given most credit for shaping his thought. Aristotle's ethics, politics, and metaphysics found fertile intellectual soil in Aquinas's thinking despite the previous centuries of suppression by the church, which considered Aristotle's teachings dangerous and unfit for serious consideration.[8] As in the case of Cassian, King's theological anthropology found resonance in the thinking of Aquinas. Confronted with the reality of social evil, King concurred with Aquinas's assessment that humanity was essentially good and that the universe was essentially friendly. At bottom, their shared desire to extend the moral concerns of the church beyond the church in a manner that was universally accessible to all of "God's children" stemmed from a common belief that "all truth is God's truth." Thus King and Aquinas were understandably eclectic in the formulation of their theological views on human nature, social justice, and community.[9] Unlike Augustine and the Reformers, King, Cassian, and Aquinas shared a noticeable optimism with respect to human capacity. Human beings created in the image of God, though imperfect and fallen, retained their ability to choose and to move toward that which is good.

In part, Aquinas's framework embraced this level of optimism because, unlike Augustine and the Reformers, he did not consider human reason and will as being utterly depraved by the Fall. While those of the reformed tradition considered human reason and will as either tragically hopeless or totally eradicated, Aquinas chose to nuance his interpretation of evil and sin. Aquinas wrote, "Sin cannot take away entirely from man the fact that he is a rational being, for then he would no longer be capable of sin. Wherefore, it is not possible for this good of nature to be destroyed entirely."[10] According to Aquinas, all that God created was essentially good, including humanity. Though human beings are fallen, the original declaration of them as good continued to describe humanity's essential nature and the capacity for human excellence. Evil was, therefore, explained as a manifestation of humanity's neglect to exercise the good that is within them, choosing rather to engage in decisions that result in unworthy and evil ends.[11] In contrast to the more orthodox views, evil was described as a dissipation or denial of humanity's goodness as opposed to understanding it as a warring against some adversarial force. As Renick explains, "Evil is never a thing. It is a privation of some of the good from a wholly good substance."[12] Aquinas would agree that Adam's sin was factual, and that human beings may do evil, but the evil that they do is not a reflection of their metaphysical makeup. If anything, it marked a denial of or a departure from the good that they by nature were inclined to do. King's basic contention, as in the case of Aquinas, was that the human condition was essentially good though fallen. Sin and evil represented more of an abnormal failure or falling away from the call to return to God and to living lives that reflected higher degrees of moral commitment to self and others. As such, social sins such as Jim Crow represented a choosing to ignore the moral good by extending sociopolitical opportunities to Afro-Americans that were just and equitable.

For Aquinas, evil existed as a human possibility because human nature was not created *immutably* good, that is to say, humanity's goodness was *created* (unlike God's) and was therefore subject to the kind of choice-making that was considered incompatible with their good nature. Thus, the good that an individual had the ability to do was always subject to the possibility of choosing wrong means to arrive at an essentially right end. Similarly, as a result of humanity's fallen condition, individuals could choose to do that which would otherwise be considered ethically correct to serve the goal of an unethical end. In either instance the outcome would be considered a gross departure from the good that could and should have been achieved had choices been made that were consistent with their true nature. King would often point out the ethical shortcoming in choices that did not allow the means and ends to stand in agreement. For example, King considered it unethical and immoral to pursue justice and community in ways that juxtaposed the desired end. He would often remind his hearers of the fact that the civil rights movement was by no means an attempt to displace one power structure with that of another. The movement could not be tainted with ulterior motives and agendas that were inconsistent with moral law. By the same token, if America's goal was to create a pluralistic democracy, segregation as a means of socialization flew in the face of that glorious and noble end. Although leaders were free to choose a specific course, a choice to suppress African Americans on the basis of race represented an immoral choice that was inconsistent with the higher good. Therefore, in their considerations of human nature, Aquinas and King took into account the idea of choice-making within the ethical context of means and ends. Although human beings were created good, as a result of human mutability they may choose not to follow the good that they know to do and as result engage in that which might be considered evil or sinful. Aquinas believed that this sort of inconsistency, the potential contradiction of means and ends, could be the only prevailing reality apart from the proper exercise of human reason.

While the eternal law was less comprehensible as a result of humanity's imperfection and need of faith, the natural law, which was readily accessible by reason, provided humanity with multiple truths concerning God, self, and the created order. For Aquinas, these truths were universal expressions of reality and could be discovered via two sources: human beings could perceive their existence as a matter of faith, or they could investigate reality through the faculty of reason. This theological distinction that existed between Aquinas and the more orthodox views that preceded and followed him may be attributed to his assessment of human nature and its capacity. Aquinas observed that human beings were created with animal-like qualities inasmuch as they had physical bodies and thus could experience the world about them through sensory perception. More than animals, however, human beings created in the image of God also shared an "angelic" quality inasmuch as they possessed an intellect that provided them with the ability to understand truth intuitively.[13]

Whereas animals were guided solely by their senses and angels by their intellect, Aquinas believed that humanity was endowed with both forms of perception to aid in drawing conclusions about God and the cosmos. Although a number of literary sources informed Aquinas's conception of reason and its significance, his thoughts were primarily shaped by the philosophy of Aristotle and certain Neoplatonist variations that had come down through Augustine.

Aquinas's substantial reintroduction of reason and its crucial relationship to faith as a means by which humanity may understand and respond to the moral requirements of natural law provided important theological insights into how King would later critique unjust laws. As a leading voice within the civil rights movement, King would rely heavily upon Aquinas's relating of faith and reason, natural law and eternal law conceptions to describe and convey the extent to which segregation and racial oppression reflected a breach of this higher moral law.[14] Essentially, he developed his anthropology by mediating the thinking of Aristotle and Augustine, such that Aristotle's reason and Augustine's faith became the primary means by which the good that was revealed in the natural law could be perceived. This merging of faith and reason was consistent with his understanding of truth as revealed through the eternal and natural laws.[15] The perception and understanding of these laws therefore required the mutual exercise of faith and reason.

In keeping with the more orthodox view held by Augustine, Aquinas first of all agreed that reason needs faith. Certainly Aquinas stood by his convictions with regard to the significance of reason. One must will to choose means that are consistent with ends, and only a will properly guided by reason could achieve a desired outcome that was in keeping with conceptions of the good. Aquinas explained, "The will cannot desire a good that is not previously apprehended by reason."[16] With the assistance of reason, Aquinas optimistically insisted that human beings could move the will to desire and achieve good ends. And yet Aquinas also believed that the good end that was achieved as a result of reason's ability to understand and comply with the natural law was occasionally in need of being informed and corrected by that which was witnessed via the eternal law and faith. In this respect Aquinas was careful to acknowledge the limitations associated with human reason and the fact that there were aspects of human existence that were inexplicable, and perhaps even unintelligible, apart from faith. Faith could interpret and comment upon aspects of human existence when reason and science were silenced because of scarcity of natural data and facts. While committed to the exercise of scientific investigation and an open-minded assessment of its findings, King wholeheartedly agreed that science could be rendered incomplete without the insights provided by faith and its theological commentary. As King understood, science left to itself could easily degenerate into the practice of pseudoscience, thus allowing reason to become co-opted by the status quo to serve the self-serving agendas of the powerful. Hence, in keeping with Aquinas's conception of human reason as limited because of limitations created by sin and one's perception of the physical world, King concurred with the need for a faith that would speak to issues that existed beyond the reach of scientific inquiry.

In an attempt to further establish Aristotle's essential nature of reason, Aquinas mediated this line of thinking by also asserting that faith needs reason, a notion that would have been rejected by Augustine, as it was in the theology of the fifteenth-century reformers.[17] For them the human faculties were utterly unreliable. Luther not only refused the idea of the image of God as having survived the Fall but also adamantly denounced the idea of human goodness apart from the saving grace of Christ. It was unthinkable that unregenerate reason or human intellect would have anything to contribute to the enhancement of one's faith. After all, insofar as he was concerned, faith elevated reason; reason could not possibly elevate or add to the quality of one's faith. Aquinas and King could not have disagreed more. Those created in the image of God retained the natural ability to reflect the God in whose image they were made by exercising the ability to understand God, self, and their natural environment via reason. If faith provided verification for science, science provided a similar verification for faith. Within this framework suggesting that all truth is in fact God's truth, truth could speak from within so-called sacred or secular contexts. In fact, sacred and secular categories became less significant here if in fact the truth of God permeated all. For Aquinas, therefore, as in the case of King, reason served faith well by radically reforming its worldview. Prior to the introduction of scientific discovery, the church held to a three-tiered understanding of the universe. While biblical thinking sought to substantiate these claims of how the universe hung together, science challenged and eventually informed this faulty faith perspective. To the surprise of many, the earth was not flat, and the cosmos was more complex and layered than hitherto imagined. Just as the newfound sciences of the Enlightenment helped to dispel some of the church's more erroneous beliefs about the natural world, so faith and its perception of the eternal law needed the insights offered by reason and its understanding of the natural law to continually align and properly focus its views.

Although it was rejected by Augustine and the Reformers, King, as did Aquinas, affirmed the dynamic relationship between the human will and reason. While distancing himself from liberal conceptions that dismissed God all too easily, King would agree with Aquinas's supposition that humanity did in fact possess the ability to respond to moral suasion as a result of their God-given capacity to reason and exercise faith. This represented an important shift in King's theological anthropology because without this assurance the adoption of a nonviolent methodology would be futile and reckless. To the question "Do human beings have the capacity to change?" King, with this premise in mind, could respond with an emphatic yes. His response, as in the response provided by Aquinas, was hinged upon the belief that humans, created in the image of God, retained the ability to reason and respond to that which was morally good. Apart from this capacity for individual and social transformation, it would have been considered futile to engage in a nonviolent protest against racial injustice. What moral victories could be gained, and what systemic changes would be made if political leaders and fellow citizens could not appreciate the reasonableness of a moral argument and desire changes that were commensurate with their new understanding? To hope for such dramatic social change would have been thought futile apart from a belief that the human will could be altered given the proper appeal. In fact, more than futile, a hope that placed the lives of others in harm's way without the assurance of change could have been considered reckless. Hence, Aquinas's anthropology implied that the will would desire and do that which was morally good providing there was sufficient understanding of the proposed good. This was a notion that would maintain currency for centuries to come. It represented a conception that was altogether reminiscent of King's anthropological view, which centuries later affirmed the presence of a "hidden goodness" in human nature that could be awakened by an appeal. King's similar assessment of human nature and his confidence in humanity's capacity to respond to moral suasion would surface in response to the needs of the civil rights movement.

The development of this idea that spoke a hidden goodness that could be appealed to represented an important theological move for King because it provided the outline on how social change could be initiated and subsequently negotiated. In his affirmation of the autonomous quality of human nature, King affirmed that social change would ultimately involve more than an adjustment in society's legal and judicial structures; indeed, it must include the adhered conviction of this internal inclination toward that which was morally just, a conviction that shall be more fully explained in the next chapter. Notwithstanding the need for just laws and sociopolitical documents in a fallen world, the "image of God" provided humanity with an internal witness. Via this internal witness, humanity was considered inherently aware of what constituted the just act even apart from the imposition of a just law. In this sense, laws simply served to *reinforce*, not simply enforce, that which humanity instinctively knew to be true and just. Whereas Luther insisted that human depravity deprived the human condition of such awareness, King emphatically maintained that it had not. The so-called fairer angels of human conscience, despite the reality of sin and evil, remained available as an internal instructive guide. This internal guide simply required the proper moral appeal, an appeal that would correspond to the movement of God in history. As in the case of Christ who arrived in a season of *kairos*, King believed that nonviolent reformers could also appeal to a "hidden goodness" in human nature. This thought is reflected in his comparison and evaluation of the theologies of Luther and Calvin:

> In the same vein we must reject Luther's and Calvin's view that man is incapable of performing any saving good, and that man can do nothing to save himself. Certainly we must agree that the image of God is terribly scarred in man, but not to the degree that man cannot move toward God. As seen in the life and teaching of Jesus, humanity remains conscious of its humble dependence upon God, as the source of all being and all goodness. "There is none good save one, even God." Yet in dealing with even the worst of men, Christ constantly made appeal to a hidden goodness in their nature. We must somehow believe that the lives of men are changed when the potential good in man is believed in particularly, and when the potential bad in man is sought to be overwhelmed.[18]

In order to effect change, one must believe that human beings possess the goodness required for such a transformation. The goodness that King spoke of was not somehow added to, or created within an individual at the point of some awakening. As such it was not considered a postconversion development of the human condition. For King, the goodness required for sweeping change was already hidden within. The idea that human beings could allow this innate goodness to surface represented a major theological move. King understood the Reformation position, which essentially denied humanity's ability to contribute in any wise to the process of redemption and salvation. For the Reformers, the image of God, particularly for Luther, was of little or no real practical value. Theologically, the determination was made that the image of God was either terribly marred or altogether lost by the Fall. If goodness in any degree surfaced, it was only due to Christian conversion and must be viewed as an expression of God's grace operating in the human heart. Short of this intervening work of the Holy Spirit, human beings have no goodness whereof they may boast. Goodness, insofar as the reformers were concerned, is not even an option until after conversion. If anything is hidden, it might be the greater dimensions of humanity's tendency toward evil. If anything, that which has been corrupted is withheld from full expression by God's grace. For them, the only reality that was hidden was the depth to which impaired human beings could descend. But as we have seen earlier in this chapter, King came to a very different conclusion as he thought through his anthropology. His determination was that the image of God, that which most defined what it meant to be human, was scarred but not severed or detached from humanity. As a result,

King believed that humanity could participate, that they could in fact decide and/or choose to move toward God of their own volition. If there is no clear evidence of humanity's goodness, it is simply a result of its hidden quality. What was hidden was not the depths of evil to which humanity might plummet but the heights of civility and nobility to which they might soar. Even the so-called worst among us have a hidden goodness in their nature. It was this belief in an individual's capacity to bring forward a level of goodness that had been obscured by a given behavior that denies the true nature that fostered King's hope during the years of the civil rights movement. Because the behavior is not self-evident does not mean that it does not exist; it is simply undetected.

Much more will be said of how King understood the place and power of moral suasion in the following chapters; here I would simply like to begin introducing the degree to which King embraced and affirmed this very big idea. Human beings were fallen but not hopelessly fallen. They simply needed for the good that was hidden in them to be believed in and appealed to. As argued in his student essay, King believed that humanity remained conscious of its dependence upon God "as the source of all being and goodness." Every human being made in the image of God, irrespective of religion or race, creed or culture, was conscious of God and that which represented the chief good in life. Every human being created in the image of God was somehow conscious of his need for God and this universal obligation "to love others as they would love themselves or to do unto others as they would have others do unto them." Basic to King's understanding of human nature was this idea of human beings as created beings, created beings who were yet connected in this way to their Creator and each other. It was this inner consciousness, this spark of inner hidden goodness, that Christ appealed to in his coming to establish the Kingdom of God. In love, Christ came to appeal to humanity's hidden goodness. In like manner ambassadors of Christ, and even individuals of goodwill such as Gandhi, were able to appeal to the goodness obscured in the lives of fellow travelers forging through their own respective generations. Admittedly, this notion that human beings would respond to a moral appeal represented yet another very big theological shift in King's anthropology. As Christ came in his appointed season to extend the invitation to return to God and live by a higher understanding of what it meant to be human, so in every age there would be God-appointed times and individuals who would announce "the acceptable year of the Lord." While all would not choose to adjust to the call of their higher nature, all could. Essentially, the theological rationale affirmed that since all were created in the image of God, all possessed the capacity and the goodness to recognize and respond to moral appeal. An appeal could be extended, and more important, humanity could choose to respond.

Key to King's anthropology, therefore, was the weight he placed upon human initiative and human involvement. Since humanity was conscious and could respond to a moral appeal by choosing to move toward that which represented a moral good, it was vital that those of goodwill not simply entertain the idea intellectually but engage it actively. As discussed earlier in this chapter, and as we shall see more fully in chapters 6 and 7, King's anthropology stood in stark contrast to those ideologies that leaned toward a gradualist view. That is, those views that endorsed a "take it easy you're moving too fast, things will change if you let everything run its course" mind-set troubled King. In Birmingham, a group of concerned business leaders, politicians, and clergy came together to inform King of how mistaken he was regarding the protest and to request his departure from their city confident that they would solve their own race problem. All they needed was time, not the annoyance of an "outside agitator." Needless to say, that sort of response to the Birmingham protest troubled King because of its apparent failure to recognize humanity's moral obligation to appeal to that which was good and to overwhelm or overcome that which was potentially bad within society. King of course understood that this kind of ethical call raised the question as to what or who determines what actually represented the moral good. While much could be debated on that account, King was clear that segregation and the social injustices that it promulgated were clearly a nondebatable wrong that was in need of being corrected. He was also very clear about the fact that the kind of entrenched social issues being addressed in Birmingham usually did not fix themselves. Although humanity possessed the capacity to change, moral change as King imagined it would not "roll in on the wings of inevitability." This was, in part, his chief concern with liberal advocates of human perfectionism. Insofar as he was concerned, humanity was not on an unavoidable evolutionary track toward perfection apart from God's grace and humanity's constructive intervention. Indeed, there was a hidden goodness in their nature. Societal change, however, must be ushered in as a result of our belief in that inherent goodness and our work to overwhelm that which is potentially bad. The good must be invited and affirmed while that which is demoralizing and socially destructive is resisted and overcome by introducing humanity to that which is potentially good.

In the final analysis, however, King's confidence in humanity's goodness was buttressed by his assurance of God's necessary, yet willing, participation in the process of human and social transformation. Although various sects within liberalism affirmed the inevitability of human progress as an evolving reality apart from God, King recognized humanity's proneness to finitude and human frailty and acknowledged the provenience of divine participation.

While not succumbing to the idea of utter human depravity, King concurred that the "brotherhood that God makes possible" was dually contingent upon humanity's cooperation with God. Oates writes, "As a student of Personalism, King was certain that man could cast out evil from the world—by confronting his own sinfulness and opening himself to the Father's incandescent love and goodwill."[19] Although humanity created in the image of God may possess and choose to exercise goodness as an aspect of their essential character, the fact and realization of "the good" is wholly dependent upon God, "the source of all being and goodness." As King acknowledged, goodness becomes a human option because of the "isness" of God. God facilitates humanity's ability to realize their choice to "do justly" as they engage, or are confronted by, the ethical or moral appeal. In this regard, King conceived of a framework in which God and humanity cooperated, as it were, in the task of facilitating humanity's progression toward being more human(e). Similar to, though certainly more generous than, Calvin's civic account of human nature, King sensed that being created in the "image of God" was to be created with the capacity to acknowledge the veracity of a moral appeal and, moreover, to respond affirmatively as God enlightened and empowered the human reason and will. To that end humanity could discover and begin to experience a life of cooperative grace. In keeping with this basic premise King writes:

> Not only is the spirit of God working that we differentiate between right and wrong, but he is also working that we will choose the right. He is forever seeking us only hoping that we will seek him. The search is a double one, and the good life is the work of both the spirit of God and the effort of man. All good that appears in men grows up under the fostering care of the Holy Spirit. . . . As the circle is narrowed from the world to the church and from the church to the individual, the work of the Holy Spirit becomes more specific and intense. In the individual human being is done the fundamental work. God, the conductor of this moral transformation, is pledged in truth and love to complete it. This moral transformation cannot take place, except by the cooperation of man with God in promoting it.[20]

King's anthropology would be incomplete without this acknowledgment of how he understood the working of God's spirit on behalf of human progression. While human beings have the capacity to choose, it is the spirit of God that is working incognito so that humanity will acknowledge and choose to do that which is right and good. More than an image of God conception for the sake of personal enlightenment, the very spirit of God, in whose image humanity was created, facilitates humanity's ability to discern and desire the moral good. The spirit of God, in this sense, is neither neutral nor unengaged. Far from disinterested, the spirit of God is both active and occupied in the business of fostering and furthering a meaningful human enterprise. Even before a judgment is made regarding right or wrong, and before a choice is made to follow the lead of the will, God is working. And King is clear: the work of God is on behalf of humanity. God, who for King is the Conductor, is ever committed to seeing the moral transformation through. This would have come as quite a shock to those who labored under the theological notion that the Holy Spirit's sole concern was the salvation of the soul. Why would the spirit of God bother to bridge the spiritual concerns of salvation with such a mundane civic concern? Perhaps, thought King, what we believed to be theologically mundane was in fact important to God.

While most theologians limited their understanding of "God's work" to the church, with little more than pronouncements of judgment for those without, King believed that the gracious working of the Holy Spirit was more inclusive than that. The church represented the clearest revelation of God's will in the world, but all those created in the image of God could begin to move and function in the realm of the divine by so deciding. All could commence their journey toward understanding the moral imperatives of what it meant to love God and to love one's neighbor because all were created in the same image of God. No one could argue ignorance of the moral truths, or that which was required of the human family, because all were created as responsible moral agents. Human beings were responsible free-willed agents that could cooperate with God. Human beings could choose. Only then would the idea of human rights be balanced with the notion of humans acting as responsible agents. Inasmuch as justice represented a human issue, not simply a Christian issue, the idea of *imago Dei*—as the primary aspect of the human condition—moved humanity beyond provincial notions of justice and its pursuit, offering the broadest possibility for human interest and participation. Beyond class, culture, ethnicity, and creed, *imago Dei* represented King's irreducible and universally inherent claim regarding human existence and its possibility. As King stated, "All good that appears in men grows up under the fostering care of the Holy Spirit."[21] To be sure, the view looks quite different at the level of the world than that of the individual, but all constructive movement in the direction of that which is right can be attributed to the work of the spirit of God.

Inasmuch as the good work, according to King, was a reflection of the work of God and the effort of humanity, it could be said that God sought humanity hoping that humanity would in turn seek him. This undoubtedly would appear theologically curious from an orthodox perspective because for them, unregenerate human beings have no apparent need or desire to seek

God in their fallen state—not to mention their inability to desire or do that which is good. Humanity's estrangement from God and God's will is the normative and even preferred state of existence. The only good, therefore, that the Holy Spirit would be interested in fostering would be with regard to the work of salvation in the individual life. Theologically, the work of the Holy Spirit within the context of a reformed framework tended to narrow the concern to that which was redemptive and salvific. Luther often rehearsed the role of the Holy Spirit and the scriptures in announcing humanity's need for God and, above all, salvation. To therefore suggest that God initiated the search would fit theologically. After all, the God of creation is also the God of redemption. It is a position that is altogether consistent with the God of prophetic pronouncement, who both rejects and passionately reconciles ruptured relationship. The incarnation is God's clearest announcement of his longing and of his work to seek and save a failed creation. Fallen human beings, however, did not and in fact could not commence their move toward God within the possibilities of an orthodox theology. This, once again, underscores the degree to which King nuanced his theological anthropology. For King, given his regard for the image of God and its place, it is not at all blasphemous to suggest that human beings possess the sensitivity and ability to seek God. As outlined earlier in this chapter, King acknowledged the reality of human sin and evil, but he refused to embrace theological notions of humanity as utterly depraved, utterly helpless, and utterly hopeless. Human beings created in the image of God retained the ability to choose God and that which is morally good.

King, therefore, as in the case of Cassian and Aquinas, embraced an anthropology that believed that the process of knowing that which is right and doing that which is right was a dual process. In the end, it was the duality that freed his conception from the error of one-sidedness. Unlike certain liberal conceptions that either ignored or explained away God and evil, King embraced an anthropological position that factored in the idea of human fallibility and affirmed God's activity in human history to assist in overcoming it. Instead of these one-sided liberal notions, however, the human choice to pursue a right course was preceded or at least accompanied by divine work. In fact, for him, without God there would be no history to speak of. For King, no real concept of human progress could disregard the presence of a loving, personal God. God sought and worked! By nature, humanity created in the image of God was invited by God to participate in an upward journey defined by the high road of moral responsibility. In this sense, King's position retrieved the idea of responsible human living and theologically placed it front and center. Unlike certain orthodox conceptions of humanity as utterly depraved, King celebrated a humanity that could exercise the freedom of choice as a result of having been created in God's image. Hence, the burden of making responsible moral choices could not be explained away as a by-product of humanity's liability due to a historical fall from paradise. As opposed to waiting for God to "fix it," King believed that God was seeking to "fix it" through the agency of human hands. At the very least, God was waiting for humanity to awaken to their sense of moral obligation and to rise to the occasion of responsible human living. King maintained that there was a distinct God-given role that human beings should and indeed could assume in order to fulfill their human destiny. In order to "make it to the promised land," human beings gifted with the strength of mind, body, and soul were expected to utilize their God-given faculties in ways that were self-determined as opposed to predetermined—not self-determined in the sense that humanity acts independent of God, but self-determined in the sense that the self comes to recognize the capacity it has been granted to know and to do the good. At most, God was willing and waiting to facilitate humanity's choice to foster a greater degree racial harmony and social justice. Although this view of humanity as good-natured and willing to adapt to a moral mandate was sobered during King's latter years (1965–1968), his belief in the capacity for human social progress was sustained by his hopeful anthropology.

One may ask whether or not the theological conclusions that King came to were just the musings of an inquisitive student who was simply experimenting with theological ideas as part of an academic exercise. Did King do theology as a matter of the head, such that the doing of theology was no more than a cognitive exercise, or was it a matter of both intellectual investment and heartfelt conviction? As King engaged his studies, wrote his essays, and participated in theological conversations, did he simply see himself as participating in an ongoing academic debate? Did his theological concepts represent no more than a contemporary collection of sermon helps, which were used by King to add interest and distinctiveness to his preaching? Or, as Chappell suggested, did King knowingly adopt certain theological positions simply to appease his professors with hopes of propping up his grades? The following chapter is provided in answer to this line of inquiry regarding King and his theological conclusions by offering an analysis of how King imagined his anthropology being worked out and applied in the real world. Far from one who engaged theology for the satisfaction of its intellectual rigor, King seems to have thought it through for the purpose of an applied end. For him theology was engaged to serve a noble sociospiritual good. Theology did not stand over, above, and in some ways against the affairs of humanity's daily existence; it informed and served to shape and correct it. The following chapter, therefore, is provided to aid us in understanding King beyond this point of potential skepticism. As such, it allows for a consideration of how King extended his theological anthropology beyond thoughts of God and humanity as a mere conversation piece. Hence, chapter 5 can be viewed as the "so what" chapter. Since humanity is created in the image of God, and since this is what it means to have been created in the image of God, this is what human existence should look like according to King. As King personally contemplated the meaning of image of God, he arrived at a theology that he could call his own. The following details the implications that grew out of his theological premise, and as such represents the core of his theological concern.

5

King's Theological Implications

From his outlook as theologian, King drew at least four major conclusions from his explication of image of God, which ultimately formed the basis of his civil rights appeal and the core of this book's development of his theological anthropology. The first two conclusions are strikingly similar to that of his early black church and abolitionist predecessors; the third and fourth advance King into new and somewhat uncharted theological terrain. First, all individuals, as children of God, were equally valued inasmuch as they were birthed with an inherent dignity. Second, human beings had an intrinsic worth that in and of itself became the requisite for the bestowal of just and fair treatment. Third, in addition to warranting just treatment by virtue of their having been created in the image of God, humanity thus created possessed the capacity to cooperate with God by living out the mandates of their moral conscience, such that the desire to choose to do that which is socially good can actually be translated into the deed itself. Fourth and finally, image of God provided the existential common ground for genuine community-building, making beloved community, in its broadest sense, a distinct historical possibility.

Each of these four considerations shall be summarized with thought given to how King related to the church theologically. In recent years, numerous references have been made to King's identification with black church theology; few attempts, however, have been made to delineate the subtle ways in which King adopted and yet distinguished himself in a theologically critical manner. Admittedly, while a work focused on King's thought and life cannot possibly be expected to provide the contoured analysis often provided by black church historians, if the claim is that King's *theology* was a product of, and therefore identifies with, the black church, greater care should be taken by all disciplines of study to then accurately convey and substantiate their respective theological orientations over a given time frame, assuming that King's and the church's theological views have, in fact, been sufficiently clarified and/or understood. The following reflects a summary of that attempt to bring such clarity to the subject.

Imago Dei and Human Dignity

The first of four implications identifiable in King's theological anthropology was the belief that all human beings were individuals of dignity. In short, everybody was somebody of significance. In keeping with arguments raised a century before his, King echoed the need to counter the false claims of human superiority and inferiority, particularly those that were premised upon false notions of race. Racial assumptions erroneously affirmed the dignity of some while systematically denying the humanity of others. As in the case of the activists who preceded him, the underlying basis for King's civil rights appeal and its emphasis on the question of human dignity was not sociopolitical but theological, although he certainly understood the relationship between the two. As King so often acknowledged, few sociopolitical documents captured and expressed the dignity of the human spirit as did those within the American political context. The language was celebrated by him for being succinct and unsurpassed in its potential to model the social good. In fact, Lewis V. Baldwin rightly acknowledges King's high regard for the ideals conveyed in the language of the nation's founding documents. According to King, the Declaration of Independence, the Constitution, and the Emancipation Proclamation were political writings that captured and communicated something of the sublime. By leveraging the democratic principles embodied by these documents, King hoped to usher America into a fuller realization of liberty and justice for all its citizens. His was not an anarchistic campaign of unconcern or disregard for democratic principle. Rather, he sought to honor and work within the legal boundaries of America's sociopolitical system, while attempting to hold it accountable to the millions of African Americans who were being denied their rights. At bottom, King rightly regarded the "sacred political documents" and the democratic governmental process that allowed for their implementation. Particularly within a social scenario that allowed for the choosing of that which was evil as a result of humanity's fallenness, the protection of human rights and human dignity via political process represented a necessary good. King, however, understood that the documents, while providing the theoretical model for democratic process, were slow to inspire a consideration of all as persons of human dignity, and therefore required a call to accountability.

If the nation's founding documents proposed to acknowledge and protect human rights on the basis of life as sacred, their proposal had not extended far enough to include the dignity and worth of African Americans. King alluded to this apparent inconsistency in his graduate student papers: "America," he explained, "gave its full pledge of freedom 75 years ago. Slavery has been a strange paradox in a nation founded on the principles that all men are created free and equal."[1] Though King presumed that the documents were written with the *potential* for a more inclusive read, the recurring self-evident fact was that the abolishment of slavery and its resulting social failings were not a real consideration in the minds of those who first conceived of an American democracy in which "all men are created equal" and therefore guaranteed "certain unalienable rights." This uneasy social climate defined King's involvement in a civil rights movement that spanned three U.S. presidencies, those of Eisenhower, Kennedy, and Johnson. As signs of resistance to the movement increased, King found himself grappling with the disheartening realization that the political documents he evoked in his earlier appeals for civil rights were not, in fact, originally written with Americans of African descent in mind. This renewed awareness of the framers' original intent and the "strange paradox" of its lingering sociopolitical ambiguities led King to conclude years later that the Declaration of Independence "has never had any real meaning in terms of implementation in our lives."[2] While referencing the Declaration of Independence, the Constitution, and the Emancipation Proclamation with obvious frequency, Lewis Baldwin and Michael Dyson are correct in their assertion that King minimized, and all but withdrew his reliance upon, the "sacred documents in American political life" during his final years (1965–1968).[3] While the documents guaranteed the protection of rights for a vast majority of Americans, those of African descent essentially remained unattended. In their original intent and, therefore, in their implementation, the documents required the kind of fluid interpretation that would one day allow for the marginalized to be brought into the mainstream.

The same, however, cannot be said of King's unswerving reliance on the theology of image of God and the ways in which he considered its original intent with respect to the human condition. Whereas the sociopolitical statements were in need of being expanded in scope with regard to meaning and inclusion, the theological narrative attached to the creation of humanity provided a self-evident expression of God's intent for all humanity from the beginning.

As such, his rationale for the bestowal of human dignity and humane treatment, like the Declaration's, was consistently centered in this theological premise that all humanity were created equally in the *image of God*. All humanity, therefore, were fundamentally endowed by God with dignity upon birth. This resolute commitment to that truth formed the basis of his appeal for civil rights from Montgomery to Memphis. As previously noted, this is not to say that King did not incorporate secular reasoning into his overall conception. As would be expected, King integrated the best ideals of his liberal democracy into speeches and addresses that were necessarily prepared for audiences that were representative of the public square.[4] His ideological center, however, was not sociopolitical but theological. His mediation of terms, political and otherwise, was unapologetically interpreted and developed through theological lenses. After all, King considered his role as a Baptist minister/public theologian foremost and the biblical text, from which his framework originated, as normative.[5] For him, as in the case of the early black church, certain liberal Protestants, and abolitionists, *imago Dei*, as the scriptural rationale for human egalitarianism, "contained real meaning in terms of implementation" despite the Declaration's failure to do so.[6]

To affirm one's place in the world as a "child of God" made in the "image of God" was to affirm one's sense of self-worth. For King, to embrace this theological statement as true was to refute the myths of racial inferiority, thereby providing a historically oppressed people with the psychological ability to move beyond centuries of oppressive socialization bent toward the creation of an impotent labor force. Few, King reasoned, would challenge a denial of their rights as long as their perceived place in the world dictated that they were somehow undeserving of, and unfit for, first-class citizenship and the rights thereof. More than a violation of law, an image of God framework brought attention to the violation of one's personhood. Lives conditioned by low thoughts of inferiority acclimated to the social status; to have been made in the image of God, however, radically reoriented that perspective. Contrary to the view that "Negroes" were destined to be "toters of water and hewers of wood," King held to the belief in the dignity and worth of all humanity. To acknowledge and affirm one's relationship to God was to assume a newfound dignity. It also called for a radical rethinking about how human beings relate to others. At bottom, his decision to assign individual meaning and worth to the disenfranchised by virtue of one's creative origin, while not degrading the worth of others, established the grounds for a proper personal assessment. Theologically, King understood the difficulty in attempting to love others apart from having the capacity to affirm and love self. In the wake of questionable sociological and biological analyses of the "Negro" plight, King offered an alternative theological analysis as a means of reorienting one's worldview toward the accommodation of a more generous regard for self. King often spoke of the damaging influences of history and the need to alter one's sense of self by reintroducing those with an incorrect sense of self to this image of God view. The primacy of this belief was presented in his description of religion's role in firming up one's sense of Somebodyness:

> Once plagued with a tragic sense of inferiority resulting from the crippling effects of slavery and segregation, the Negro has now been driven to re-evaluate himself. He has come to feel that he is somebody. His religion reveals to him that God loves all His children and that the important thing about man is not "his specificity but his fundamentum, not the texture of his hair or the color of his skin but his eternal worth to God.[7]

If individuals were deserving and worthy of rights that were civil, it was a result of divine declaration, not simply the Declaration of Independence. "The Negro," as King explained, "came to feel that he was somebody. His religion revealed to him that God loves all of his children and that every man, from a bass black to a treble white, is significant on God's keyboard."[8] Apart from this profound sense of basic human worth, which was common to all, a movement for rights that were civil seemed less plausible, given the alarming record of sociopolitical reluctance and resistance to integrating African Americans into the social mainstream. King, therefore, saw in this theological description of the human condition an occasion to raise the once latent hopes of those considered "the least among us." If no other doctrine or creed spoke definitively to the question of human identity, the idea of existing as a "child of God" made in the "image of God" certainly did. Human life has been infused with meaning, significance, and dignity. As a result, when King confronted power with love, he did not do so with a "hat-in-hand" approach. An appeal for civil rights was not a matter of social service panhandling. Rather, it represented an engaging moral discourse on the basis of an egalitarianism that theologically warranted the assurance of civil treatment for all. In his estimate, every human being was a deserving recipient of justice and goodwill because, simply stated, every human being was equally recognized as a child of God. And it was this sense of "being in the world" that essentially fostered a spirit of restless determination to carve out a sociological reality that would catch up with this theological hope. King explains: "And that's all this whole thing is about. We aren't engaged in any negative protest and in any negative arguments with anybody. We are saying that we are determined to be men. We are determined to be people. We are saying that we are God's children. And that we don't have to live like we are forced to live."[9]

In its most basic form, King's appeal for civil rights was premised upon the theological fact of "Somebodyness," the understanding that everybody was "somebody" because everybody was created and conceived in the image of God. Irrespective of ethnic origin, persons defined by this shared sacred origin merited serious unbiased acknowledgment inasmuch as the image of God assigned the highest degree of Somebodyness and worth upon all human life. The idea of humanity created in the image of God provided the basis for attempts to level all provincial ideas that were developed with the intent of systematically devaluing certain populations within a given society. For King, this immoral tendency toward the insidious assignment of artificial stereotypes not only eroded human personality but also stifled the potential creation of just and caring relationships within a given society. As such, the image of God represented King's chief argument against the racially induced claims of *Negro* inferiority and all the associated acts of systemic discrimination. In essence, this concept of human life as dignified represented the bottom line insofar as the idea of mutual regard was concerned. It served as the universal invitation to fulfill the so-called Golden Rule by treating others as they themselves would want to be treated. In keeping with this idea, Rufus Burrow writes, "The universe is created in such a way that everybody ought to be treated with dignity and respect just because they are."[10] Beyond a narrow, and at times faulty, biological analysis of the self and others, King understood that one might entertain a more thoroughgoing account of human being by acknowledging humanity's essence. In the final analysis, an individual's worth and dignity were discovered in consideration of who they essentially were, not in what they may or may not have possessed materially. King explained: "This innate worth referred to in the phrase the 'image of God' is universally shared in equal portions by all men. There is no graded scale of essential worth; there is no divine right of one race which differs from the divine right of another. Every human being has etched in his personality the indelible stamp of the Creator."[11]

If segregation and racial discrimination helped foster the institution of inferior and unequal social categories on the basis of race, an image of God conception offered an alternate worldview through which alienated members of the human family could view themselves and others as ontologically equal. This sense of connectedness provided the precondition to the development of relationships defined by their sense of genuine regard for the other. In so doing, the affirmation of one's genuine self and one's true place in the world consequently created the intellectual space for one to imagine new possibilities for relationships. In King's estimate, individuals were not somebody over others but somebody with or among other somebodies, and as such there could be no "graded scale of essential worth." Hence, to affirm the idea of our likeness to God was to affirm the idea that no one was essentially "less than." To suggest that all were created in the image of God was to establish a baseline with regard to human self-understanding. As such, he interpreted the sociopolitical in theological terms, with an imagining of *imago Dei* and its implied meaning for the fundamental adjustment of all social relations.[12] For King, this kind of far-reaching shift in the way the other was viewed established the locus, as in the case of the antislavery advocates preceding him, for the development of his mid-twentieth-century social justice framework. From Montgomery to Memphis, one could readily recognize Douglass's passionate appeal for the abolishment of slavery and justice similarly voiced in the "image of God" language appropriated by King a century later. Basic to King's appeal was the shared sentiment that injustice could no longer be viewed as being compatible with their reaffirmation of God's work in the nation and world. Persons were expected to march, protest, and participate at the dictate of human dignity. At bottom, all individuals were deserving of just social dealings, in response to and as an expression of their innate human dignity. As such, human dignity called for a response to life's indignities.

In his book *Somebodyness: Martin Luther King, Jr. and the Theory of Dignity*, Garth Baker-Fletcher provides helpful insights into King's understanding of what it meant to have been created in the image of God. While there are clearly a number of language similarities, the emphasis of the present work tends to be considerably nuanced. Whereas Fletcher appears to place the idea of human dignity as the centerpiece of King's image of God conception, this work sees King's explication of human dignity as one of several complex implications for image of God and its meaning for human(e) living. As opposed to reading human dignity as the center, this work develops the idea of human dignity as a logical starting place for the way in which King argued at least three additional progressively related positions. (Hence, King could say, since we are created in the image of God, therefore. . . .) Also, Fletcher presents the idea of human dignity as an ideal that King somehow hoped humanity would work toward achieving. This work, however, contends that King understood human dignity as a matter of human awareness and not one of human attainment. While civil issues requiring the desegregation and integration of society were in need of being attained and realized, human dignity simply required an awareness of a given human quality. King believed that human beings, those who were made in the image of God, were by nature persons of worth and dignity. For King, human beings did not have to march and protest to somehow achieve dignity. They engaged in marches and protest as a result of the dignity that defined their human existence, with hopes that the more favorable social circumstances external to their lives would catch up with their inherent spiritual condition.

Instead of striding to achieve human dignity, as one would stride toward freedom, they were simply in need of cooperating with the Eternal by acknowledging and living with an awareness of that which they possessed upon birth.

Hence, in seeking to undergird the denigrated and disenfranchised with a philosophy of "Somebodyness" that was universally and unconditionally accessible, King offered his image of God concept with a theological understanding that one's sense of human worth was not ultimately derived from the conjecture and status claims of our horizontal existence.[13] The assignment of human worth was not a product of human agency. Human agency could describe and define human worth, but it could not dictate who the recipients should or, as in the case of African Americans, should not be. For King, all human beings were individuals of assigned value simply because God deemed them so. Human beings were created as the objects of God's love and holistic concern. The indelible reflection of God's image was the sublime characteristic that most distinguished the state of being human and was thus considered the quintessential affirmation of human personality and the fundamental explanation of one's personal worth.

Imago Dei and Human Rights

As discussed in chapter 4, King's understanding of human nature suggested that human beings, while born with a propensity toward evil, were also birthed with an inherent sense of worth and human dignity. Moreover, he reasoned that all of "God's children," inasmuch as they have been birthed with inherent worth, should have a basic threshold of justice made available to them. In this nonprovincial sense, King concurred with a *broad* Jeffersonian interpretation of the ideal that "all men are *created* equal, and that they are endowed by their *Creator* with certain unalienable rights." Prior to any natural consideration and apart from any politically administered social contract, human relations warranted a high degree of social parity as a result of the moral law and the sacred nature of human existence. Unlike Tocqueville, who in the 1830s observed that the American colonizers were "born equal instead of becoming so,"[14] as a result of their "state of democracy," King essentially embraced an appeal that associated civil rights with birthrights that were validated as a result of having been birthed in the image of God, irrespective of geographic locality or political affiliation. In so doing, King imagined civil rights as a divine endowment that was in need of being equally protected inasmuch as all human beings were equally created. That is to say, the circumstances of one's birth should not obviate or occasion his experience of the basic rights to life, liberty, and the pursuit of happiness. As such, the enjoyment and/or denial of rights that were civil could not be based on race, class structure, or religious persuasion and be considered morally correct. In contrast to egregious regimes and states typified by feudal and caste systems, the Declaration of Independence provided King with a political framework that indiscriminately protected the basic rights of every human being of American citizenship, irrespective of class, culture, or creed. Irrespective of the original intent, or the lack thereof, that document of independence gave voice to the disenfranchised masses as well. King affirmed this truth when he wrote:

> For in a real sense, America is essentially a dream. . . . One of the first things we notice in this dream is an amazing universalism. It does not say some men, but it says all men. . . . And there is another thing we notice in this dream that ultimately distinguishes democracy and our form of government from all totalitarian regimes that emerge in history. It says that each individual has certain basic rights that are neither conferred by nor derived from the state. To discover where they came from, it is necessary to move back behind the dim mist of eternity, for they are God-given. Very seldom if ever in the history of the world has a socio-political document expressed in such profoundly eloquent and unequivocal language the dignity and the worth of human personality. The American dream reminds us that every man is heir to the legacy of worthiness.[15]

This rudimentary belief in the American dream, and in human beings as persons of worth, established the theological rationale for bridging theoretical and practical aspects of just living. His was a theology that bridged the hope for justice with a working methodology to achieve greater degrees of justice. For King, theory and application merged within a social context defined by mutual regard and acts of unrequited benevolence. As King explained, "And when we truly believe in the sacredness of human personality, we won't exploit people, we won't trample over people with the iron feet of oppression, we won't kill anybody."[16] In other words, when we genuinely believe the dream, when we believe that all are created by God with certain basic rights, our creeds will be translated into constructive action plans that are designed to elevate the least among us. In this respect, King thought it not inappropriate to involve himself in so-called political affairs. After all, he understood himself to be advocating and advancing the rights chartered for children of God, not simply citizens of a nation. More than local citizens, the elderly who were discriminated against on Montgomery's buses and the disgruntled sanitation workers who were denied fair wages and working conditions in Memphis represented God's precious "children."

As such, the Constitution could not *justifiably* withhold the bestowal of rights that it did not, and in fact could not, originally confer. In his confrontation with injustice, as in the case of the antislavery and pro-Reconstruction voices that preceded him, King resorted to a theological anthropology that related the dignity of human worth to the guarantee of certain basic rights.[17] In this regard, King appropriated and followed the freedom tradition of the early black church and its nineteenth-century interpretation of *imago Dei* quite closely. As King reminded his Memphis hearers:

> We don't need any bricks and bottles, we don't need any Molotov cocktails, we just need to go around to these stores and to these massive industries in our country, and say, God sent us here, to say to you that you're not treating his children right. And we've come here to ask you to make the first item on your agenda—fair treatment, where God's children are concerned.[18]

The appeal to the city officials was simply for the exercise of fair treatment. Fair treatment, said King, not simply where the taxpaying citizens of Memphis were concerned but fair treatment insofar as the plight of "God's children" was concerned. If colonial citizens once revolted over the idea of taxation without representation, certainly there should be a massive outcry over the mistreatment of those who were also created to experience a destiny of dignity. As such, image of God represented one of the civil rights movement's chief cornerstones. Rightly understood, it was an insight that centered the conversation's premise for the fair treatment of others in the arena of theological fact. While recognizing the potency of political documents to describe the idea of human dignity and to protect the notion of fair treatment through judicial process, King joined abolitionists of earlier centuries in centering his hopes for the granting of civil rights in the sublime yet pragmatic idea of having been created in God's likeness. While making frequent reference to political jargon as a means of shaping his public discourse, ultimately he understood that the idea of fair treatment as a moral condition was derivative of yet another realm of meaning. As theologian, King grasped for ideas, language, and concepts that for him reflected ultimate and even universal meaning. Beyond the question of constitutionality, King, not unaware of the historical debate, viewed civil rights as the championing of human treatment that was God-granted. Fairness, as an expression of just dealings in human relations, was expected by virtue of humanity's relatedness to God and one another as persons created in the image of God. On the eve of his assassination, a fatigued King, unapologetic in his insistence that one's inherent human dignity warranted civil and humane treatment, called for an additional march to advocate and further protest the unjust treatment of those fashioned in God's image. The level of suffering among many African Americans could no longer be ignored and, insofar as King was concerned, could no longer be tolerated. Upon his arrival in Memphis, King said: "Now we are going to march again, and we've got to march again, in order to put the issue where it is supposed to be. And force everybody to see that there are 1,300 of God's children here suffering, sometimes going hungry, going through dark and dreary nights wondering how this thing is going to come out. That's the issue."[19]

That was the issue for King, as it similarly was the issue for those who preceded him—advocating the rights of individuals made in God's image, individuals abandoned to "wonder how things were going to come out." Whether the circumstances spoke to the inevitability of emancipation or the fair employment of sanitation workers, the issue remained the same: humans created in the image of God warranted civil treatment. For King, an anthropology developed upon an image of God premise could not ignore the cause and effects of human suffering, nor could it dismiss the complex discussions related to ways of minimizing it. By no means did King live under the illusion that human suffering could be eliminated altogether. He did, however, believe that human beings should genuinely work toward an existence that would bring the human family closer to an expression that more perfectly reflected what it meant to be created in God's image. To accept, therefore, the theological fact that all were made in the image of God was also to suggest that the disadvantaged, voiceless, and powerless among us should not be overlooked, neglected, or, worse yet, exploited by the advantaged. While the poor and suffering were said to "be with us always," the issue raised by King suggested that they did not have to be the same poor always. Those who were of considerable means and influence were compelled to consider the plight of the poor, particularly those who were impoverished as a result of intentional denial and/or restricted opportunity. As King traveled the country and witnessed the disparities in housing, health care, education, and economics, it was clear that not near enough attention was being directed to narrow the gap between rich and poor. His concern, while national, also took on a global perspective, making King's scope in this regard was quite broad. At bottom, King supposed that the material wealth and resources of the world were sufficient to benefit the residents of the world, not simply a privileged population that seemingly benefited most from their demise. Whether citizens of America, Asia, South America, Africa, or wherever poverty was perpetuated, fellow travelers created in the image of God should neither morally justify nor comfortably adjust their conscience to that desperate condition.

Much more was at stake than the denial of basic human goods. King believed that much more was involved than the fundamental denial of food, clothing, shelter, and health care. More than the neglect of human services and material goods, to neglect the poor was to neglect an aspect of self. Since life was understood as being interrelated, to deny others was to deny self, even though that act of denial may have been thought to be done in the interest of so-called enlightened self-interest. King would argue that injustice and the neglect of the poor are rarely if ever reflections of enlightened activity, and certainly not in accordance with one's self-interest. Irrespective of one's social status, although separated by an economic gulf, all members of the human family were considered morally bound by the tie of their common humanity, and moreover by their common sacredness, having been created in the image of God. The social implications of this theological anthropology were profound. To ignore the poor was to concurrently ignore self; it was to ignore a deeper spiritual impulse that defined what it meant to be human(e). To do harm to another was to harm and debase oneself. In a 1962 address prepared for an annual church conference, King spoke to this issue of sacred worth and the degree to which an embrace of the idea ought to translate into meaningful, nonoppressive interrelationships. To do otherwise was to violate, and to even do violence to life as intended along the horizontal social plane. King said, "So long as the Negro is treated as a means to an end, so long as he is seen as anything less than a person of sacred worth, the image of God is abused in him, and consequently and proportionately lost by those who inflict the abuse."[20] More than judicial debate about the ethics of civil treatment, one's soul and the soul of the nation were at stake. King, therefore, believed that the bestowal of rights was a necessary implication of what it meant to be made in the image of God not simply for the good of the one who became the recipient of that right to life opportunities but for the sake of the advocate as well. In short, to come to aid, to protect and preserve the rights of others, was to aid, protect, and preserve the soul of that individual, that community, and that nation.

Having considered the role of the advantaged and their relationship to the less-advantaged and the disadvantaged, King also gave thought to the role and responsibility of the recipients of injustice. Not only did the privileged need to see the less privileged as worthy recipients of justice, the less privileged, those often stereotyped as somehow inferior, had to see themselves as persons of worth and great dignity. In so doing, King understood the relationship between self-esteem and self-determination. He understood the relationship between one's ability to translate a healthy sense of self-worth into a distinctive form of self-help. In this regard, the image of God assertion represented that internal dynamic that could favorably empower and direct one's destiny when affirmed. As outlined in the previous chapter, King believed that human beings possessed the ability to choose, and that those who were oppressed could choose to

celebrate their humanity by asserting their shared right to life. Notwithstanding the absence of an affirming social infrastructure external to oneself, "image
of God" informed individual awareness via this internal deposit of human dignity. Persons could affirm, "I am somebody" because of who they intrinsically
were and in direct proportion to that reality consider themselves worthy of certain basic rights. American citizens who realized their true place in society
could also realize the significance of their stand for first-class citizenship in a
first-class nation, despite the maltreatment that might have suggested that they
were otherwise undeserving. King, therefore, reasoned that a "child of God,"
made in the image of God, possessed sufficient standing in and of himself to
commence and determine a reordering of his own social paradigm. The relationship between self-awareness and self-determination, therefore, came as a
reminder that relationships with others could be altered due to one's relationship with God. As a child of God, one had the civic and moral obligation to
oppose laws that were inconsistent with the moral law and its prescribed sense
of justice. To acquiesce was to deny one's "birthright" and to essentially become
complicit with the conveyors of injustice.

For King, to participate in the civil rights movement was to participate
in a modern-day great awakening of sorts. Unlike Rip Van Winkle, the fable
character whom King often referenced to illustrate the tragedy of sleeping
through a great revolution, those who struggled against the injustices committed against them were likened to those awakened from the slumber of willful nonresistance. While King understood that persons conform to oppression
and injustice for a variety of complex reasons, their break from that cycle of
victimization began with an embrace of self as created in the image of God.
Persons who understood the profound implications of life as sacred became
weary of tolerating life's injustices. Instead of accommodating the abuses of
humanity against humanity, those who assigned to their own existence a status
of Somebodyness could no longer take the abuses in stride. As persons worthy of unalienable rights that were God-granted, those created in the image of
God were called upon to be "true to oneself" by engaging in the discipline of
passive nonviolent resistance against the evils of human oppression. Above all
else, it was their identification of self as one created equally among others that
insisted upon challenging and resisting injustice. While attempting to avoid
all forms of violent resistance, believing that violence begets violence, King
refused to compromise with, or conform to, any social standard that did not
support and further the cause of human dignity and decency. As a final resort,
the decision to dramatize the reality of injustice by engaging in civil disobedience corresponded to King's desire to reconcile ruptured humanity by merging familiar activist strategies with certain innovative theological conceptions

of liberation. His 1968 address to Memphis sanitation workers was clear and emphatic. King announced that as children of God, "we are determined to be." For King, a reconsideration of one's self and the state of one's social existence should translate into a reconsideration of one's "place" in the world and hence a fuller realization of and intolerance for the unacceptable experiences of injustice. King understood that a proactive, nonviolent determinism could ensue as persons embraced definitions of themselves through the lens of an image of God theology.

Imago Dei and Human Capacity

The first two of four implications delineated earlier in this chapter placed King's theological anthropology in sync with that of the early black church in America. King, as did the early black church, believed that all human beings are individuals of worth and dignity, and should therefore enjoy the safeguard of basic human rights. His hope in human nature, and its capacity for good, however, began to move King in a different theological direction. In contrast to the less optimistic view of the early black church, King's theological approach to this carefully framed anthropology was developed by resorting to liberalism as the school of thought offering the broadest possibilities for optimism about human nature.[21] While not necessarily committed to a specific liberal ideology, it could be said that King, unlike his ancestors, demonstrated an unapologetic allegiance to a distinct *process* of liberal methodology that resulted in not only a firm commitment to reconciling intersecting truths but also to integrating racially, socially, and economically divided populations. This theologically mediated anthropology, while providing King with a basis for his civil rights appeal, theologically distanced him from a number of traditional views regarding human nature and its capacity.[22] King examined the veracity of this theological assumption, which essentially asked whether or not human beings were *collectively* capable of exercising moral judgment on behalf of others, even when doing so did not appear to serve their immediate economic and social interests.[23] Was the human capacity such that nonviolence, moral suasion, and direct action could effectively bring about the necessary societal changes given these various ideological distinctions? Or would social progress, as in the case of mid-nineteenth-century emancipation, require the additional exercise of violence (a struggle alternative embraced by Frantz Fanon) and physical force?[24] What were human beings capable of achieving insofar as the transformation of the social landscape was concerned? What kind of capacity do human beings have in this regard? Could the theory of human worth and rights premised upon that fact actually become translated into a society characterized by the realty of freedom and justice for all?

This line of inquiry led King to a thorough analysis of the complex relationship between his understandings of human dignity, the subsequent demands dignity required of one another, and humanity's ability to exercise this moral obligation to "love thy neighbor as thyself." King needed to determine what that level of human capability looked like. Unlike the romanticized visions of utopian society, King acknowledged humanity's capacity for evil and developed an anthropology that accounted for the kind of individual and societal sins that were both historically and experientially self-evident. Humanity was created in the image of God and as a result of their intrinsic worth became recipients of rights that were God-granted. The bestowal of rights, however, did not somehow exempt members of the human family from the power and penalty of human corruption. While not fully convinced of reformed conceptions that described humanity as utterly depraved and utterly helpless, King did agree with the basic doctrinal conclusion that human beings were fallen creatures. He embraced the idea of human imperfectability, although his sense of what it means to have "fallen" was considerably nuanced, as we have seen in the previous chapter. Conversely, and unlike the overly pessimistic assessment of human nature provided by proponents of the Reformation and Neo-orthodox thinkers of his day, King concluded that the greater propensity of the human will created in the image of God was toward a realization of the *good* and that which was most attuned to God's good intent for the human family. Although humanity was flawed and hence prone to evil, King fostered an anthropology which declared that many of these stifling contradictions could be overcome as a result of God's work through the agency of human efforts. Not even Niebuhr's argument regarding the possibilities of "moral man" and the impossibilities of "immoral society" could dissuade King. For King, both the individual and the societal group possessed the capacity to consider, desire, and do that which is morally good. As such, King held to a position that allowed fundamentalism and liberalism to overlap, thus creating a reconstituted theological center that merged aspects of both positions. In the end, King arrived at a theological center that still provided a rather generous assessment of the human condition and human possibilities.

This interest in the discovery of "truth wherever it may be found" provided King with a perspective regarding human capacity that was informed by a number of sources. In seeking to determine the extent of humanity's capacity to perceive and achieve the good, King consulted theological as well as historical, psychological, and biological sources. His primary interest was in determining where the intersection occurred, that place that most nearly approximated an understanding of human potential. If an overreliance upon God to correct social maladies represented a fundamentalist barrier to social activism, the essence of King's criticism insisted that "to believe that God will do everything while we do nothing, is not faith but superstition." By the same measure, if humanism's liberal assumptions regarding human perfectibility denied the place of Divinity within the process of human progression, King theologically tempered its too naive assumptions regarding humanity's *inevitable* evolution toward the perfect society with a slightly more neo-orthodox view of evil and sin. In the end he includes the idea of human failure, but he does so without totally rejecting the spirit of optimism attached to the idea of human capacity. Hence, King's optimism regarding human nature and its capacity for community was developed to include concepts of sin and evil. His hope, however, in humanity as good-willed and capable of dramatic change was not relinquished. As such, his theological outlook could best be described as a cautious celebration of human possibilities. He affirms and celebrates humanity's ability to creatively forge a future that is in keeping with what it means to have been created in the image of God, but he does so with the understanding that human beings also have the ability to make choices that are contrary to the good. For King, God was that one who initiates the transformation of the social landscape; human beings created in God's image are simply in need of sensing the movement of God and exercising their capacity to choose to cooperate with God's transforming will for human society.

To be sure, there are several similarities that might warrant the identification of King's thought with that of the church's traditional belief system, although even here we must not run the risk of oversimplifying the idea by suggesting that there was a "single" belief system that defined all churches in each historical period. The church was far from monolithic in its observance of doctrine and practice. Thanks to a number of authors, the gradual development of the early black church during the eighteenth and nineteenth centuries, with its nuanced theology and cultural practices, has been thoroughly documented. If there is a common theme that places King and the church on the same page, as it were, it may be found in the fact that neither labored under the illusion of inevitable human progress. Carol George, Ronald Walters, Lewis Perry, Michael Fellman, Albert J. Raboteau, Evelyn Higginbotham, C. Eric Lincoln, Vincent Harding, Gayraud S. Wilmore, and Henry H. Mitchell are a few who concur in their views that the black church rarely, if ever, bought into the liberal assumptions of humanity's inevitable evolution into kinder, gentler beings. Overall, the content of biblical and sociopolitical documents associated with America's religious and political independence was diffused through the experience of African tradition and struggle, as church converts during the previous two centuries sought to bring a sobered blend of theological meanings that would make sense of the duration and nature of their egregious suffering. As in the case of King, the themes of "American dream" that were gleaned from this glowing ideology, though clearly appropriated from Western visions of a liberal democracy, were culturally adjusted and recast to distinguish them from those of the concept's original presentation. Both King and his predecessors came to certain theological conclusions that were informed by the material of their experiences and cultural traditions. Henry Mitchell explains:

> The most important African survivals of all may very well be in the belief systems, African traditional religious doctrines, as closely related to and merged with the orthodox Christian faith. At some points, the parallels are amazing, as with the omnipotence, justice, omniscience, and providence of God. None of these attributes of God had to be learned first in slavery. And all of these cross over [into] African beliefs so amazingly well in America because they served so well to support African American psychic survival under oppression.[25]

With this as the presumed theological orientation of the early black church, it would not be surprising that *certain* basic epistemological and theological similarities did, in fact, exist between King and the *early* black church. Their mutual tendencies toward eclecticism, the avoidance of liberal ideologies that pointed to the inevitability of human progress minus God, and the embrace of a holistic theological bent that affirmed God's liberating character are evident. God was embraced as the liberating God of the Exodus. Consistent with his nineteenth-century appropriation of *imago Dei*, King reached back to recapture some of these aspects of the early church's "black sacred cosmos."[26] The black church's recasting of the raw theological material from within its context of suffering led to an emphasis upon God's liberating work and a corresponding cynicism concerning the slaveholders' nineteenth-century reluctance to oblige this divine mandate to set the captive free.[27] Although President Lincoln was widely revered and celebrated for his political role, ultimately the early black church believed that it was the Lord, not Lincoln, who graciously intervened in history and secured their emancipation from slavery; a reflection of the degree to which human capacity was minimized. Polly, a slave of Barbara Leigh Smith Bodichon, eloquently expressed to her mistress the meaning she derived from religion: "We poor creatures have need to believe in God, for if God almighty will not be good to us some day, why were we born? When I heard of his delivering his people from bondage I know it means the poor African."[28] With little or no thought of inevitable human progression, the early black church in essence confessed, "If it had not been for the *Lord* on my side, where would I be?" The black church primarily held to a theology of hope in God and God's work in the world. Their optimism and hope for deliverance rested squarely upon their belief in the omnipotence, justice, omniscience, and providence of their God.

Many of these shared expressions of liberation, however, were significantly eclipsed by King's nuanced anthropology. Whereas King aligned himself with his predecessors by denouncing liberal positions that denied God's involvement in humanity's forward journey, he moved beyond them by also embracing a view of human capacity that is much more generous than they would have allowed. His conclusions concerning that which constituted human being placed him well beyond the theological scope of his contemporaries and the black church from earlier periods.[29] For King, there seemed to be sufficient cause to vest considerable hope in humanity's capacity to do the moral good. Given the proper conditions and circumstances, human beings have the ability to make choices that are compatible with the aspirations of freedom and justice for all. Unlike the theological models developed by the early church, and even the church of his own era, King held to a shared optimism in both God and humanity. Richard Lischer is correct in concluding that "the black experience in America left no room for optimism about human nature."[30] In keeping with the early black church, King affirmed the centrality of God's role in human emancipation, but he did so while "leaving room" for the place of human participation in a manner that had rarely been done hitherto. Carol George records such an account: "In his Episcopal address to the AME conference in 1851, Bishop Quinn charged his listeners to honor their commitment to preach despite the difficulties created by 'prejudice and persecution.' Advising cooperation, he said, 'We should work together. Nine times out of ten when we look into the face of a white man we see our enemy. A great many like to see us in the kitchen, but few in the parlor. Our hope is in God's blessing on our wise, strong and well directed efforts."[31] While King shared their emphasis upon God's liberating work, he did not share their cynicism concerning the conversion of Pharaoh, especially during the earlier years of the civil rights movement. It was not simply the release from Egypt's oppressive clutch that interested King. He was ultimately interested in a theological anthropology that imagined Pharaoh and Moses sitting together "at the table of brotherhood." For King, the idea of liberation included the reconciliation of Egypt with its former oppressed citizenry.

As we, therefore, consider King's thoughts about human capacity, we can see the careful ways in which his theology was differentiated. It is over this question of human capacity that King begins his departure from some of the more common anthropological views adhered to in the ecclesial mainstream.

His thoughts are more attuned and more readily shared by his academic mentors and peers with whom he studied. It was a framework that captured the theological tone and tenor of a school of thought known as Personalism. As he contemplated human capacity, King imagined the results of free-willed beings who could choose the direction of their chartered path, a view clearly rejected in the more fundamental circles from which he was accustomed to seeing during his youth. As McKanan explains, "Many social reformers had to conclude that their understanding of God's presence in humanity was at odds with traditional Protestant doctrine, which stressed God's difference from humanity and the awesomeness of divine power."[32] Despite the dogmatism in either theological camp, King explored concepts that stood the test of time, consulted the findings of recent scholarship, and developed his theological anthropology. He was not bound by the thinking of his Baptist tradition or the unbridled optimism of the pacifist or evolutionist. While hearing, and at times even borrowing, concepts from both, his would be a position that docked in neither. While King believed that integration, voting rights, decent affordable housing, educational equity, and economic justice were in society's best long-term interests, not simply that of African Americans, he also understood that there were a host of segregationists who failed to embrace his vision of human life as interrelated and inextricably bound, gradualists who scoffed at his sense of urgency, and liberals who affirmed his goals but denounced his process. King, however, believed in the inherent goodness of the human condition and despite these evidences of opposition held to his theological hope in the conversion and redemption of human society.

As indicated in chapter 1, the early church, abolitionists, and antislavery proponents drew upon the idea of humanity created in the image of God to frame arguments for the discontinuance of slavery. That human beings were created in the image of God and were therefore justified in their pursuit of just treatment were views that were fairly consistent in both King's and his predecessors' positions. In this respect King and his predecessors stand in close agreement regarding the meanings that were attached to how they understood human existence and its possibilities. However, unlike the black church of the preceding century, King proceeded to develop a scholarly explication of human nature so as to personally determine whether or not human beings actually retained sufficient capacity to desire, pursue, and realize the genuine well-being of others. It was, after all, one thing to say that humanity "merited" and therefore should be moving toward a more perfect union, in which justice was experienced by all. It was quite another to suggest that that kind of theological theorizing was indeed humanly possible within the context of a pluralistic society.[33] As King contemplated what it meant to be human through the lens of an image of God theology, he concluded with an anthropology that celebrated humanity's capacity to desire and do that which is morally constructive. As a result of having been made in the image of God, this idea regarding human capacity represented a significant shift in King's thinking. King would often liken the social climate through which he journeyed to days that were both "dark and difficult." Notwithstanding the serious challenges, King maintained a theological orientation that affirmed humanity's ability to experience change and to then participate in the process of ongoing change that would be redemptive and reconciling in nature.

Imago Dei and Beloved Community

This fourth and final implication of King's image of God conception continues to demonstrate his distinctiveness from that of the black church by broadly identifying beloved community as an intended goal of the civil rights movement, a position that stood in stark contrast to Booker T. Washington's concession with segregation and the more Garveyian voices who later saw emigration and black separatism as the only viable alternative for genuine black independence, a notion that did not escape the early black church. As Carol George explains, "By the 1850's, a separatist undertone pervaded the message of most black churches, which is not surprising given the increasingly oppressive racial climate of opinion."[34] More than black independence and separatism, however, and even more than American independence, for that matter, King ultimately became interested in an idea of human independence that necessitated a reconfiguration of the narrow ways in which the idea of community was viewed and defined. Robert Franklin illustrates the extent to which King sought to modify the provincialism that so characterized his faith tradition: "Not content with merely inheriting his 'Daddy's' religion, he [King] reached intellectually beyond it into other great world religious classics and traditions to discover the true height and depth of a universal God."[35] His belief in the idea that individuals were created in the image of God, led King to consider the promising implications of humanity's interrelatedness and the tragic consequence of this unacknowledged possibility. As detailed in the following chapter, King imagined an existence beyond the realization of a desegregated just society, wherein individuals chose to work toward the imminent creation of a community of the beloved, and they did so in terms that sought broad, universal accessibility.[36]

As we think about this final implication, it is important to note that King's concept of beloved community moved beyond the boundaries of traditional church life. That is to say, his sense of community was not circumscribed or strictly defined by church membership. While believing Christianity to be the clearest revelation of God to humanity, King also believed that there was sufficient overlap in our common status as persons made in the image of God for unjust societies to adjust and move toward a harmonious whole.[37] As Franklin points out, King was interested in describing and discovering the "true height and depth of a universal God," a universal God who was concerned with the universal suffering of humanity. If human suffering and disenfranchisement represented the tragic "isness" of life, the freedom struggle's emphasis upon the creation of beloved community signaled an equitable and hopeful move toward the "oughtness" in life. In this sense, beloved community represented the epitome of human possibility. For King, the prevalence of oppression, exploitation, and separation did not have to be the normative indicia by which human existence was measured. Rather, beloved community implied that "the disconnected aspects of reality" could be brought "into a harmonious whole," with broad application and currency that reached across religious, race, gender, class, and cultural lines. A beloved community premised upon the principles of mutual regard thus collapsed the ways in which superficial social categories were allowed to create a rationale for the provincial assigning of worth and the subsequent manner in which individuals could adversely be viewed and disengaged. At bottom, the image of God as a theological construct provided King with an engaging, inclusive social framework, in which a collective vision of mutual regard could be practiced.[38]

As in the case of the previous implication regarding human capacity, King's concept of community also created a place of ideological and theological departure from conventional thinking. Whereas a community of the beloved was restricted to the fellowship of the converted that were located within the circle of congregational and church life, King defined community to include every member of the human family. Every human being was made in the image of God, every human being was birthed with a degree of dignity, every human being possessed the capacity to desire and do good, and therefore every human being was viewed as having been invited to participate in the community of the beloved. While the "choice" to work toward beloved community may have required a conversion of one's attitude and will, King certainly did not have an evangelical Christian conversion in mind, no more than he would have expected Mohandas Gandhi, Kwame Nkrumah, or Abraham Heschel to convert to Christianity as a prerequisite condition to sharing in the commonwealth of this community and working to further its goal of global goodwill. While thoroughly Christian in his *personal* theological conviction, King anthropologically understood the image of God to be that universal condition that interrelated all humanity at its most basic level.[39] In this sense, image of God preceded religious belief inasmuch as individuals were birthed with the former and developed the latter at some given point in one's life. As King often stated, "All humanity is involved in a single process, and all men [and women] are brothers [and sisters]."[40] Although belief in a particular religious tradition may vary from person to person, all persons created in the image of the one God could affirm the employment of nonviolent resistance in the cause of freedom, justice, and the creation of global community.

> Consequently, the believer in nonviolence has deep faith in the
> future. This faith is another reason why the nonviolent resister can
> accept suffering without retaliation. For he knows that in his struggle
> for justice he has cosmic companionship. It is true that there are
> devout believers in nonviolence who find it difficult to believe in
> a personal God. But even these persons believe in the existence of
> some creative force that works for universal wholeness. Whether we
> call it an unconscious process, an impersonal Brahman, or a Personal
> Being of matchless power and infinite love, there is a creative force in
> this universe that works to bring the disconnected aspects of reality
> into a harmonious whole.[41]

The faith, therefore, that constituted this fraternal tie within the context of the civil rights movement could not have been a reference to the evangelical saving faith preached from most mainstream pulpits (although King genuinely embraced this aspect of his own Baptist Christian experience), but another more universalized faith that he believed was commonly available to all humanity everywhere as "children of God" made in the image of God. It is here that Lischer may have overstated his claim regarding King's retreat from liberalism. While King's views were clearly chastened by the sheer weight of defiance to the civil rights movement, his eschatology remained a testament of his reluctance to abandon the liberal framework altogether.[42] In fact, King's eschatology described the degree to which he remained theologically connected to liberalism, contrary to Lischer's suggestion that the "liberal optimism was blown away," and the degree to which he remained theologically distanced from the black church, contrary to Lischer's assertion that King returned to "the bedrock of black eschatology." King's eschatology, though approaching the "bedrock," was actually quite distinguishable from that of his contemporaries and his nineteenth-century ancestor's more radical view.[43] After all, his was not a view that subscribed to the violent overall destruction of this evil world and the creation of another; rather, King continued to envision a period *in history* when the "lamb would lay down with the lion, and nations would study war no more." The latter allowed for a social order that held forth the possibility of being salvaged and reconciled as opposed to destroyed and re-created. This, unlike the theology of the church, was an eschatological outlook that King embraced, particularly during the earlier days of the movement; that was not interested in retribution but rather in reconciliation and the formation of beloved community. His shift to a position not commonly held by those within his faith tradition is further evidenced in his affirmation of an eschatological view that remained committed to a belief in the possibility of a reconciled community "in time" as contrasted to the more orthodox and even violent eschatological visions of divine judgment and the subsequent creation of a new heaven and earth.

As such, the theological distinctions between King and the church can be said to have been subtle, yet extremely significant. In contrast with positions that uncritically identify King's theology with that of the black church, King's appropriation of the black church was actually less cognitive and more intuitive, less literal and more visceral, less theological and more practical. Although he never abandoned the influences of his youth, insofar as many of them were synthesized into his overall conception, King's conclusions suggest that his theological anthropology was far-reaching and more dissimilar than similar particularly with respect to the degree of confidence he placed in human nature and its capacity to cooperate with God's desire for the created order. Hence, while not undercutting his belief in God's primacy in the historical development of any human progression, King's theological anthropology explicated image of God and its relationship to civil rights in a manner that substantiated a kind of generous optimism in humanity. Moreover, King acknowledged the universal significance of beloved community as the civil rights movement's ultimate goal and humanity's chief common destiny. In time, however, this glowing theory, despite its dramatic successes through 1965, would have to be reconciled with the agonizing realities of human regression that would follow. Although King did not concede altogether to the growing skepticism witnessed during the final three years of his life, with their increase in violence and drastic decline in support of the civil rights movement, he does moderate the measured optimism of his earlier years with a return to the less optimistic views of human nature espoused by the early black church of the nineteenth century. In so doing King rediscovered a recast theological view that minimized his focus upon human efforts, emphasizing instead the time-proven trust in God's Providence and justice.

As indicated at the outset of this chapter, King's sobered appreciation for the Declaration of Independence and the Constitution coincided with the revision of his anthropology, which later necessitated the introduction of a more eschatological interpretation of the movement and its uneven progress. With his ties to the White House all but severed (due largely to his unpopular stand against the Vietnam War), King continued to envision the realization of beloved community via the organization of an interracial, cross-cultural, international community of the dispossessed. In keeping with his high hopes for humanity, King looked toward edging the nation and world closer to the ideals of a liberal democracy and a fuller realization of freedom and justice for all via his organization of the Poor People's Campaign.

PART III

Practical Application

6

Beloved Community

Although King assisted in popularizing the idea of beloved community during the mid–twentieth century, earlier usage of the term is attributed to late nineteenth-century philosopher and Harvard professor Josiah Royce (1855–1916), often credited with having developed the phrase into a philosophical framework upon which later community conceptions were hung.[1] In keeping with the evolved "fatherhood of God and brotherhood of man" conceptions that preceded him, Royce conceived of a community that, in effect, addressed the redemptive upward mobility of the human race. McKanan writes, "The common fatherhood of God, of course, made all humanity brothers and sisters, and all liberals taught that God's love enables each person to form family ties with all people."[2] While not uncritically aligned with this view, King was undeniably influenced by nineteenth-century Protestant liberalism and the degree to which its idea of community was broadly typified. As explained in chapter 5, even if one considers the contribution of the church to King's thought, it cannot be said to have had significant theological influence apart from the pervasive influence of this "other than orthodox" stream of thought.[3] Though distinguishable from one another, Royce's account, as in the case of King's, made room for similar concerns with regard to the unfortunate fragmentation of human society along racial lines, and mutually emphasized the urgent need for the introduction of a social reform that would foster the creation of a more just and equitable society. While recognizing humanity's propensity to produce and perpetuate social conflict, King also acknowledged the extent to which human beings could realize community as a result of having been created in God's image. As such King's commitment to beloved community was seen as being vested in a reality that, at bottom, spoke to humanity's common ground. This worldview regarding beloved community informed every dimension of King's social and theological reflection.

In so doing, image of God not only provided the initial basis for the recognition of humanity's common dignity but ultimately resulted in King's premise for humanity's common claim to community as well. This ground for King's abiding confidence in the human capacity for community, as suggested in chapter 4, was initially established by the belief that *all* individuals were children of God, uniquely made in God's image, and universally created with the capacity to choose relationships that build community instead of creating chaos. The essence of King's community concept is explained by Allen Boesak, who writes: "At the center of what Martin King believed about humanity and human relations stood the Social Gospel doctrine of the Fatherhood of God and the Brotherhood of man."[4] For King, this worldhouse offered a global living environment in which each member of the human family could be housed and sustained by his Creator. As Cartwright explains, "Much as the *imago Dei* becomes the basis for the individual's dignity and worth, created relatedness becomes the basis for community. Since we are all children of the same Father-Creator, we are all one family, one community, inseparably bound together."[5] Although King reflected his specific cultural and creedal influences, he also fervently believed that this common tie to God could bridge benevolent relations between individuals, groups, and even nations. If the philosophic mind of Royce conceived of a community whose origin was linked to the idea of absolute mind, or Logos as world-mind, King would later contemplate beloved community as a theologically mediated possibility that had its origin primarily grounded in the familiar soils of his faith tradition, particularly as the history of that tradition related itself to the theological analysis of a harsh social climate and an ever-hopeful cure. Fluker cites this tradition and its centrality in the development of King's community conception:

> It can be argued that while evangelical liberalism provided the
> theological content and Personalism, the coherent methodology
> and philosophical formulation for King, the black church tradition
> of protest for equality and justice provided the source and the social
> context in which he worked out his conception of community and the
> method for its actualization.[6]

As such, King's thoughts concerning the parameters of community were not ultimately determined by the theory of liberal thought alone but by the experience of his black church tradition and the nation's divided social predicament. Charles Marsh is correct in asserting, "Apart from these beliefs, King would have acted quite differently."[7] His beliefs were a by-product of society's attempts to depersonalize and objectify blacks by the enforcement of Jim Crow following the conclusion of slavery's brutal era. This comprehensive system of legalized social stratification deepened racial polarization, further rationalized black inferiority, and considerably dampened and delayed all genuine attempts toward the creation of Royce's broad-based pluralistic society of the beloved. Hence, King's was a concept of community, though obviously shaped by various ideological influences, that was worked out of the center of his intimate acquaintance with the struggle tradition. Community was no ivory-tower conception for King; rather, as Marsh further contends, "the spiritual energies of the movement were born of particular forms of theological expression."[8] His, therefore, was not a concept created purely in academia but rather one that was developed as a result of the composite influences outlined in chapter 3. King's theological thoughts regarding the nature of community were born of a theological thinking rooted in God, Jesus Christ, and the church. His concept of community was conceived within the context of his specific social circumstances and its relationship to the past. In this regard, many of King's lessons regarding beloved community were gleaned from the real-world classroom called life. For him, beloved community was a concept filtered through the lens of struggle. As King sought to build community, he was altogether aware that efforts to mitigate this social stratification prior to the turn of the century were severely compromised as the exaggerated complexities of a desegregated society were debated and at times bitterly contested. The conception of beloved community, inclusive of former slaves and slave owners, was both feared and resented by segregationists, establishing an immeasurable gulf between the two communities, which were separated by clearly defined boundaries and rules of engagement. As King, therefore, considered the meaning of community, he did so fully aware of those who could scarcely imagine an existence beyond the uneven realities of slavery and a society severely segregated by stagnant race relations. Burrow writes:

> What King learned about human dignity, the need for self-love, cooperative endeavor, and the beloved community he learned from the Bible, from behavior modeled by his parents and grandparents, and from what he knew of the black struggle and contributions of black foreparents since the time of slavery. These things were not

learned primarily through reading philosophy and theology books, and listening to highly refined lectures. They were etched into King's bones while he was struggling in the hot cauldron of racial oppression.[9]

King, of course, did not follow the lead offered by all of his black forepar-ents since the time of slavery. His position on nonviolence would not allow him to attempt the liberation tactics of a Nat Turner, the conforming tendencies of a Booker T. Washington, or the Pan-Africanism of Marcus Garvey. In the final analysis King was not interested in replicating Turner's methodology for the attainment of freedom, Washington's compromise, or Garvey's disengage-ment. None of these positions would have been fully compatible with King's beloved community conception. While King understood the circumstances and conditions that may have warranted their respective responses to slavery and racial suppression, he saw himself as being able to model a new activist para-digm. His was an activism that called for the radical reorienting of community, the establishment of beloved community. Charles Henry explains:

> Beyond their attempts to develop black respect, Garvey and King share another fundamental project. Both attempt to construct a civil religion. . . . The historic difference, however, is that Garvey's civil religion has as a goal the unification of the black race while King's is directed toward a reconciliation of white and black Americans and eventually the human race. Garvey's goal does not preclude the use of violence, or at least self-defense, while King is unalterably opposed to violence.[10]

Violence was seen by King as the antithesis to community. Hence, vio-lence was deemed unacceptable for him because the means and objectives of the movement had to reflect the desired end. Since beloved community was seen as that end, the process required an approach that remained conducive to the creation and long-term goals of such a community. A violent response to violence could not satisfy the call to authentic community building. Similarly, complacency to and complicity with systems that encouraged the polarization and alienation of certain populations within the human family were in need of careful critique. Community could not flourish under social conditions that oppressed and legally separated human beings from one another on the basis of race.

Toward the close of the nineteenth century, attempts toward Reconstruction were stifled and stalled by a kind of social accommodationism that endorsed the compatibility of a "separate but equal" society, most notably illustrated by

Booker T. Washington's (1856–1915) analogy of the "hand and its fingers" in his Atlanta Exposition Address of 1895. "In all things that are purely social," said Washington, "we can be as separate as the fingers, yet one as the hand in all things essential to mutual progress."[11] Though fundamentally aware of the interrelatedness of national social life and the degree to which black impoverishment impoverished the nation, Washington yet conceded to separatist ideology while maintaining a long view toward racial assimilation following the educational development of those emancipated after the Civil War. One year after Washington's concession with segregation, the U.S. Supreme Court provided the corresponding judicial sanction with its 1896 decision in the *Plessy v. Ferguson* case. Segregation was viewed as an acceptable interim social arrangement, providing the oppressed were extended comparable opportunities for social advancement, a reality rarely experienced. Notwithstanding the obvious differences in era and social climate, Washington adapted to living terms in a manner that King would have considered altogether troubling nearly a half century later. King considered the system of segregation appalling for at least two reasons. First, it created a social arrangement that allowed for the neglect and exploitation of African Americans and other minorities who remained "out of sight and out of mind." To restrict access to educational and economic opportunities was to assure the perpetuation of social disadvantage and the availability of a domestic underclass that would service the whims of an expanding nation. Segregation fostered and facilitated a climate of fear, mistrust, and miseducation. This system of racial separation spawned social conditions that could give rise to the creation of myths and the kind of social stereotyping that justified concepts of inferiority and superiority. The racial categorizations, in part, attempted to offer a calculated way of explaining the way things were, and moreover, why things shouldn't change. But more than that, segregation was viewed by King as the practice of a social system that defied God's intent for human relations.

In stark contrast to that Washingtonian affirmation, King viewed Jim Crow and the segregationist's ideology of social separatism as symptomatic of humanity's alienation from God, others, and self. For King, this separatist ideology was considered theologically untenable and was interpreted as a manifest expression of sin as estrangement. As in the case of Paul Tillich's and Reinhold Niebuhr's explication of sin, salvation was not simply a matter of individual redemption and personal piety; it was a reflection of ruptured relationship. Considered at a more fundamental level, it vividly reflected the cause and effects of human disaffection in the instance of both personal and group relations. At bottom, segregation was considered intolerable because it threatened relationship, and in this sense, to threaten relationship was to deny the laws by which the moral universe was created and governed.[12] If Thurgood Marshall of the National Association for the Advancement of Colored People challenged the illegality of Jim Crow by emphasizing the negative psychological impact that segregation had on the oppressed community, King provided a theological analysis of the system's harmful impact and offered "beloved community" as an antidote to this increasingly dysfunctional global condition. Within this theological framework that viewed sin as a ruptured relationship along both the horizontal and the vertical plane, it was altogether conceivable for God to both will and participate in the creation of a beloved community. Therefore, for individuals created in the image of God, there was a sense that the complexities of civil rights struggle could, in fact, graduate into the creating of a reconciled nation and world as humanity exercised its innate ability to cooperate with God's projected intention for human society. If America possessed the moral will to abolish Jim Crow and advance monumental civil rights legislation, surely, King thought, it could continue its progressive move toward justice and ever fuller realizations of beloved community.

Unlike some of the more accommodating voices of the preceding century, King the theologian viewed his hope for community through an image of God construct that was less tolerant of the status quo. Instead of simply offering an analytical description of how to adapt to what was, King imagined and spoke of what society could look like and how it could behave. Despite the incongruity created by the lingering effects of Jim Crow's separate and *unequal*, King envisioned the transition from E. Franklin Frazier's "nation within a nation" existence to one that could be merged into an integrated whole, the creation of a diverse "community of the beloved." In the final analysis, King's urge for community was guided by a belief that God desired community and that he and others of like mind were merely cooperating in the work of God. If the existing human suffering that was created by intentional acts of injustice represented the "isness" of human life, the civil rights movement represented an equitable invitation toward the "oughtness" discovered within the range of life's human possibility and God's participation. In this sense, his appeal for civil rights was not considered a mere complaint on behalf of a disenfranchised minority; rather, it was set forth as an invitation to experience the "oughtness" in life, as prescribed by divine intent. Marsh correctly asserts, "In King's hands, the idea of beloved community was invigorated with theological vitality and moral urgency, so that prospects of social progress came to look less like an evolutionary development and more like divine gift."[13] As he envisioned the future, King projected the prospective development of a global community that moved beyond the isness of senseless suffering while contemplating and working toward the hopes of beloved community. For King, the theological fact of *imago Dei* necessarily led to the eradication of a legalized system of racial segregation, which remained as the most apparent vestige of an institutionalized slave past, and the earnest formation of beloved community as the most hopeful indicator of America's (and the world's, for that matter) promising future.

What made King's theological proposition for community rather profound, therefore, was that he genuinely sought to explicate and envision the prospect of beloved community from the unlovely perspective of those living under the seemingly insuperable burden of imposed second-class citizenship (at best) and a relegated sense of noncitizenship or nonbeing (at worst). Essentially, King affirmed and embraced a view of community despite all the glaring contradictions that stood against him and it. He imagined a juncture in human history that could be characterized by human collaboration and cooperation from within a context he often described by its degrees of conflict and controversy. This was an enormous undertaking, considering the extent to which the historic discourse on race and its attending phobias had become entrenched and systematically translated into laws and policies that reinforced pro-separatist arguments. Cook explains, "The conclusion that black men have been, for the most part, outside the performance and ethos of the liberal tradition in America—in terms of the premises, norms, and promises of that tradition—is inescapable."[14] The marginalized black mass, while having limited interaction with the American mainstream, rarely participated as social equals. In most instances, the occasional community interactions, particularly those of a domestic nature, served as strange reminders of black folks' ambiguous outsider status, and the stigma associated with their involuntary racial polarization.[15] King's imagined paradigm, therefore, underscored the extent to which he essentially read, wrote, and worked to transform the theory of community into the actuality of beloved community. Remarkably, he does so from within a social context once described by E. Franklin Frazier as the alienated "nation within a nation." In the final analysis, it was his generous account of human nature created in the image of God with the possibility God had given for brotherhood that would ultimately represent the basis for King's qualified optimism in the formation of the beloved community. As such, King imagined an existence toward which individuals could move forward with the hope of experiencing reconciled relations and the eventual creation of beloved community. Within this context of beloved community, individuals could exercise mutual regard because they essentially wanted to and could, not simply because they had to and were thus compelled. While hatred and bigotry were common current realities, those realties were by no means ultimately definitive, nor could they ultimately determine the fate of human destiny. King alluded to this point in his 1961 address to the Fellowship of the Concerned:

> And so the nonviolent resister never lets this idea go, that there is something within human nature that can respond to goodness. So that a Jesus of Nazareth or a Mohandas Gandhi can appeal to human beings and appeal to that element of goodness within them, and a Hitler can appeal to the element of evil within them. But we must never forget that there is something within human nature that can respond to goodness, that man is not totally depraved; to put it in theological terms, the image of God is never totally gone. And so . . . the worst segregationist can become an integrationist.[16]

While familiarizing himself with the antislavery writings of Douglass and others at an early age, King entered the academy drawn to studies that would facilitate the task of discerning and developing a theological rationale for the social gospel he witnessed and deemed morally compelling as a youth. But he did so with a growing understanding that any long-term hope for constructive social transformation would prove futile apart from a clear determination that moral suasion could, in fact, awaken sufficient goodwill and courage to amend and reform the remaining vestiges of the nation's inequitable social condition. Long-term hopes for constructive social change required the implementation of a relevant social gospel that would lead to the development of a sustainable community of the beloved. As chapter 4 indicates, King's studies led to a theological anthropology, much like the fifth-century conceptions developed by John Cassian, and later embraced by Thomas Aquinas, which associated the image of God with humanity's capacity to reason. It was that attribute within human nature that provided human beings with the ability to distinguish between, and the free will to choose, that which was either good or evil. Leaders could choose to establish despotic regimes, or as in the case of Jesus could be compelled to participate in and experience a community in which persons exercise their capacity to love others as self. Hence, King concluded that human nature was neither wholly depraved nor wholly innocent but, rather, that it possessed the faculty for both. Jesus could appeal to the element of goodness within humanity's nature while Hitler could appeal to an element of evil. Inasmuch as either behavior was thought to be determined largely by external influences and circumstances, King was of the mind that moral suasion and nonviolent direct action could eventually result in the constructive transformation of an individual and the eventual integration of society. At bottom, "image of God" as a theological construct for the envisioning of community provided King with an inclusive, comprehensive social framework from which the efforts of God and humanity could result in a social condition characterized by society's move toward increased mutual regard.

If, however, King had come to understand anything during the brief course of his years, it was that society certainly did not represent "perfected place." Guided in part by Niebuhr's Christian realism and Barth's neo-orthodoxy, not to mention his own personal encounters with the social struggle, King avoided the error of engaging the idea of community creation under misconceived utopian illusions. King shunned notions that led to one-sided, overtly optimistic conclusions regarding the human tendency. For him, community represented a place that was in perpetual process—creating and reacting to the prevailing sociopolitical conditions, never static, always capable of experiencing either greater degrees of brutality or increased suggestions of the beloved. Short of beloved community, in its truest sense, King acknowledged that a semblance of just or desegregated community was indeed achievable via the route of judicial and legislative means. Notwithstanding humanity's capacity for evil and brutality, his high hope for the exercise of an equitable pluralistic society within the context of a liberal democracy was notable. If, in fact, all men were created equal and were endowed with certain inalienable rights by their Creator, the realization of these rights, despite humanity's propensity toward evil, remained a high probability. In this sense, the acknowledgment of life's duality deeply influenced King's methodology. His was a wide view that acknowledged the semblance of just community merely as an initial stage in the social progression. For King, adherence to legal mandates did not necessarily equate to what it meant to experience beloved community. Justice could assure that persons would be protected under the law, adequately housed, educated, and employed, but it could not assure that persons move beyond their distrust and disdain for one another. While the achievement of justice was notable and necessary, it was not community's final commentary. Beyond the achievement of justice, King remained committed to the realization of beloved community as the logical next step. In the view of many, the nuclear arms race had chartered a course for global chaos; it was this hope of community that would ultimately guide humanity from a climate of societal disharmony to one of societal cooperation. This view of God's intent for creation and its specific relationship to the formation of a human community was generally embraced by the black church by the early to mid–twentieth century and followed some of the more holistic concepts adhered to by preachers from previous centuries. For them, the creation narrative prescribed the degree to which human beings could experience liberation from bondage and oppression. James Cone writes:

> According to black preachers, Christianity is a gospel of justice and love. Believers, therefore, must treat all people justly and lovingly—that is, as brothers and sisters. Why? Because God, the Creator of all, is no respecter of persons. Out of one blood, God has created all people. On the cross Jesus Christ died for all—whites and blacks alike. Our oneness in creation and redemption means that no Christian can condone slavery or segregation in the churches or the society. The integration of whites and blacks into one community, therefore, is the only option open for Christians.[17]

Cone's rather generalized assessment of where preachers biblically positioned themselves was clearly affirmed by King, who agreed that "no Christian can condone slavery or segregation in the churches or the society" primarily because of the social arrangement's inconsistent witness with God's good intent for humanity, and its devastating effects on societies at large. Cone is also correct in assuming that few dissenters were to be found among the pew or pulpit of the black church to that which they deemed the "only option open for *Christians*." Considerable discussion, however, ensued along the lines of two directly related inquiries, particularly during the era of the modern civil rights movement: Who does the beloved community represent, and how shall the reality of beloved community be brought about? King held to a concept of beloved community that was distinct from—though inclusive of—the church, one that was in need of reflecting the *universality* of humanity because of life's undeniable intricacies and interdependencies. While he was unapologetically Christian in his worldview, it is of interest to note the extent to which King's theological position on beloved community follows and yet moves beyond conceptions of the traditional church. This broad-based analysis gave answer to the "whom" of beloved community. As King conceptualized community, he was certainly cognizant of the church's obligation to model genuine *koinonia* on a global stage, but his response to the question of "whom," while including the church, necessarily reached beyond. This stood in contrast with the church. Although much of the black church typically agreed on a standard of what was considered socially, ethically, and theologically correct within the context of church, there was little or no expectation that those who lived their lives beyond the "arc of safety" would or could willingly comply to Christianity's code of conduct. This growing skepticism with regard to civil rights advocacy was undoubtedly sustained and reinforced by the white church's continued resistance to blurring racial distinctions in secular and/or sacred space. Instead, the white church, with the exception of a sympathetic minority, unapologetically broached its biblically based anti-integrationist arguments in defiance of the movement's reconciliatory attempts. Lewis Baldwin explains:

> This was particularly true of the South, where most of the King-led civil rights campaigns occurred and where many white Christians viewed segregation as a Godly ordained social order. When King went to St. Augustine, Florida, in 1964 to lead a major crusade "against segregation in public accommodations facilities" he and his followers were met with white mob violence of unspeakable proportions, and with a city mayor and Biblical fundamentalist who tolerated such lawlessness while insisting that "God segregated the races when he made the skins a different color."[18]

Given this level of bitter opposition within the twentieth-century church, could non-Christians realistically be held to the same high standard of social accountability as those who claimed conversion and yet resisted the broadening of Christian community? That is to say, if persons who professed to have known and experienced the love of God behaved in this manner, how would those who were believed to be unregenerate assist in the creation of beloved community? Could persons who existed beyond the context of this "ordained social order" known as the church bring order to society? And if not, as typically espoused by the reformationist claim, how could non-Christians be expected to benevolently participate in the formation of genuine community? While in general agreement with the idea of a faith-based fellowship, a number of popular views that countered that of King's suggested that the idea of community at best was, in fact, restricted to a Christian communion of saints. Two decades prior to King's civil involvement, Roger Lloyd maintained his belief in a strict account of beloved community as church. "Communities," he said, "must become a part of the true church, within which sacred and secular cease to be terms having meaning . . . the church is the beloved community."[19] Contrary to Royce and others of like mind, the church was considered by many to be the only community of the beloved to speak of. In keeping with this distinguishing of sacred and secular, it was thought that civic groups should engage the social and political affairs of those *outside* of the church, with the view that God would ultimately eradicate the current social arrangement upon the establishment of a new heaven and earth. "Under no circumstances can it be in this world, because this world comes to its destined dissolution and end," writes Lloyd.[20] Essentially, the thought of social disengagement was attached to this view of a declining social order over which God had already decreed judgment. To renovate, refurbish, and restore this world and its kingdoms would be to interfere with God's business. The church's spiritual duty, therefore, was primarily to *pray* for the stir of revival and reconciliation, and to subsequently "wait on the Lord" for the miraculous transformation.[21] Any additional direct-action efforts assumed by the church toward social and/or civil transformation represented a radical and, in some sense, heretical departure from the faith and its precepts. As Baldwin notes:

> King's "consistent adversary" and greatest nemesis among the clergy
> in Chicago was Joseph Jackson, who maintained that the proper role
> of the church and its leaders involves spreading God's word to the
> flock, saving souls for Jesus, and effecting change through exemplary
> conduct. . . . Moreover, the National Baptist president dismissed King's
> nonviolent direct action campaigns as premeditated actions designed
> to cause "civil disruption" and charged that King's challenge to local
> laws and court authority "was not far removed from open crime."[22]

This certainly seemed to be the church's general consensus upon King's arrival in Montgomery in 1954. Observing that the "two communities moved, as it were, along separate channels,"[23] King commented on the ministers' unresponsiveness to the disturbing social condition, explaining that it "stemmed from a sincere feeling that ministers were not supposed to get mixed up in such earthly, temporal matters as social and economic improvement; they were to preach the gospel and keep men's minds centered on the heavenly."[24] Matters of the "social kind" were best delegated to civic groups and organizations specifically developed and funded, following the close of the nineteenth century, to provide the ongoing legal support so often required by an indifferent judicial process that increasingly seemed altogether evasive. James Cone explains, "The organized fight for justice was transferred from the churches to secular groups, commonly known as civil rights organizations, especially the NAACP, the National Urban League, and CORE. Each came into existence for the sole purpose of achieving full citizenship rights for African Americans in every aspect of American society."[25] Although at given intervals within the life of the early black church there were noted periods of resistance, protest, and organization, some would suggest that that was not normative for the life of the church, particularly as it approached the mid–twentieth century. Beyond the push that came with Reconstruction hopes, there appeared to be what King often referred to as a "cooling-off period." As in every period, there were those congregations, pastors, and individuals who were noted for their activism, who voiced their prophetic discontent over the social injustices of their day. In this sense, there have always been those persons who may have

held membership with a church and yet engaged the community as an activist independent of direct congregational association. Overall, however, it was
expected that the church would not interfere with the work and mission of
civic organizations specifically birthed to give voice to their sociopolitical concerns. Many did not. While remaining sympathetic to the movement, and at
times offering indirect support to the work of local civic groups by housing
meetings or financing organizations, the church and its leadership generally
understood that the normative posture of the black church in the South was
one that frowned upon the church's involvement in *outside* affairs and insisted
instead that preachers and their congregations remain in their "place." Baldwin further writes:

> Conservative Christians and other defenders of the status quo
> in Montgomery denounced the bus protest as un-Christian and
> accused King of "bringing trouble there where we've always had
> peace." . . . The Reverend E. Stanley Frazier, "one of the most
> outspoken segregationists in the Methodist Church," urged King and
> other black preachers to "bring this boycott to a close and lead their
> people instead to a glorious experience of the Christian faith." . . .
> Throughout his 13-year career as a civil rights leader, King found
> himself in conflict with Christian conservatives, white and black, who
> did not share his understanding of the Bible and the faith, particularly
> around the question of the essential character of Christian witness.[26]

Notwithstanding the conservative-led opposition to racial desegregation,
King understood that the church, at least in part, based its laissez-faire views
upon long-held traditions, its perceived relationship to society in general, and
a narrow interpretation of Pauline regard for governmental affairs in particular. The church, generally speaking, was expected to assume a supportive role
of government, to pray for its officials, and to sustain societies that allow for
its existence. The primary mission of the church was considered spiritual,
the evangelization of lost souls. As assumed by Lloyd, the church's sole purpose for being in the world was to reconcile humanity to God through the
redemptive work of Jesus Christ, thereby creating space for a uniquely Christian fellowship "in but not of the world." In this regard, the church defined
what it meant to exist in authentic community; any discussion of community beyond that context was considered a gross misrepresentation of biblical truth. As Lloyd indicated, "Christianity in particular and the spirit of the
beloved community in general are therefore untrue to themselves in so far as
they fix their final aim upon the things that are capable of being realized in
the world, however distant they may be."[27] King, however, envisioned a kind

of society that embraced, appreciated, and even celebrated diversity of ideas and tradition while maintaining genuine respect and regard for the other as equal, a society that in fact could give evidence to even greater degrees of civil community in this world. In some respects church dogma, with its emphasis on the predestination of the *chosen few*, may have presented ideological barriers that were antithetical to the broad-based community that King envisioned and sought to achieve. Within this school of doctrinal thought, an individual was either saved or unsaved, wheat or tare, sheep or wolf, included or excluded. In any event, the latter was always viewed as the outside *other than*. In this position's most antagonistic form, marginalized non-Christians could conveniently be viewed as the potential adversarial other, the dreaded foe instead of members of the one dedicated faith family. These theological convictions were widely embraced during the years of King's civil rights campaign and reflected a reformed tradition that historically dichotomized, as Baldwin explains, the essential roles and relationships of church and society:

> Questions concerning the proper relationship of the Christian to the
> state permeate the entire history of the church. . . . Martin Luther
> King, Jr., was keenly aware of how the issues of church-state relations
> had unfolded in intellectual and practical terms, up to his time,
> and his knowledge of that history informed his sense of his own
> responsibility as a Christian in the American society.[28]

Despite these pressures to concede to the theological provincialism of his day, King held to a more generous description of community in response to the inquiry regarding who should be included. For King the answer was simple: "everybody." While everybody might not have been equally lovable, everybody was equally deserving of one's love, not simply as a result of what they do or have but as a result of who they are. All human beings were creatures created in the image of God. As his anthropological conception of humanity readily suggests in chapter 4, King included all. If the traditional idea of Christian community found sanction in the commonality of fellowship in Christ, the Eucharist, and the *mystical union* of the church via the Holy Spirit, King intentionally broadened his community conception by emphasizing the commonality discovered in the reality of *imago Dei* and its unique implications for the formation of the beloved community, resistance and reconciliation. For King, beloved community was not to be strictly equated with the church but was inclusive of the whole world as the object of God's love. Ultimately, his concept of beloved community included those within and without the context of church proper. It could, therefore, be said that King's distinctive view of the beloved community was undoubtedly inclusive of, but not limited to, the church. While he remained committed to the idea that the church provided the clearest revelation[29] of God's intent for humanity, and that it could therefore be best suited to model this kind of social cohesion for the nation, his anthropological outlook and certainly his awareness of the white church's ambivalent, and oftentimes complicit, history, suggested the need for an alternate vision. Hence, King's theological anthropology suggested that the boundaries that defined beloved community could be located beyond context defined as church. Ivory explains:

> King identified the church as the most segregated major institution in American society. It harbored a chasmic internal division in its soul that simply had to be closed. This moral schizophrenia caused the church to lag woefully far behind the Supreme Court, trade unions, factories, schools, department stores, athletic gatherings, and virtually every other social organization in terms of integrating its own body.[30]

While never abandoning hope in the replication of the socially active church that he had experienced as a child and later helped foster in Montgomery during the 381-day bus boycott, King refused to relate to the nonchurched as exempted, nonparticipating others. He believed instead that the church would rediscover its prophetic ministry as it moved beyond its stained glass walls and allowed its authentic orthodoxy to be translated into an authentic orthopraxis. At that point, it could be said that faith and works had genuinely merged. Beyond a strict ecclesiological account of an exclusive faith community, as in the case of Lloyd, King envisioned vast potential for inclusive human fellowship in its broadest theological sense, one that obviously transcended race and religion in fulfillment of humanity's inherent desire to relate to others as like individuals, created in the image of God. In a very real sense, the line of demarcation between created relatedness and being created in the image of God was blurred by the fact that the former was so intricately linked to the latter in King's thought. "However varied the interpretations are," King explained, "it is probably commonly agreed by all Christians that God's final purpose is the building of a regenerated human society which will include *all mankind* in a common fellowship of well-ordered living."[31] To understand human nature as having been created in the image of God was fundamental to his appeal for civil rights, but moreover it provided humanity with the requisite capacity to progressively experience "a common fellowship of well-ordered living" as a historic reality, irrespective of creed, class, or culture. For King, the human family, in its entirety, could choose to fulfill the requisite for full-fledged participation in the beloved community by virtue of their inherent solidarity and universal urge to be in relationship, despite the haunting histories that would suggest otherwise.[32] Howard Thurman, a renowned theologian/lecturer at Morehouse, Howard University, and Boston University, though far less direct in his use of image of God language, moved along the liberal edge of this Judeo-Christian doctrine as a means of describing his similarly broadened understanding of human community and its several implications for social equity. Although the phrase "image of God" finds only occasional use in Thurman's writings, much of the meaning inherent in this traditional doctrine of the church was implied throughout his numerous descriptions of human existence, with an emphasis always upon humanity's profound relatedness. Thurman captured the essence of King's hope for beloved community, particularly during the years following his receipt of the Nobel Peace Prize in 1964:

> There is a spirit abroad in life of which the Judeo-Christian ethic is but one expression. It is a spirit that makes for wholeness and for community; it finds its way into the quiet solitude of a Supreme Court justice when he ponders the constitutionality of an act of Congress which guarantees civil rights to all citizens; . . . it kindles the fires of unity in the heart of Jewish Rabbi, Catholic Priest and Protestant Minister as they join arms together, giving witness to their God on behalf of a brotherhood that transcends creed, race, sex and religion. . . . It is the voice of God and the voice of man; it is the meaning of all strivings of the whole human race toward a world of friendly men underneath a friendly sky.[33]

Although the mystic language of human transcendence is not quite as evident in King's writings, he clearly understood image of God in terms of its metaphysical implications so that the essence of that which made for universal human commonality principally became a function of that non-material human quality.[34] With an image of God emphasis similar to that of Thurman's, King reasoned that humanity possessed the capacity to desire and direct its will toward community. Despite all that potentially divided the human family, Thurman's image of God concept reflected a theological truth that also spoke of this essential common thread. As such, the image of God represented the datum, the starting point, the point of departure, if you will, in one's search for common ground, inasmuch as it reflected that which was most universally kindred to all. For Thurman, as in the case of King, the image of God was viewed as that nexus in humanity that was irreducible, existent beyond creed and culture, and that pointed to a common human origin while commencing social possibilities existent beyond all of the superficial barriers often assigned to human socialization, such as status, nationality, religion, and race. All human distinctions necessarily collapsed at the level of *imago Dei*; this was the level at which community commenced. King's great and unyielding hope was that the church, with its truths of redemption, liberation, and reconciliation, would eventually lead in the struggle against injustice, and, moreover, in the modeling of true community wherein is "neither Greek nor Jew, male nor female, bond nor free." Hence, King's basis for beloved community and the provision of an equitable social existence were discernible within this framework of what it meant to be in mutual possession of the *imago Dei*, which ideally bound all persons inseparably together at humanity's deepest level. King writes, "Whenever this is recognized, 'whiteness' and 'blackness' pass away, as determinants in a relationship and 'son' and 'brother' are substituted."[35] As such, King's anthropology was a theology of community, a community in which all persons were made in the image of God, and, more important, all persons were created to be in relationship. In this regard, beloved community represented the logical progression of King's theological anthropology.

While careful to never reduce human existence to some vague, abstracted, metaphysical universalism, to the neglect of real physical, cultural, and theological distinctions, King understood image of God as basic to his understanding of *human*. At bottom, King was a third-generation Baptist minister, with particular theological convictions that unapologetically viewed the church as having the capacity to offer the clearest revelation of God to humanity. While never abandoning this hope for the church, King understood that God's love for the world did not discourage the idea of beloved community amid rich cultural and ideological diversity. With his keen awareness of humanity's interconnectedness, King explicated the church's doctrine of *imago Dei* to underscore how persons of goodwill from "every kindred and every tongue" might genuinely experience God's intent for human(e) being. More than some philosophic or natural formulation of humans as reasonable beings, King held to a belief in a single human family made in the image of God. This commonality, which had its ground in humanity's relationship with God, as creator and sustainer, ultimately became the foundation for harmonious societal interaction. Hence, the implications of this less philosophical and more pragmatic approach to beloved community were understandably reflected in King's critique of the nation's inconsistent alignment with its constitutional ideals and less than broad-minded bestowal of society's God-granted rights. As King, therefore, pondered the meaning of beloved community and its scope, he was not simply interested in the independence and well-being of a specific population, as perhaps in the case of Oliver

Cromwell and those colonists inclined toward the idea of eschatological sectarian Protestantism. Rather, King was genuinely concerned about the liberation and freedom of the social order in its entirety. In this sense, the civil rights movement was not simply a black movement; it was a movement that celebrated the human interconnectedness between individuals from every ethnic background; it was a move toward community's fuller meaning. Enoch Oglesby directs our attention to this aspect of King's theological view when he explains:

> In the black man's struggle for racial justice in American society,
> Dr. King held the conviction that ultimately our loyalties must
> transcend the narrow confines of race, class, and nation. In striking
> a universal note, he suggested that men of conscience must be
> concerned about developing a "world perspective" in the cause of
> freedom, justice and love—the genuine hallmarks of the beloved
> community.[36]

If the aforementioned analysis describes King's broadened sense of where the beloved community's boundaries were located, and "whom" he considered the beloved community to be, the following addresses his response to concerns about the actual logistics that were connected to the idea of community formation. "Since you cannot find the universal and beloved community," Royce had said, "create it."[37] The perennial question, of course, was how. Once assured that community is indeed a "good" worthy of global pursuit, how does one, in fact, go about the task of effectively pursuing and creating it? How do members of a pluralist society and/or a world, for that matter, progressively assume responsibility for one another as children of God in a manner conducive to a universally shared conception of beloved community? Having determined that humanity created in the image of God remains inherently capable of such coexistence, King then was in need of giving thought to how this kind of community could be created and sustained. King understood that the creation of a community of the beloved involved much more than mere assent to human capacity and one's aspiration to integrate. It was one thing to imagine beloved community and another altogether to attempt its implementation. Humanity had been imagining, theorizing, and describing the ideal society from the early days of ancient philosophy, and while that looked good on paper and possessed the ring of truth in the classroom, how did one go about translating that theory of community into actuality? This was King's great challenge. King's attempt to move from mental assent to methodology further reflected the complexity of his theological anthropology. King's move toward beloved community, therefore, was in need of being carefully embarked in full view of humanity's finitude and freedom so as not to succumb to the unbridled optimism of his pacifist predecessors or to the overstated pessimism espoused by fundamentalists. For him, a society governed by principles of reconciliation and equality required some form of legal measure that would realistically match methodology with mission. Having reconciled himself to the realism of sin and evil, King clearly understood that any community conception with promised longevity could not be naively framed; it would require faith and fortitude, capacity and commitment, desire and unusual dedication. Burrow makes note of this in his observation of King:

> King believed that there was no lack of human and other resources
> to solve the problems being created to undermine the human dignity
> of blacks. What was lacking, he believed, was the will to make the
> effort to eliminate this problem. . . . If one has the will to do the right
> thing, one can usually find a way to do it. But it requires effort. King
> himself held firm to the conviction that human progress never rolls
> in on the wheels of inevitability.[38]

Consistent with this theological anthropology, King developed a civil rights methodology that took account of society "as is" in expectation of what society "could be." The distinction was an important one inasmuch as it underscored his awareness of the need to address humanity's dual capacity for good and evil. He does so with an assurance that the implementation of just and civil laws, as a first step in the direction of beloved community, would ultimately serve as the catalyst for society's willing adherence to the principles of inclusivity and reconciled community as growing social realities. If the bestowal of rights were considered God-granted, the protection and equitable perpetuation of human and civil rights could ultimately become a function of free-willed human cooperation. "True integration," said King, "will be achieved by true neighbors who are willingly obedient to unenforceable obligation."[39] Insofar as King was concerned, the nation and world did not lack the resources needed to correct the "problems created to undermine blacks" and other members of disenfranchised communities. God had graciously provided sufficient resources to supply every member of the human family with the basic life necessities. The challenge, therefore, was not one of depleted material resources but one of depleted human will. If society simply willed to overcome its injustices against others, it could discover the resources to do so. King, however, also realized that justice could not wait for that adjustment in societal goodwill and considered methodologies that would facilitate progress in that direction. While acknowledging the shortcomings of civil process and judicial coercion, King nevertheless understood the sociopolitical process as essential to the creation of beloved community.

As King explained, "Desegregation is the necessary step in the right direction, if we are to achieve integration."[40] This necessary step, as King understood it, was initiated through legal recourse and directed by the courts, with desegregation as its desired outcome. The subsequent transformation of the social landscape would be inspired by love (agape) and directed by the Creator with integration as its final goal (although in the final analysis King would, of course, view both as the result of God's loving intervention). King writes:

> Court orders and federal enforcement agencies are of inestimable value in achieving desegregation, but desegregation is only a partial, though necessary step toward the final goal which we seek to realize—genuine intergroup and interpersonal living. Desegregation will break down the legal barriers and bring men together physically, but something must touch the hearts and souls of men so that they will come together spiritually because it is natural and right. . . . Those dark and demonic responses will be removed only as men are possessed by the invisible, inner law which etches on their hearts the conviction that all men are brothers and that love is mankind's most potent weapon for personal and social transformation.[41]

Additionally, if King understood that legislation was a necessary step, he also understood that it was not the only step. If the instituting of legislation and laws provided the legal grounds for society's gradual desegregation, which was required as a result of humanity's *finitude*, the image of God guided by the influence of agape could result in the social integration and the formation of beloved community. As Niebuhr explained, "The fence and the boundary line are the symbols of the spirit of justice. They set the limits upon each man's interest to prevent one from taking advantage of the other. A harmony achieved through justice is therefore only an approximation of brotherhood. It is the best possible harmony within the conditions created by human egoism."[42] While legislation commenced a process of community, King believed that the remaining barriers were in need of being resolved on the basis of love. As King, therefore, sought to understand the relationship between civil rights and community, he was also compelled to reckon with the awkward though necessary relationships between justice and love, liberation and reconciliation.[43] Garber explains how King understood that relationship between liberation and the creation of community when he writes, "King was arguing that liberation and reconciliation are, in fact, bound up together, and that you cannot have one without the other. Liberation is never, in King's view, only from oppression; it is for community."[44] As such, beloved community represented the goal toward which all appeals for civil rights were consistently directed and upon which they were hinged. King carefully balanced his desire for a society minus segregation and injustice with his hopes for beloved community by attempting to implement methodologies that were relevant to the circumstances. Ultimately, the creation of an integrated beloved community was not a matter of dependence upon an either-or scenario; it would clearly require the collaborative efforts of both legislation and love. In his view, legislative intervention provided an initial legal basis for interracial socialization, while love consequently appealed to humanity's capacity for transcendence with hopes of engendering a pervasive long-term spirit of genuine mutual regard. In this sense, the government and faith community were ideally seen as compatible, though functionally distinct, allies in the creation of a community of the beloved. Niebuhr writes:

> The harmony of communities is not simply attained by the authority of law. *Nomos* does not coerce the vitalities of life into order. The social harmony of living communities is achieved by an interaction between the normative conceptions of morality and law and the existing and developing forces and vitalities of the community. Usually the norms of law are compromises between the rational-moral ideals of what ought to be, and possibilities of the situation as determined by given equilibria of forces.[45]

In no small way King's vision of the beloved community underscored the significant link between law and the furtherance of social harmony, and as such clearly positioned beloved community as the movement's projected end. In the final analysis, the attainment of laws that made for civil rights, while a necessary precondition for true community, was viewed as a proximate objective, not as an ultimate goal—a means and not an end unto itself. King explains: "It is true that as we struggle for freedom in America, we will have to boycott at times. But we must remember . . . that a boycott is not an end unto itself. . . . But the end is reconciliation; the end is redemption, the end is the creation of the beloved community."[46] With a conception informed by a number of intersecting disciplines, including psychology and science, King extended the theological idea of *imago Dei* employed by eighteenth- and nineteenth-century activists by projecting society beyond the short-term attainment of social justice. More than the realization of justice for its own sake, a community of the beloved was contemplated as the quintessential expression of humanity's capacity for love and goodwill. While King clearly recalled the "image of God" tradition in a manner similar to his activist predecessors, his desire to broaden the appeal to include opponents of the movement required that he view the "image of God" in terms of its reconciliatory capacity. His position was assumed as a result of the theological distinctiveness he brought to his understanding of *imago Dei* and the distinctive manner in which he applied the concept to the issue of civil affairs. Whereas abolitionists may have sought freedom and justice as an end unto itself, King sought reconciliation and beloved community as fuller expressions of a way of "being" beyond justice. Justice, while serving as a necessary first step, could not be the overarching goal. The introduction of social integration into the civil rights equation necessitated that the final goal be something other than justice. While authentic community could not exist apart from the exercise of just relations, King distinguished himself by subordinating his prophetic request for liberation and justice to the idea of community, thereby establishing community as his priority.

Much more than a nicety, beloved community represented life's most urgent and vital necessity. For King, community pointed to the interrelatedness of all human life, not to mention humanity's relatedness to the rest of creation. Human destiny was interrelated and inextricably bound such that the demise of some, in one respect or another, diminished all, and to injure any aspect of the other was to do injury to oneself. "All humanity," King commented, "is involved in a single process, and all men are brothers. To the degree that I harm my brother, no matter what he is doing to me, to that extent I am harming myself."[47] Insofar as King was concerned, the granting of rights that were civil was not simply a unilateral consideration for those long deprived of their birthright; the realization of rights as a by-product of beloved community was ultimately viewed as the only multilateral means by which the progression of a society's hopeful future could be ensured. To deny the "least of these" was, in fact, to deny and stall the larger social project, the actualization of a more perfect union. For King, the union could not be perfected simply for the sake of the privileged few. More than an economic imbalance, the glaring gap between rich and poor was suggestive of a spiritual deficiency. King would often allude to the fact that economic strength could not translate into moral and spiritual strength. In this respect, beloved community became an absolute requirement, not simply for the benefit of those whose lives would improve materially but for the sake and benefit of society as a whole. More than pure economics or sociology could comprehend, the soul of the nation and the very survival of the world were at stake. As an alternative to hate, oppression, unjust wars, the imbalanced consumption of global resources, and the growing threat of human annihilation, King prophetically forewarned that the global community "must learn how to live together as brothers, or perish like fools."[48] For King, a society that neglected the poor and exploited the powerless was ultimately a society on the decline. No individual, nation, or empire could indefinitely sustain its growth and expansion while failing to acknowledge and empower the least among them. In this sense beloved community served to ensure the healthy and harmonious future of a given society. King further explains the unavoidable fact of human interrelatedness:

> The real reason that we must use our resources to outlaw poverty goes beyond material concerns to the quality of our mind and spirit. Deeply woven into the fiber of our religious tradition is the conviction that men are made in the image of God, and that they are souls of infinite metaphysical value. If we accept this as a profound moral fact, we cannot be content to see men hungry, to see men victimized with ill-health when we have the means to help them. In the final analysis, the rich must not ignore the poor because both rich and poor are tied together.[49]

For King, this notion of human interrelatedness represented the critical underlying imperative for nurturing and fostering a community wherein "the fears of insecurity and the doubts clouding our future will be transformed into radiant confidence, into glowing excitement to reach creative goals, and into an abiding moral balance where the brotherhood of man will be undergirded by a secure and expanding prosperity for all."[50] Beloved community needed to become more of a reality while poverty became increasingly intolerable, because as he understood it, "the rich and the poor were tied together." Far greater than any social tie could suggest, humanity was joined by their mutual existence as creatures made in the image of God and their common destiny. The nation and world, as King saw it, would essentially rise and fall together. As such, he believed that persons, societies, and nations with means to assist others should never be content to witness those who are hungry, victimized, or suffering from ill health due to lack of human resources. Such human suffering should be inexcusable considering humanity's interconnectedness. Ultimately, the claims of just community, and even beloved community, were forged by this sense of spiritual relatedness and *common* interest. As such, the U.S. Supreme Court's decision in *Brown v. Board of Education* (1954) and the gradual abolishment of Jim Crow with the passage of the Civil Rights Act of 1964 and Voting Rights Act of 1965 were considered mutually beneficial legal achievements, inasmuch as the nation and its citizens both gained some greater semblance of human dignity from the enactment of these watershed measures. King, therefore, did not consider the civil rights appeal, issued on behalf of the overlooked and neglected, in terms of self-interest but rather as an expression of his profound sense of mutual regard for the other. To deal justly and to authentically extend the socioeconomic bounds of society by correcting the nation's historic ills was to hasten the day of the beloved community's glorious arrival.

King describes the concrete manner in which society would be collectively improved through a fuller realization of civil rights:

> One aspect of the civil rights struggle that receives little attention is the contribution it makes to the whole society. . . . Eventually the civil rights movement will have contributed infinitely more to the nation than the eradication of racial injustice. It will have enlarged the concept of brotherhood to a vision of total interrelatedness. On that day, Canon John Donne's doctrine, "no man is an island," will find its truest application in the United States.[51]

As King, however, would come to understand, this shift in societal civility was always contingent upon overcoming new levels of challenge and new manifestations of evil upon the realization of each new success. Niebuhr writes, "No traditional attainment of brotherhood is secure against criticism from a higher historical perspective or safe from corruption on each new level of achievement."[52] While humanity may stride toward a social place that is kinder, gentler, and more just, humanity also has the capacity to make choices in the interest of self with little or no regard for others. This characteristic of human corruption would continually challenge each new level of the beloved community's growing prospect. As King increasingly realized, this opposing element required continual vigilance and the perseverance of goodwill. It also necessitated the ongoing practice of direct action. As McKanan explains:

> The many scholars influenced by Michel Foucault have proposed a rather different critique of American liberalism. Like the Niebuhrs, Foucault viewed the attempt to purge society of all forms of coercion as essentially unrealistic. Indeed, he believed that each epoch of human history has its own distinctive form of coercion.[53]

Although the Civil Rights Act and the Voting Rights Act created long-awaited legislative milestones, the achievements on "the Hill" rarely trickled down into the valleys in which the masses continued to suffer. Garrow writes, "Martin King came to a deep and very painful realization, a realization he had had inklings of before, but that never had crystallized: those acts of Congress, no matter how comprehensive, really did very little to improve the daily lives of the poor black people across the rural South."[54] This growing realization forced King to deepen his analysis of the relationship between community and corruption as he encountered new dimensions of both white and black backlash. If image of God represented community's chief hope, the relentless resistance to integration represented community's greatest threat. Though King never abandoned his hope for beloved community, the harsh realities of the powerless required that he continue to explore new means and methods to reconcile and adapt his beloved community conception to the multifaceted needs of a shifting civil rights movement.

Walter Fluker is correct when he claims that much of King's formulation of community, particularly during the earlier years of the movement, was in fact theoretical.[55] Short of the model provided by Gandhi's nonviolent campaign and activist mentors such as A. Philip Randolph, King had few, if any, historic models suggesting that his civil rights conception could succeed on the scale that he had envisioned. Although his work in the academy afforded him a theoretical working knowledge of human nature and its capacity, King's intellectual progression was more the by-product of a trial-and-error process than that of the systematic theoretician. While he never forsook the idea of beloved community and the benign transformation of human nature through the efforts of nonviolent direct action and love, a growing awareness of the need to address institutional structures and their relationship to the inequitable powers that govern them developed. Cook points to this important development in King's thought when he writes, "After 1967, King began to see that America was built on the corrupt social values of inequality, and that this corruption made it virtually impossible for the oppressors to be morally persuaded of the injustice of their actions. History has shown that oppressors never voluntarily give up power."[56] This, of course, did not come as much of a surprise to King, who was altogether familiar with Fredrick Douglass's reminder of the oppressor's unwillingness to concede power without struggle. What did surprise King was the extent to which the church was unwilling to participate in the advocacy of the disadvantaged minority, unwilling to facilitate the development of beloved community, and unwilling to embrace the notion of shared power structures. It is most interesting to note that while society discouraged the involvement of the black church in the affairs of politics and economics, it encouraged the white church to reinforce its separatist ideals for the sake of power consolidation. The idea of beloved community threatened the imbalance of the status quo, and even King could not fully anticipate society's response. As such, King embraced a theological worldview that defied the prevailing logic by essentially envisioning an inversion of that which historically represented America's inequitable sociopolitical norm, insofar as its disadvantaged citizens of "Color" were concerned. C. Eric Lincoln explains:

> The institutionalization of perceived differences and interests
> established a racial hegemony which limited all power, all political
> and all human rights to itself. Whatever their separateness in other
> interests, Church and State were co-joined and mutually re-enforcing

in the establishment of a rigidly defined racial order. Since there was no place in either church or state for the meaningful participation of blacks in the perceived destiny of the nation, their alienation from those institutions was, or should have been, predictable by any logic, had logic been in vogue.[57]

In time, this disproportionate access to and exercise of sociopolitical power and its impact upon civil rights and beloved community, respectively, would become King's central focus and the leading cause of his increased concern. Thus King observed, "So often it [the church] is an arch defender of the status quo. Far from being disturbed by the presence of the church, the *power structure* of the average community is consoled by the church's silent—and often even vocal—sanction of things as they are."[58] Instead of providing an alliance that would edge society within closer proximity of beloved community and the more equitable balance of power, the church and state continued to ally in a fashion that seemingly perpetuated the established racial hegemony. Particularly during the final years of his life, King would discover that legislative intervention on behalf of beloved community might not have been as effective an instrument of change as once imagined. Short of actual empowerment, legislation could provide the illusion of progress without assuring the concrete realization of its promise.

7

Beloved Community
and Beyond

In several of my recent conversations about Martin Luther King Jr.,
I have observed, more often than not, that the general perception of
King has been significantly formed, fashioned, and even fixed by a
single moment in time, his August 1963 "I Have a Dream" speech.
As momentous as the March on Washington was, the reality is that
many of the presumptions about who he was, what he thought, and
what he hoped to achieve are often based on that single King caption,
a mere sound bite selectively gleaned from an extremely complex system of thought, much of which was articulated and published prior
to and beyond that historical moment. For many, "I Have a Dream"
has come to represent the "essence of King," notwithstanding that
this very narrow window, though symbolic in and of itself, is far from
exhaustive. A full accounting of King's evolved dream is far more
extensive and for some, perhaps, far more difficult to appreciate and
affirm. While the speech fosters that congenial sense of human solidarity that is often associated with a vision of humanity joined by this
common spirit of altruistic goodwill, King in fact never suggested
a philosophy of "going along, to get along." Prior to concluding his
address with the hopefulness of his dream realized, King provided a
chronicle of the unsettling conditions that precipitated a painful past
and persistent present. In contrasting the social reality of 1863 with
that of 1963, King celebrated that the Emancipation Proclamation was
signed but in the next breath went on to lament the fact that a hundred years later, the Negro still was not free. Thus while his dream

envisioned a future date when racial, social, political, and economic issues would be reconciled and resolved, that vision was imagined against a contrasting current reality that was very much foreign to that noble vision. His concluding thoughts captured the essence of his hope for beloved community, and yet it was clearly a hope that emerged out the context of a less hopeful social reality.

Coretta Scott King said of the March on Washington, "It was as though heaven had come down." If it did, it descended only for a moment. Within weeks of that dreamlike historic gathering, a 10:22 A.M. bombing of Sixteenth Street Baptist Church in Birmingham, Alabama, killing Denise McNair (age 11), Addie Mae Collins (14), Carole Robertson (14), and Cynthia Wesley (14) shattered that tranquil vision of things hoped for. The four girls had been attending Sunday school classes the morning they were murdered by members of the local Klan. As the *Washington Post* reported on September 16, 1963, "Dozens of survivors, their faces dripping blood from the glass that flew out of the church's stained glass windows, staggered around the building in a cloud of white dust raised by the explosion. . . . The bomb apparently went off in an unoccupied basement room and blew down the wall, sending stone and debris flying like shrapnel into a room where children were assembling for closing prayers following Sunday School. Bibles and song books lay shredded and scattered through the church." Within hours Governor George Wallace reinforced the Birmingham police patrols with the deployment of 300 state troopers and 500 National Guardsmen to quell the social unrest created by that senseless tragedy. Although the names of the killers were rumored and reported, the detainees were released and returned to society only to be tried and convicted decades later. Needless to say, the Birmingham bombing sobered King's conception of the American dream and tempered the timetable by which he had hoped for its imminent arrival. Theologically and experientially, King understood the broad range of human behavior and its capacity for both good and evil. If August 1963 provided a glimpse of humanity at its best, September 1963 reminded King, the nation, and the world of human capacity at its worst. While the heinous 1954 murder and mutilation of fourteen-year-old Emmett Till shocked the nation, the death of Birmingham's four innocent girls outraged and headlined the viciousness of an irrational racism. To describe the act as horrific was to understate the sense of loss and disbelief. Although King never dismissed the probability of his dream fulfilled, the idea of Langston Hughes's "Dream Deferred" certainly invited a rethinking of his approach to the civil rights movement and its methodologies. What does beloved community look like in the wake of unbridled ruthlessness and unrestrained acts of irrationality? While that August 1963 image of beloved community undoubtedly represented authentic King thought, the escalation of violence forced him to reconsider and contend with the social perplexities that lingered well beyond that promising moment in American history.

Hence, even though the denial of beloved community never became an option for King, his thoughts regarding its approach and achievement certainly were nuanced. And that is not to say that King did not anticipate resistance and struggle prior to the tragic bombing in Birmingham. Evident in the development of his theological anthropology was the idea that humanity possessed the capacity to plumb the depths of hatred and evil. As such, King was careful not to overidealize or romanticize beloved community by projecting the arrival of some surreal utopia. In fact, King concurred with Frederick Douglass's observation regarding the need for struggle from the early days of the Montgomery bus boycott. The intensity and duration, however, of that modern-day freedom struggle could not be presumed. King, therefore, needed to compensate for both. Having established the need for beloved community as a distinct historical possibility, King moved beyond that image to give additional thought and credence to its coming. This concluding chapter, therefore, considers the ways in which King was required to imagine measures that would have to be taken post–March on Washington to arrive at the promised land of beloved community. For King, the issue was not one of whether or not such a community should materialize; the recurring thought was one of exploring how long it would take for that vision to become a growing national reality given the new levels of violence. How does a society of individuals created in the image of God choose to transition into a kinder, gentler social space? How does the promise of August 1963 expand on the heels of September 1963? The civil rights movement encountered several setbacks, and, therefore, the logistic of dream fulfillment was in need of being adjusted accordingly. Whereas King previously spoke of the human capacity to choose the social good and embrace measures that would lead to greater degrees of just community at the movement's outset, beyond 1963 his outlook began to shift. Beyond the successful March on Washington, his optimistic reliance upon humanity's inherent goodness and moral fortitude was tapered. In *Where Do We Go from Here: Chaos or Community?* (1967), King wrote, "However lamentable it may seem, the Negro is now convinced that white America will never admit him to full rights unless it is forced into doing so."[1] This sentiment is clearly contrasted with the King of earlier years who spoke of humanity's ability to replicate Jesus' capacity to alter human life by simply appealing to their inner goodness. Scholars are therefore correct to note the shift in King's oratory during the final three to five years of his life as the more prophetic overtones of redemption and pending judgment were announced to an unyielding nation. While King never questioned his earlier theological presuppositions, he did recognize the ongoing need to reconcile his optimism with the slow and often stagnant march toward the promised land.

With hopes of beloved community remaining intact, King overcame his reservations by reconciling his dream with the stubborn social realities that created ongoing resistance to the civil rights movement. He realized that the sweeping transformation he had hoped for required a fundamental restructuring of the ways in which underprivileged minority populations were empowered. King would also come to realize that beloved community would require shifts in basic social structures that were far more systemic than even he originally imagined. He witnessed, and came to understand, the function of social systems and the ways in which they facilitated specific social outcomes. In fact, King became increasingly aware of the sociopolitical dynamics that made it possible for pockets of people to be cordial while unjust political, educational, economic, employment, and housing conditions remained virtually unchanged. If King learned anything from his bout with Mayor Daley's political machine in Chicago, it was to be found in his observation of how expeditiously one could mask human exploitation with a facade of human cordiality. Of this relationship and its effect King said, "The plantation and the ghetto were created by those who had power, both to confine those who had no power and to perpetuate their powerlessness. The problem of transforming the ghetto, therefore, is a problem of power—confrontation of forces of power demanding change and the forces of power dedicated to preserving the status quo."[2] Racism was not always blatant and overt; at times it could be subtle and nonconfrontational. Racial segregation was simply another way of systemically structuring and rationalizing the imbalance of power. As Fairclough points out, "More and more, King saw racism as an instrument of class privilege, a means of dividing the working class by giving whites marginal economic advantages and encouraging their psychological pretensions to superiority."[3] Therefore, instead of continuing to emphasize the role of love and the power of moral suasion to inform and influence society, King emerged with a conception of community that also took into account the delicate and often overlooked relationship between social harmony and power. In consideration of this shift King wrote: "Equally fallacious is the notion that ethical appeals and persuasion alone will bring about justice. This does not mean that ethical appeals must not be made. It simply means that those appeals must be undergirded by some form of constructive coercive power."[4]

King came to understand that appeals to one's moral conscience, though necessary, were insufficient in and of themselves. As Otis Turner commented, "King began speaking more and more about the need for power, the power to force change, not to beg for it. Moral persuasion is simply not enough."[5]

Ethical appeals and persuasion alone could not accomplish the goals of the civil rights movement. No matter how logical the arguments were, no matter how noble and decent the goal, King witnessed the degree to which discriminatory practices defied reason. In some instances, it appeared that an appeal for sisterhood and brotherhood on the basis of a human family created in the image of God would not suffice. The systems that perpetuated injustice were so entrenched and pervasive that King came to appreciate more fully the need to employ the use of "constructive power" in the struggle for justice and community. Thus King wrote, "Power, properly understood, is the ability to bring about social, political or economic changes. In this sense power is not only desirable but necessary in order to implement the demands of love and justice."[6] King did not understand love and justice as acting in isolation from one another. Rather, the relationship between the two necessitated the discouragement and disruption of injustice. A dialogue regarding the relationship between love and justice concluded with a realization that change of any real magnitude relied on the constructive use of power. King believed that humanity created in the image of God had the ability to choose to implement the moral demands of love and justice; when these moral choices were denied, however, there was a need to resort to power as the means by which constructive change could be achieved. Although the elements of struggle and opposition were factors from the outset, King could not fully fathom from his perspective in Montgomery the ways in which the entrenched forces of opposition would rally and escalate despite his commitment to nonviolence as a movement philosophy and methodology. As he discovered, that unanticipated counterresponse to moral suasion would have to be engaged more proactively. King realized to a far greater extent that change would come through struggle, and that the struggle would call for and require the unapologetic use of power. In so doing, King would spend much of his final years attempting to further understand and articulate the significance of power and its relationship to love and justice. Unlike human rights, that were thought to be God-granted and deserving by virtue of one's birth, power was organized and developed by individuals and groups who understood its workings. King said of power:

> Now power properly understood is nothing but the ability to achieve purpose. It is the strength required to bring about social, political, and economic change. Walter Reuther defined power one day. He said, "Power is the ability of a labor union like UAW to make the most powerful corporation in the world, General Motors, say, 'Yes' when it wants to say 'No.'" That's power.[7]

This, then, was the first of at least three observations King made beyond his initial hope for beloved community. Beloved community required more than a mere sharing of physical proximity in the form of desegregation. For King, it called for a more equitable redistribution of privilege and power. As such, riding at the front of the bus and drinking from water fountains that were once illegal to drink from were but symbolic gestures of social progress. Without the ability to effect systemic change, however, they were mere symbols. Essentially, they would represent little more than the token gestures that allowed African slaves to sit in the balconies of white antebellum churches. While creating an appearance of fellowship, these kinds of social tolerances accomplished little in the way of diminishing the systemic sociopolitical structures that affirmed the slave's pain and prolonged their years of insuperable suffering. One who was enslaved could not determine his personal future, or the fate of his family, much less participate in the shaping of the nation's future. As King stated, "Integration is meaningless without the sharing of power. When I speak of integration, I don't mean a romantic mixing of colors; I mean the real sharing of power and responsibility."[8] If segregation was seen as a way of sustaining power and privilege by perpetuating pockets of powerlessness, beloved community at its best represented the removal of the barriers that prohibited the empowerment of societies least advantaged citizens. Communities that failed to harness the ability to effect social, political, and economic change were considered powerless and remained essentially underprivileged. As King saw it, it was this kind of ill-intentioned powerlessness that resulted in poverty and many of the related social ills that prohibited the establishment of beloved community. In contrast to arguments that attributed poverty to race inferiority, King responded by considering the ways in which inequities in power created predictable inequities in privileges. According to Niebuhr, "Privileged members of the community invariably use their higher degree of social power to appropriate an excess of privileges not required by their function; and certainly not in accord with differences of need."[9] In fact, King held that the imbalanced exercise of power by one group over another was a practice that was altogether inconsistent with the stated ideals of a just American society. King wrote:

> What is needed is a realization that power without love is reckless and abusive and that love without power is sentimental and anemic. Power at its best is love implementing the demands of justice. Justice at its best is love correcting everything that stands against love. There is nothing essentially wrong with power. The problem is that in America power is unequally distributed.[10]

King's evolved conviction suggested that authentic community presup-posed a balance in power. There needed to be a greater leveling of the so-called field of opportunity in ways that balanced persons' "ability to achieve their purpose." Within the context of beloved community, King believed that per-sons should experience real empowerment as a result of the real economic, political, and social opportunities afforded them. Segregation and racial dis-crimination were obvious barriers to the achievement of such possibilities. Insofar as King was concerned, one could not truly experience beloved com-munity while being relegated to places of powerlessness that were designed to position persons outside of the societal mainstream solely for the benefit of the privileged few. Beloved community, for King, assumed the idea of provid-ing the disenfranchised with access to opportunities that led to the engage-ment and constructive control of power structures instead of being controlled by them. Particularly in the northern centers, the ghetto existed as a result of a kind of social conditioning whereby the powerful intentionally restricted and exploited the disadvantaged urban masses. The discriminatory redistrict-ing practices, along with the inequitable annexing of neighborhoods to the political and economic advantage of the privileged, further aggravated living conditions among those who were impoverished, serving as a modern means of lower-class entrapment. "New methods of escape," King noted, "must be found. And one of these roads to escape will be a more equitable sharing of political power between Negroes and Whites."[11] Insofar as King was con-cerned, the tenets of mutual regard invited the provision of mutual opportuni-ties to participate in shaping and accessing the power structures of society.[12] The ability, therefore, for all to participate in the process of social, political, and economic change was critical to the formation of a beloved community com-mitted to edging toward greater realizations of both love and justice. This kind of empowerment, according to King, was akin to the construction of authentic community:

> When a people are mired in oppression, they realize deliverance
> only when they have accumulated the power to enforce change. The
> powerful never lose opportunities—they remain available to them.
> The powerless, on the other hand, never experience opportunity—it
> is always arriving at a later time. . . . We must frankly acknowledge
> that in past years our creativity and imagination were not employed
> in learning how to develop power. . . . Now we must take the next
> major step of examining the levers of power which Negroes must
> grasp to influence the course of events. In society power sources can
> always finally be traced to ideological, economic and political forces.[13]

As King explained, persons who were oppressed did not experience deliverance merely as a result of desegregating society, although he certainly considered the outlawing of segregation and Jim Crow a major sociopolitical accomplishment. The desegregating of society represented a critical first step toward beloved community inasmuch as it allowed for the dissemination of accurate information and the dismantling of long-held myths and rumors regarding race. Desegregation opened the doors for the commencing of a new kind of social discourse that primarily sought to make the content of one's character the real focus, not the color of one's skin. In this sense, desegregation served as an unmistakably important move toward the realization of integration and beloved community. More, however, than a seat at a Woolworth's lunch counter was needed; King understood that the poor ultimately needed power in order to participate in a social course considered upwardly mobile. In the end, deliverance from oppression was not assured via a desegregated society; true deliverance from oppressive living conditions could only come in proportion to the accumulation of power needed to create and "enforce change." King observed that the desegregating of society that came in part as a result of judicial and legal mandates needed to be followed promptly by an understanding and free exercise of sociopolitical power. As Robert Franklin so poignantly stated:

> In King's judgment, democracy as the status quo defined it
> (freedom and power for white male property owners) was an
> "anemic democracy." In order to achieve the authentic democracy of
> which W. E. B. DuBois wrote in *The Gift of Black Folk*, political and
> economic power would have to be redistributed to empower the poor,
> minorities, and women.[14]

Short of participating in the structures of power, the powerless never really experienced opportunities commensurate with the prevailing standard of living. Opportunity, in King's view, was always in the process of "arriving at a later time." And this was not always due to some deprivation in one's work ethic. As in the case of the "working poor," opportunity did not evade the experience of some due to their slothfulness or lack of work ethic. As King observed in Chicago, it was not unusual for persons to work two or three menial jobs to merely maintain their substandard living arrangements. Honesty, hard work, and determination did not always translate into greater opportunities for social advancement.

King determined that the problem of poverty was not necessarily the result of one's personal inferiority or deficiency; the problem of poverty was one of powerlessness. King understood the complexities contributing to conditions of poverty. He was aware of the ways in which poor education, diet, and health contributed to poverty. He understood the relationship between the family and the child's social development and success. He often addressed the ways in which lack of economic opportunity fostered crime and incarceration and deepened the plight of those who were poverty-stricken. In the final analysis, however, King attributed the inability to understand and/or exercise power as the leading cause of poverty in America. The underprivileged, the destitute, the homeless, the powerless poor were tracked into predictable patterns of disenfranchisement and desperately needed to learn how to engage and exercise the so-called levers of power that fueled the sociopolitical system. In part, the challenge, then, was to inform those in need of empowerment of the ways in which they could empower themselves. King clearly understood that those who needed advocacy the most were also those who were least informed of the dynamics that were at work in the world around them, and more important, of how those dynamics affected them. In personal interviews done to assist with the organizing of the Poor People's Campaign, King realized that the lack of information and misinformation had a profound impact on the extent to which the poor were able to make informed decisions about their future. In those instances where the facts were available, the doors of opportunity were closed. Efforts, therefore, had to be initiated to both inform and correct the sociopolitical barriers that prohibited the progress of our nation's poorest citizens. This effort, as King saw it, was in need of being supplemented by appeals to the political and judicial systems to assure that equal access to the corridors of opportunity was granted. Every American citizen needed to be able to exercise the right to vote; every child deserved the right to access and experience educational excellence. Basic access to health care and economic opportunity needed to be the critical partners in that fight for freedom. At bottom, every citizen needed to be aware of and have access to the "levers of power" that shaped and guided their destinies. According to King, this provision of information and opportunity also required considerable organization:

> Another basic challenge is to discover how to organize our strength
> in terms of economic and political power. No one can deny that
> the Negro is in dire need of this kind of legitimate power. Indeed,
> one of the great problems that the Negro confronts is his lack of
> power. From old plantations of the South to newer ghettos of the
> North, the Negro has been confined to a life of voicelessness and
> powerlessness.[15]

More than moral suasion and the petitioning of citizen rights, more than protest marches and mass meetings, the poor were in need of discovering how to organize their "strength in terms of economic and political power."

King was absolutely certain that underprivileged populations from America to Africa could be organized and instructed to participate in the various systems of power. Indian and Ghanaian independence, in 1947 and 1957, respectively, were not granted on the heels of moral suasion alone; King understood the degree to which these nations freedom from colonial rule came as a result of shifts in power. He also observed the manner in which the oppressed masses could be organized into forces of nonviolence that had to be reckoned with. Reinhold Niebuhr discussed the significance of this kind of power sharing when he wrote, "The domination of one life by another is avoided most successfully by an equilibrium of powers and vitalities, so that weakness does not invite enslavement by the strong. Without a tolerable equilibrium no moral or social restraints ever succeed completely in preventing injustice and enslavement."[16] During the latter years of the civil rights movement, with beloved community yet in view, it was this idea of empowerment that intrigued King most. While desegregation could be legislated, the successful passage of legislation without an acquiring of power fell short of his beloved community hopes. The passage of a bill did not guarantee shifts in power structures. As King commented, "Power is not the white man's birthright; it will not be legislated for us and delivered in neat government packages. It is a social force any group can utilize by accumulating its elements in a planned, deliberate campaign to organize it under its own control."[17] While the right to life, liberty, and the pursuit of happiness were God-granted, power was considered a "social force" that groups needed to harness and control to their benefit. In that sense, rights were a given whereas the power to exercise those rights was in need of being identified, organized, and exercised.

King clearly found the gap between his own deepening radicalism and the political powerlessness of the masses frustrating. He hoped that black clergymen could, through education and training, be oriented toward his own radical values, enabling them to occupy the vanguard in a struggle for economic justice just as they had been in the forefront of the civil rights movement in the South. "We must develop their psyche," he told a planning meeting of SCLC's Ministers Leadership Training Program. "Something is wrong with capitalism as it now stands in the United States. We are not interested in being integrated into this value structure . . . a radical redistribution of power must take place."[18]

Throughout the years of his public commitment to the civil rights movement, King had long hoped that the clergy would be among the first to appreciate the relationship between social justice and their theological beliefs, so as to assist with the promotion and organization of the masses. Beyond the pledge of their prayers, presence, and financial support of the movement, King welcomed and encouraged the full participation and support of the local pastor. As a fellow pastor, King understood that few were as well positioned to articulate and advocate the needs and hopes of the poor in their midst as the clergy. Few were as poised to organize and structure plans and strategies to initiate and sustain the empowerment of community organizations as were the local pastors. The challenge as King saw it, however, was twofold. The clergy had to possess the ability and the willingness to enable others. As King discovered, some were willing but incapable of providing the kind of community leadership necessary for that level of organizing, and others were undoubtedly capable yet clearly unwilling to support King and the movement because of ideological differences. Still others would deny their need for assistance from "outside agitators" and labored under the belief that they could address and resolve their own local issues, their way. Ministers, however, such as A. D. King, Bernard Lee, Ralph Abernathy, Fred Shuttlesworth, C. T. Vivian, Andrew Young, Walter Fauntroy, Howard Creecy Sr., Jasper Williams, Fred Legarde, Jesse Jackson, Joseph Lowery, John Lewis, James Lawson, Thomas Kilgore, James Bevel, Otis Moss, Charles Booth, Wyatt Tee Walker, and Gardner Taylor were invaluable to the movement. King desired tens of thousands who, like them, could and would empower communities at their respective levels. During the final years of his life it became increasingly apparent that this sort of intentional organizing on the part of local and national leadership was a vital element in the furtherance of justice and beloved community. In addition to the ongoing moral appeals that were made to awaken national and individual conscience, persons, communities and the nation were in need of campaigning in ways that empowered and enabled the poor. Notwithstanding the effectiveness of the sit-ins, marches, and protests, the voiceless and powerless people of protest were in dire need of political and economic power.

Second, in addition to realizing that moral suasion must be combined with the use of coercive measures, King increasingly realized that power was not voluntarily divested by those who possessed it. In other words, gaining the ability to sit and eat next to whites at a lunch counter did not necessarily create a shift in the structures of power that determined their respective fates. As difficult as it was to desegregate lunch counters, King would discover that the greater struggle existed in the meaningful integration of blacks into places of genuine power. Not simply the occupation of the dining room, but also a presence in executive boardrooms and classrooms of higher education was needed. The places of power that were primarily defined by closed doors and glass ceilings, insofar as blacks were concerned, were in need of becoming places of shared opportunities for social advancement. All too often, court orders to desegregate the public square did not translate into comparable transfers in power. In fact, efforts to organize and power-share were often met with greater degrees of resistance as King clarified his understanding of the ways in which he related concepts of power to what it meant to exist in beloved community.

There is little doubt that King suspected the limitations of moral appeal early on in his campaign for civil rights. As early as the Montgomery bus boycott, King emerged from that negotiating table with a fuller realization akin to that of Douglass, who often said, "No one gives up his privileges without strong resistance." King's perceived need to incorporate concepts of massive civil disobedience and his attempts to develop additional economic and political alliances were certainly indicative of this need to challenge the resistive tendencies of the powerful. Consistent with his critique of liberalism, progress would not "roll in on the wings of inevitability," but it would rather require a synthesis of moral fortitude and the creative implementation of nonviolent direct action. As Robert Franklin explains, "In short, King realized that in order to eradicate racism, economic exploitation, and militarism, a revolutionary transformation of American society and values was required."[19] The question, of course, was in terms of how that transformation would occur given the extended history of racial domination and the extent to which that form of exploitation would be relinquished. In this regard, Cook writes:

> White America suffers from three-and-a-half centuries of the exercise of the tyranny of power which victimized, brutalized, and dehumanized black America. Power over blacks has been irresponsible (in the sense that the exercise of that power did not have to answer to blacks) and, at critical points, absolute (the only limitation being white self-restraint). Inevitably, this situation bred arrogance, insensitivity, and a sense of "divine prerogatives."[20]

King contemplated the prospect of beloved community as a growing new social reality, but he did so with an acute understanding of the many ways in which the social milieu had been entrenched and perpetuated by the given hegemony. Essentially, King proposed to shift, in little over a decade, an accepted societal arrangement that developed over the period of some three and a half centuries. To some this may have seemed like an outrageous proposition; to King, however, such a proposition seemed altogether plausible given the nature of his theological anthropology. Overcoming a sometimes violent system of racial segregation was indeed possible, yet not without due consideration for the historical evidence that confirmed theories of unrelenting group dominance. It was here that King reckoned with his need to contend with society's reluctance to part with the accruements of its accumulated power and privilege. Less than a glance at the receding efforts of nineteenth-century Reconstruction hopes served as that sobering reminder. The withdrawal of Federal troops along with the reinstatement of racially biased laws quickly faded the hopes cast by freedom's bright star. This refusal to willfully divest and share the levers of power with persons who were formerly enslaved is commented upon by Hanes Walton, who remarks, "Throughout the South the whites recaptured their former position of power and quickly saw to it that all means at their disposal were employed to maintain their authority."[21] Long-held beliefs, myths, customs, and social traditions suggesting that blacks were both unworthy and incapable of understanding and managing sociopolitical power served to rationalize resistance to appealed shifts in the power structures. Additionally, an underlying concern continued to spring from questions about how those who were previously oppressed would use and/or abuse their newfound power. Both considerations spawned a climate of gradualism that pushed issues of black advancement and the idea of real power sharing to the social periphery. It was this denial of power and the nation's unwillingness to expeditiously balance the scales of power that prompted King's need to forge a collaboration of massive civil disobedience among grassroots leadership organizations. In addition to his national network of clergy colleagues, King sought to develop economic and political alliances among labor unions and civic associations that would join forces to challenge the patterns of resistance established by the brokers of sociopolitical power. Walton further comments upon the relationship between struggle and the attainment of power:

> A glance at human history, King believed, reveals that the pursuit of justice and equality requires not only continual exertion, concern, and dedicated individuals, but sacrifice, suffering and struggle. Time, together with perseverance, becomes a powerful force for motion and social progress. As he saw it, no privileged group would give up its position without resisting strongly.[22]

While his understanding of how the intricacies and complexities of power were exercised and guarded developed over time, King's awareness of the nation's uneasiness to adjust the scales of power did not go unnoticed, even at the outset of his involvement with the civil rights movement. This kind of nagging realization was occasionally set against the more optimistic view King held of humanity. As observed in the previous chapters, King affirmed an unmistakably generous theological assessment of the human condition. Although human beings could choose either the social good or evil, the urgings of those created in the image of God would be inclined toward the original goodness with which humanity was created. According to King, the tragic historical commentary did not necessarily dictate an unlikely prospect for future progress; rather, human beings could overcome their painful past. In contrast to beliefs that pointed to the utter depravity of humanity, King embraced a theological framework that affirmed humanity's dignity and freedom of choice. More than mere material matter; human beings were created beings that bore the very image of God, a theological truth that for him underscored the scope of human possibility. Nevertheless, the recurring reminder of there being "some difficult days ahead" was the reality with which King continually had to contend. Although humanity could choose to divest power and privilege such that the least, last, and lost among them would benefit, all too many, it seemed, chose not to empower those whom they were routinely accustomed to exploiting. Apart from some form of direct action, progression toward the land of promise seemed most impractical and, moreover, improbable. Moral suasion, appeals for social justice, and invitations to travel the high social road of human civility were clearly in need of being supplemented by organized acts of protest. In this sense, nonviolent protest served to provide those at the bottom of the social class with the sociopolitical power to direct the course of events that had direct bearing on the quality of their lives. As Garber rightly observed:

> At the very beginning of his [King's] civil rights role at Montgomery, he resorted to an economic boycott in his effort to accomplish his goal, insisting that "no one gives up his privileges without strong resistance," and at the end of his career he planned a campaign of massive civil disobedience in Washington, D.C., and wrote that "we must subordinate programs to studying levers of power Negroes must grasp to influence the course of events."[23]

Insofar as King was concerned, if in fact privileges were not usually divested and shared without strong resistance, what then were certain social programs for the poor actually designed to accomplish? Why would the privileged sanction the availability of social services that came woefully short of empowering the powerless, if not to further their disadvantage and deepen their dependencies? By the mid-1960s, King was already questioning the usefulness of the kinds of social programs and government initiatives that failed to genuinely empower the powerless, viewing such efforts as paternalistic attempts to simply appease the stifled masses. Sociopolitical exploitation in the garb of programming that failed to foster authentic upward mobility fell short of King's understanding of what it meant to participate in beloved community. Such programs were in need of being subordinated, in terms of their value and importance, to opportunities that accessed the social levers that would affect real and lasting social progress. While King ultimately understood that it was not a question of either-or, inasmuch as constructive programs and power were two distinct yet related necessities, he also understood that the goals associated with any program of social uplift must be genuine empowerment. In the short run, social initiatives that were not connected to long-term empowerment strategies could conceivably serve as the necessary interim measure, a welcome initial lift from the substandard living conditions that generally polarized the poor. In the long run, however, they could not replace the dire need for access to the sources of real economic and political power. If prolonged reliance upon certain forms of welfare programming fostered dependence, it was believed that an awareness of and access to the levers of power facilitated the real kinds of power sharing King envisioned. His, therefore, was a gospel of social pragmatism that took into account the many complexities of social change. For King, this national reluctance to willfully adjust the social infrastructure necessitated the pressures applied by the civil rights movement. As King observed, social struggle sought to move the country toward greater expressions of social equity in ways that the nation's willful divestment of power would not have considered otherwise. King writes:

> Nothing was done until we acted on these very issues, and
> demonstrated before the court of world opinion the urgent need
> for change. It was the same story in voting rights. The Civil Rights
> Commission, three years before Selma, had recommended the
> changes we started marching for, but nothing was done until, in
> 1965, we created a crisis the nation couldn't ignore. The same kind of
> dramatic crisis was created in Selma two years later. The results on
> the national scene were the Civil Rights Bill and the Voting Rights
> Act, as president and congress responded to the drama and the
> creative tension generated by the carefully planned demonstrations.[24]

Notwithstanding the dramatic legislative gains, contemporaries such as Reinhold Niebuhr held to neo-orthodox conceptions of community that insisted upon the need for continued vigilance at each new pinnacle of social progress. As such, any divestment of power could never be viewed as an irreversible gain. Although the wheels of desegregation were set in motion during the outset of the civil rights movement due to judicial and legislative means, any relinquishing and sharing of power certainly could not be taken for granted. Niebuhr insisted that any struggle advanced to adjust the scales of power would result in increased social tension and efforts on the part of the powerful to reclaim and reinstitute the status quo. Social reforms could suffer painful reverses as in the case of the withdrawn Reconstruction hopes that were proposed for those who had long awaited their full emancipation on the heels of the Civil War. Insofar as Niebuhr was concerned, social regression and the reentrenchment of corruptive social practices remained an imminent possibility apart from sustained struggle. According to Niebuhr, "No traditional attainment of brotherhood is secure against criticism from a higher historical perspective or safe from corruption on each new level of achievement."[25] If by brotherhood Niebuhr was referencing humanity's capacity for mutual regard and a semblance of just community that approached, or at least moved in the direction of, the beloved, his identification with the reformed tradition quickly reminded readers of society's stubborn insistence to reclaim structures that were potentially countercommunity. For Niebuhr, then, the stride toward brotherhood was always at risk of being thwarted by societal tendencies that thrived as a result of the polarization, alienation, and exploitation of the other as opposed to pursuits of a more perfect union via the liberation, salvation, and education of the powerless.

This was particularly true with regard to how he differentiated individual capacity from that of group and societal capacity. While morality held some limited possibility in terms of person-to-person relations, there was little if any possibility for that kind of moral formation at the level of the larger group. Hence, at best, Niebuhr believed that social groups could possibly edge toward greater degrees of what it meant to become a more just and civil society. Although the theological idea of mutual regard as an authentic expression of love held some promise for individual development, authentic divestment of privilege and power for the sake of others was impossible in the case of the "immoral society" without tension and struggle. The vocabulary of love and its possibilities were necessarily abstracted and skewed at the macro level of society. By distinguishing the capacity of the individual from that of the group, Niebuhr came short of affirming love as a possible guiding principle for community formation, tending to emphasize humanity's proclivity toward the group's corruptive character. In keeping with this skeptical view of humanity's social capacity, Niebuhr wrote, "Thus the pinnacle of the moral ideal stands both inside and beyond history; inside in so far as love may elicit a reciprocal response and change the character of human relations; and beyond history in so far as love cannot require a mutual response without losing its character of disinterestedness."[26] What held some possibility for interpersonal relationships could not help but fail to realistically transfer at the level of group relations. For him, language, meaning, and accountability for and to the ideals espoused all became skewed and distorted at that level of group discourse and experience. Moreover, authentic love could not be realized if appeals for divestment, justice, and mutual regard were made with the intent of securing benefits for self. Agape love could not be the by-product of human motivations that were considered self-serving and/or self-seeking. From this theological vantage point, Niebuhr attempted to articulate a rationale for humanity's involuntary surrender of power to the so-called powerless. Niebuhr writes:

> In this sense an equilibrium of vitality is an approximation of brotherhood within the limits of conditions imposed by human selfishness. But an equilibrium of power is not brotherhood. The restraint of the will-to-power of one member of the community by the counter-pressure of another member results in a condition of tension. All tension is covert or potential conflict.[27]

King, however, moved in a decidedly different direction theologically and saw no apparent contradiction in calling the privileged to power-share with the underserved and underprivileged of the nation and world. For King, this call to an equilibrium of power was seen not simply as a call to an approximation of justice but as a mandatory prelude to brotherhood. Under such conditions, a just struggle against an unjust assertion of oppressive power represented the embrace of prophetic tradition at its best. The imposition of legal measures upon those who would not voluntarily divest power was ultimately viewed as an invitation to reconciliation and the furtherance of beloved community. Both Frederick Douglass and Reinhold Niebuhr agreed that social progress depended upon the use of soul force and moral struggle. This growing awareness that power would not willingly divest its place of privilege for the benefit of others provided King with the ideological basis for the kinds of coercive strategies that were then in need of being resorted to. King increasingly realized that desegregation would become a futile social exercise apart from a real integration of power throughout the social fabric. The opponents' discomfort with desegregation was not simply one of racial interaction—a *subservient* black presence troubled few; the real discomforting reality was one of having to introduce the powerless to the levers of political and economic power. It was a question of what the place of privilege would resemble on the other side of shared power. In the final analysis, if the powerful were not naturally inclined to relinquish their power without struggle, additional methodologies of social change were required. A novel theological approach that was contextual in nature was required. An additional read of the gospel and its meaning from the perspective of the oppressed was necessary. As King grappled with the emerging social reality beyond his initial vision of beloved community, he discovered himself in need of reconciling that noble hope with the nation's reluctance to provide the powerless with corridors of equitable access to positions and places of power and privilege. Despite Niebuhr's acknowledgment of humanity's propensity for corruptive policy shaping as a means of preserving privilege, King held to a view that unapologetically refused to accept the allowance of massive abject poverty for the purpose of sustained economic exploitation. Whereas Niebuhr criticized the possibility of beloved community as a historical reality, King forged forward with thinking that underscored its imperative.

Beyond the glowing micro-image of community that assembled at the foot of the Lincoln Memorial in the summer of 1963, King later found himself having to contend with his opponents' ongoing reluctance to acknowledge society's advantage in functioning as an integrated whole. Despite his earlier conceptions of beloved community and the initial enthusiasm sparked by legislative concessions, King observed that desegregating public places did not necessarily assure the voluntary dissemination of power. More than access to a "white only" water fountain, restroom, and/or lunch counter, the disinherited required access to genuine levers of political and economic power. The cohabitation of physical space had not been the shortcoming historically. The enslaved occupied plantation households, raised their owners' children, prepared meals, labored in their fields, and even attended their churches on occasion. The shortcoming rested in the enslaved community's inability to exercise power, to determine their future, thus exercising the ability to inform, shape, and guide the destiny of their nation and world. Shared public space, while offering blacks an opportunity to more readily contribute to the gross national product, did little to translate their former state of oppression into one of promised land dwelling. In the end, integration had to mean more than mere physical proximity. Beloved community could never rise to the noble standard of *beloved*, nor could it reflect the true character of humane *community* apart from this bold adjustment in the structures of power.

Additionally, King observed that it was this attempt to create shifts in places of power that ultimately represented the catalyst for societal tension and racial struggle. Desegregation without an authentic integration of economic and political power simply led to further social frustration. Ironically, if beloved community would be experienced in any measure, it would be achieved in keeping with Frederick Douglass's analysis of struggle as the necessity for social progress. In this regard, King concluded along with Niebuhr that the social struggle that ensued at each new level of civil rights success was a result of society's involuntary divestment of power. The need, therefore, was to understand the relationship between racial struggle and humanity's struggle to secure and sustain a shared social power base. While the problem of racism dominated much of the civil rights conversation, King came to understand that the underlying tension, debate, and phobias were also centered in questions of power. Race was conveniently attached to anti-integration sentiments as a surface issue when in fact much of the struggle had to do with King's audacious move toward making access to the levers of power more inclusive. To ignore the struggle for power, as an ongoing social dynamic, was to settle for a kind of pseudocommunity and the inevitable regression to resegregated society.

Finally, as King's dimmed hopes for beloved community continued to fade, his thoughts consequently turned to the ill effects fostered by the imbalance in power and the adverse effects that were created as a result of humanity's interrelatedness. For King, this was a critical insight, since humanity's fate, as he so often remarked, was bound together by a common thread of destiny. This shared journey assured that the human family would ultimately rise or fall collectively. In contrast to John Donne's "No Man Is an Island" and its affirmation of human ascent, King saw the nation's imbalance in power as resulting in the inevitable decline of a nation and world motivated by greed and its exploitive abuses of power. The basic question regarding power sharing essentially awaited a response that would determine directions that would lead nations along paths of social chaos or community. Increasingly, King believed that the privileged could not avoid the inescapable diminishing of themselves in proportion to their impoverished populations. To conclude that no individual, community, or nation could view itself as existing independent of the other also implied that the continued abuses of power, and the furtherance of polarizing social structures that unjustly disadvantaged persons on the basis of race, would only further the extent of humanity's national and global dysfunction. As a result of this irrevocable bond, King argued that to advocate the cause of the least was in fact to assure the future of the most fortunate.

Contrary to Niebuhr's concern that a pursuit of justice somehow abandoned the principles of love as disinterested, King viewed the struggle for justice and power as a fulfillment of love's requirements. For the sake of love one could never participate in evil by becoming its silent partner in the name of disinterest. Allowing the oppression of self for the purpose of giving expression to a kind of love that overlooked one's consideration of his own personal interests failed to grasp the ramifications of the individual's impact on the whole. Permitting the slings and arrows of injustice and unmerited suffering for the sake of others actually resulted in the suffering, if not the diminishing, of others, as a result of humanity's interrelatedness. In this sense, to act in the interest of self-empowerment ultimately translated into the well-being of others, including the advantaged and privileged of society. Altruism in the truest sense of the word was not denied, violated, or compromised as a result of one's pursuit of justice and civil equality. Instead, one's pursuit of justice, in an attempt to balance the scales of power, was viewed as an authentic expression of concern for the other. Hence, the assertions of the oppressed and the concessions of the oppressor were viewed as two sides of a single coin. In this regard, King wrote, "Power at its best is love implementing the demands of justice, and justice at its best is power correcting everything that stands against love. And this is what we must see as we move on."[28] To, therefore, permit a permanent underclass so as to assure the perpetuation of a permanent upper class was both morally wrong and socially untenable. For King, abject poverty could never be viewed as a necessary evil. Instead, those who were hopelessly impoverished and left to languish in isolation, far from being isolated, always had the effect of eroding the mainstream's pursuit of life, liberty, and happiness. Niebuhr picked up on the significance of this inescapable bond between the individual, society, and their mutual need for community when he wrote:

> The obligation to build and to perfect communal life is not merely forced upon us by the necessity of coming to terms with the rather numerous hosts, whom it has pleased the Almighty Creator to place on this little earth beside us. Community is an individual as well as a social necessity; for the individual can realize himself only in intimate and organic relation with his fellowmen.[29]

For King, the prospect of an "intimate and organic relation with his fellowmen" was seriously threatened by the ways in which power had been diffused through the mainstream's unjust sanction of racial discrimination. Beloved community was being deferred by ignoring the need to empower the restricted Negro masses. More than a nicety, revisiting the intent of Reconstruction by empowering those who were little more than a generation removed from their egregious past was viewed as a moral imperative. As King, therefore, contemplated the meaning of power sharing, he was compelled to do so from within the context of humanity's essential interrelatedness. From that perspective, social systems that fostered the illusion of class superiority aided only in hastening the demise and deterioration of the whole societal fabric. The social unraveling at the fringe would inevitably work its way to the center irrespective of the so-called safeguards and barriers designed to insulate and buffer the haves from the have-nots. To narrowly define the idea of community along the lines of exclusive racial and class boundaries was to deny humanity's interdependence and hasten the decline of civil society. The welfare of the individual and that of society were, in this sense, knitted together. King understood that whites could never fully realize their conception of the American dream apart from the realization of their constructive relation to Americans of Afro descent. While the conveyors of injustice appeared to be prospering economically as a result of the various inequities, King called attention to a more profound measure of social wellness. Beyond this material measure, the state of the Union's health was also in need of being assessed in terms of its wellness of soul. In the final analysis, it was the moral measure of the individual, nation, and world that was ultimately at stake. For King as in the case of ancient biblical wisdom, to gain the world and lose the soul was in fact to eventually lose it all.

As such, King aspired to bring leadership to a civil rights movement that was designed to empower all Americans by rallying a trickle-up trend that empowered the least among them. Convinced that sustained imbalances in power invited the social malfunction of both the oppressed and the oppressor, King called for a redistribution of power with the presumption that human beings created in the image of God could harmoniously cohabit their created order. Even Niebuhr, though theologically distinguished in other respects, appears to overlap on this question of human capacity when he writes, "The capacity of communities to synthesize divergent approaches to a common problem and to arrive at a tolerably just solution proves man's capacity to consider interests other than his own."[30] King believed that in time the powerful, though not without struggle and conflict, would genuinely consider the interests of the poor within their borders. A first-class nation could not remain as such indefinitely with an expanding lower class. It was, therefore, imperative that the correction of America's substandard living conditions, which included education, housing, health care, and employment, become the priority. The 1960s domestic agenda, however, had to contend with the feared escalation of a global nuclear arms race, a growing mistrust in international affairs, and a fierce redirection of national resources that further challenged King's appeal on behalf of the nation's poor. Despite the disdain of his critics, King continued to advocate that although distinct in class, culture, creed, and color, humanity remained coupled by the ever-present demands of divinity and human destiny. Despite the political and social crosswind, he pressed forward with undaunted prophetic persistence.

The recurring question, however, was "How long?" How long will it be before the "arc bent toward justice" arrives at its long-awaited destination? How long, before calloused hearts journey beyond the restrictions imposed by racial discriminatory practices? How long, before the American dream becomes a dream for all Americans? How long, before the concept of accessibility to the levers of power becomes a reality? While no specific date could be offered with any sensible precision, the process could be facilitated and hastened by employing the right approach. Short of any immediate long-term solution to the problem, King recognized that there was an alternative kind of power in the methodology of nonviolence. The proper appropriation of nonviolence could successfully create access to these other means of constructive social participation without employing the levels of violence exercised by their opposition. He sought to avert much of the conflict by this strict espousal of nonviolence as the accepted movement methodology. This, he supposed, would minimize the threat of sustained, long-term conflict. Nonviolence sought the development of a just and beloved community while avoiding the criticisms of complicity and anarchy. As King explained, "Nonviolence is power, but it is the right and good use of power. Constructively it can save the white man as well as the Negro."[31] King realized that power could be successfully harnessed among the powerless to create this coalition of determined nonviolent change agents. In this sense, even the destitute could not be considered completely powerless. Dramatic global shifts, resulting from the decline of colonialism in India and Africa, led King to believe that "the coalition of an energized section of labor, Negroes, unemployed and welfare recipients may be the source of power that reshapes economic relationships and ushers in a new level of social reform."[32] In the final months preceding his assassination, King organized the Poor People's Campaign as a means of dramatizing the vastness of poverty and commenced the building of a broad-based coalition that would reform and heal the nation. More than racial integration, as an iconic symbol of community, the poor of every culture were organized to give presence and voice to the challenges of injustice. King addressed these debilitating social structures and society's collective need to overcome them when he wrote: "The dispossessed of this nation—the poor, both white and Negro—live in a cruelly unjust society. They must organize a revolution against that injustice, not against the lives of . . . their fellow citizens, but against the structures through which the society is refusing to take means . . . to lift the load of poverty."[33]

Inasmuch as King partially understood power as that "ability to achieve purpose," it only followed that his concept of human interrelatedness would also shape his views on the relationship between one's sense of human purpose and power sharing. Power, as in the case of human purpose, could not be shared in isolation. Power needed to be balanced and shared in community. To that end, an individual's purpose would be achieved in concert with others attempting to realize and experience purposeful lives. In short, King concluded that the improved social order that he and others imagined could not be realized amid the exclusive shouts for power. As King implored, "Let us be dissatisfied until that day when nobody will shout 'White Power!'—when nobody will shout 'Black Power!'—but everybody will talk about God's power and human power."[34] White power could not successfully coexist in contention with black power. Properly understood, power could not be successfully trumped by whites or blacks. Because of humanity's interrelatedness, hence interdependence, power and purpose were necessarily shared human experiences. King's desire, therefore, was to reconcile his conception of community with the more radical demands for black power and the recurring radicalism witnessed in the assertions of white power. As King explained, "Black Power's legitimate and necessary concern for group unity and black identity lies in the belief that there can be a separate black road to power and fulfillment. Few ideas are more unrealistic. There is no salvation for the Negro through isolation."[35] As in the case of his harshest critique against the claims of white segregationists, the cry of black power, though valid in and of itself, could not be successfully polarized or purposefully directed within a beloved community conception that affirmed humanity's common ground. King writes:

> What has happened is that we have had it wrong and confused in our country, and this has led Negro Americans in the past to seek their goals through power devoid of love and conscience. This is leading a few extremists today to advocate for Negroes the same destructive and conscienceless power they have justly abhorred in whites. It is precisely this collision of immoral power with powerless morality which constitutes the major crisis of our times.[36]

With the brightest days of the movement seemingly behind him, King reconsidered what the pace of, and price for, social progress toward the promised land would be when he asserted, "This is where the civil rights movement stands today. We will err and falter as we climb the unfamiliar slopes of steep mountains, but there is no alternative, well trod, level path. There will be agonizing setbacks along with creative advances. Our consolation is that no one can know the true taste of victory if he has never swallowed defeat."[37] In tending to this level of Christian realism, King avoided the utter disillusionment that often attended more liberal visions of human progress as an inevitable social function. Unlike the overly romanticized versions of utopian society, King had already escaped the naive assumptions of human perfectionism during his student years. In fact, beyond the 1963 March on Washington, that moment when the beloved community seemed most imminent, King had to contend with the bitter erosion of those earlier and more hopeful indicators of society's progress. Challenged by heightened resistance to the civil rights movement, King was forced to further plumb the depths of his theological-well with regard to humanity's capacity for beloved community. Consistent with the need for additional confrontation in the form of protests, marches, boycotts, sit-ins, and legislative amendments, King increasingly viewed the difficult uphill struggle for the attainment of justice, power, and civil rights as the prelude to and the sustainer of beloved community.

Beyond August 1963, however, King increasingly realized that a distinction must be made between the hegemonic systems that perpetuated human suffering and the personalities that managed them. The complex goal was to dismantle the oppressive structures that diverted wealth and opportunity from the least advantaged of our nation while redeeming the perpetrators of this social dilemma. Beloved community needed to be pursued and sustained by a moral commitment to share power within the context of a diverse American population that included 'all' not just the 'fortunate few.' King reiterated this thought in his final publication of record, entitled "Where Do We Go from Here?" when he wrote, "America must be a nation in which multiracial people are partners in power."[38] The good use of power could only be realized in and through human partnerships that sought to empower the least advantaged in American society by introducing them to opportunities to discover and exercise political and economic power. Amid accusations of being an anarchist, socialist, and even accommodationist, King reaffirmed this commitment to beloved community by addressing the issues of economics and power from within this theological framework of human interrelatedness. As an avowed integrationist, King saw beloved community as the movement's goal, with social justice and access to power as the movement's essential by-products. Beloved community would emerge in proportion to the decline of discriminatory practices that resulted in the socio-economic disenfranchisement of American citizens. Moreover, community would begin moving in the direction of a society of the "beloved" in proportion to the degree to which persons genuinely regarded the social interests of the discriminated while preserving the dignity of the discriminators'. Samuel D. Cook writes:

> We must, Dr. King insisted, make careful distinctions between persons and things, men and systems, human beings and institutions, individuals and objective structures. . . . The goal is to change objective conditions, to alter and to correct the retentions of power phenomena—the structures and processes responsible for the current distribution of rewards and burdens, benefits and deprivations. Even as we seek, with all our heart, to get rid of the cruelties and miseries of "the system" we are obligated to respect the humanity of the agents and defenders of "the system," our opponents, our enemies. The end is, after all, redemption, reconciliation, a better social order, the beloved community.[39]

It was King's understanding of the universe as moral which dictated that the means could not contradict the overall objective of the civil rights movement. If beloved community was the intended goal, as it was, any action deemed contrary to its formation could not be embraced. In the end, the building and preservation of the 'more perfect union' was the chief goal. As America was being ushered through an era of unprecedented social change, the goal was not to further alienate any citizen of the American democracy, but to redeem and reconcile the entire nation to the wisdom and morality of an integrated society, a beloved community. King, by word and deed, gave expression to the movement's goal when he wrote, "The end is, after all, redemption, reconciliation, a better social order, the beloved community."[40] The same theological center that called for the rejection of unjust structures and systems, called for the redemption of its unrelenting opponents. King clearly underscored this unwavering commitment to community formation in a July 13, 1966, article in *Christian Century*, by reaffirming the ultimate goal inherent in his quest for the beloved community: "I do not think of political power as an end. Neither do I think of economic power as an end. They are ingredients in the objective that we seek in life. And I think that end or that objective is a truly brotherly society, the creation of the beloved community." With beloved community as the overall goal and nonviolence as the operative methodology, it was critical for King to constantly remind America that the intent of the movement was to do no harm to the foes of racial reconciliation, but rather to alter and amend their unjust sociopolitical structures. The struggle against antagonistic power structures, although proving more inflexible than first imagined, could not be carried out with the intent to displace and destroy the defenders of those unjust and outdated social systems. As political and economic influence was gained by those who were historically withheld from mainstream benefits, it was to be achieved in ways that did not seek to victimize the previous vanguard.

From that theoretical and moral center, King continued to map out the movement's strategies with beloved community as the intended goal and love as the intended guide. Clearly, beloved community was impeded by the gross imbalances in power, and yet, these imbalances in power could not be overcome apart from the exercise of genuine love and a moral conscience that affirmed both oppressed and oppressor. Since community was hinged upon the concept of human relatedness, justice confronted the unjust socio-political structures while agape compelled King and advocates of the civil rights movement to "love their enemies and to pray for those who would despitefully use them." Remarkably, King's commitment to and hope for the realization of beloved community remained intact, despite the sobering levels of resistance to and regression of the civil rights movement. He would not be deterred. Instead, his tempered optimism regarding the realization of beloved community, and it's imminent arrival, was offset by the assurance of his deep and abiding faith in the God of his ancestors who often spoke of the God "who may not come when we want him, but who's always on time." King wrote, "The eschatological thinking of the Christian religion is not without its social emphasis...Whether it comes soon or late, by sudden crisis or through slow development, the Kingdom of God will be a society in which all men and women will be controlled by the eternal love of God."[41] Community, he believed, may be temporarily delayed, but not permanently deferred. King possessed a theological anthropology that saw beloved community as a distinct human possibility. Blacks and whites could reconcile. The vestiges of racism and injustice could be reduced to historical footnotes instead of continuing to make the current headlines. Today's poor could become tomorrow's power brokers. Human beings created in the image of God, he fervently believed, could choose to cooperate with God in the creation of that much needed society. More than a mere dreamer of beloved community, King had to *be*, as Gandhi admonished his followers decades earlier, the beloved community he imagined would one day emerge as a dominant reality. He was determined to be the model of love that would discount the sociopolitical darkness. He was resolved to be the voice of reason that would rise above the chorus of irrationality. King essentially committed his life to being the loving neighbor that even his foes would come to appreciate and perhaps one day also become. Though hindered by numerous setbacks, King's proleptic hope for humanity continued to be expressed in passionate oratory, in discomforting truisms, in fearless confrontation, in untiring commitment, but always in love. Though rarely discussed these days, many had become very uncomfortable with Martin Luther King, Jr.'s prophetic call to justice and community, yet he remained uncompromised in his theological conviction that the human family, created in the image of God, could be improved. For some it is hard to hear King unplugged, unedited, and unfiltered by the final lines of "I Have a Dream" in our modern day. And yet if we are to "hear something new," something that transforms old dreams into new realities, we must hear him now as he spoke then.

Epilogue

On the eve of his assassination, King asserted, "I may not get there with you. But I want you to know tonight, that we, as a people will get to the Promised Land." King's emphatic last word of exhortation to a weary people in a weary land appropriated language, originating in the Old Testament hope, of a people's exodus from a land of oppressive limitations that resulted in their eventual entrance into the land of promise, a land outfitted with all the accoutrements of freedom. In that land envisioned by King, the enjoyment of life, liberty, and the pursuit of happiness would become distinct realities irrespective of one's color, creed, or cultural origin. His prophetic pronouncement to Memphis sanitation workers, this nation, and this world on the eve of his murder affirmed the possibility of a successful promised land pilgrimage. "We as a people will get there," was his unwavering declaration of emancipation. Admittedly, the journey to that land of promise was marked by difficult days, and yet, beyond the challenge of that obstructed sociopolitical pathway, King claimed to have been elevated to the mountaintop. From the mountaintop, he looked over the symbolic Jordan River to capture and convey a sight that most could not see, that parting glimpse of promised land possibility, beloved community, an America characterized by greater capacities for humane consideration, cooperation, and compassion. The exodus from the plantations of segregated society had commenced; the entrance into the promised land of beloved community was the eminent hope.

Not to make more of this applied biblical metaphor than we need to, it is of interest to note that 2008 marks the fortieth anniversary of King's tragic assassination. King envisioned that promised land entrance forty years ago, the same period of time that preceded the fulfillment of Israel's ancient hope. Following their wander through the Sinai, *they as a people got into the promised land.* It was on the fortieth anniversary of their exodus out of Egypt that they crossed over into Canaan, thus entering into their new sociopolitical space. It is the fortieth year since King envisioned our nation's arrival into this new place in which judgment would become character based instead of color based; and for the first time in American history an African American candidate has been elected to serve the office of president of these United States. Needless to say, we "as a people" have witnessed a historical moment of unprecedented proportion. The fortieth anniversary of King's assassination has become a pivotal year in American history with regard to this major shift in the national consciousness. Reminiscent of the racially diverse audience that gathered for the 1963 March on Washington to hear King's "I Have a Dream" speech, and rivaling the two hundred fifty thousand that were in attendance then, Barak Obama supporters assembled in anticipation of the favorable electoral results. One observer likened the scene to "an ocean of people, awash in happiness and pride." That gathering, which represented the epicenter of similar gatherings across the nation and around the world, was the nearest approximation of beloved community since 1963. Given the complexity of our modern day, one could not help but describe the moment of president-elect Obama's speech and the new social space that we had crossed over into as surreal.

Had the epilogue to this work, explicating King's theological anthropology, been written three years ago, on the thirty-seventh anniversary, or as recently as a year ago, on the thirty-ninth anniversary of King's "Been to the Mountaintop" address, the closing narrative to this book would have stood in stark contrast to the current monumental leap beyond the boundaries of our nation's race matters. The marvel of an African American president in the fortieth year is made all the more surprising against the backdrop of the not so distant memories of Katrina and Jena. They form the uncomfortable backdrop to this amazingly progressive sociopolitical climate we are now witnessing. The Katrina catastrophe of 2005 forced new questions regarding the old problems of race and class discrimination in America, as the nation witnessed tens of thousands of predominantly black and poor Americans gather in the New Orleans Superdome and Convention Center without food or supplies. Within hours, a gulf storm that had been forecast, with disastrous implications for the structural integrity of the levee system and the safety of the surrounding communities, struck the southern Louisiana shore, displacing thousands and taking the lives of at least 1,800. For the victims and their families, "hope unborn had died" for the abandoned masses who lacked the basic resources to mobilize in an attempt to dodge what proved to be the costliest storm in American history. A disbelieving nation tuned in as images of the elderly left to die and children left to suffer the indignity of severe human neglect haunted the corridors of their collective national conscience. Many raised the question as to how aid, evacuation, and sophisticated resettlement programs could be provided for some 20,000 Albanian refugees who were transported from the war-torn country of Kosovo to America in 1999, while the least fortunate in Louisiana were left to linger and die within the borders of their home. As shock gave way to frustration and anger over the government's poor response to the one of nation's greatest natural disasters, conversations with respect to race and class inequities emerged in answer to the multilayered inquiries.

Two years later, in September 2007, the state of Louisiana made headlines once again as more than 15,000 protesters converged on the small town of Jena in a march the Reverend Al Sharpton called "the beginning of the 21st-century civil rights movement." The march on Jena stemmed from a 2006 incident involving three white teens who hung nooses from a tree near the local high school. The day prior to the display of the nooses, black students had received permission from school administrators to sit under the "white tree," a location customarily reserved for white students only. Three months later, six black high school students, later coined the Jena Six, were charged with attempted murder and conspiracy to commit murder following the brutal beating of a fellow white student. The charges, which were deemed extremist by some and racist by others, ignited a national protest strikingly reminiscent of the sixties and sparked a national backlash of at least fifty reported hate crimes involving a proliferation of noose hangings in locations as common as Home Depot and as prominent as Columbia University.[1] More than a prank, Federal Bureau of Investigation agents and other federal officials concluded that the Jena incident had "all the markings of a hate crime" but could not be prosecuted as such because it did not meet the federal guidelines required for certifying teens as adults. Immediately following the march on Jena, thousands of organizers and protesters gathered in Washington, D.C., to further denounce the district attorney's stubborn stand and to present their collective appeal for federal intervention in a case that seemed little more than a throwback to the infamous days of Jim Crow. What was happening to our "kinder, gentler Nation, to our Beloved Community, or as Rodney King once inquired, to our capacity to "just get along together"?[2] Exactly when would we as a people get to the promised land, thus ridding ourselves of the sin of racial intolerance and bigotry that seemingly continued to polarize society on the basis of skin color? When would "we as a people make it to the promised land"?

If 2007 was noted as the most contentious year since the days of the civil rights movement, and as the one most likely to draw America back into a mode of racial confrontation and subtle yet deeper forms of social stratification, 2008 has become the most euphoric. Although it appeared to some as though America was on the verge of unraveling over the question of race less than twelve months ago, this year, on the fortieth anniversary of King's assassination, America not only entertained but has elected its first African American president, to the amazement of many. Months ago, following the nomination of Senator Barack Obama of Illinois, interviewers turned to Georgia congressman John Lewis with hopes of gaining a firsthand perspective on the significance of that moment in U.S. history. "If someone had told me this would be happening now, I would have told them they were crazy, out of their mind, they didn't know what they were talking about," said Lewis, who was president of the Student Nonviolent Coordinating Committee when he stood with King on the steps of the Lincoln Memorial in 1963. "I just wish the others were around to see this day. . . . To the people who were beaten, put in jail, were asked questions they could never answer to register to vote, it's amazing."[3] In another interview, Lewis who was ruthlessly beaten by a violent white mob in Montgomery for his participation in the 1961 Freedom Ride, reflected, "To think a few short years ago blacks and whites could not board a Greyhound bus or a Trailways bus in [Washington] D.C. and travel together through the Deep South without the fear of being arrested, jailed, beaten or even facing death."[4] By stark contrast, not only were whites and blacks boarding buses together forty-seven years later; they were voting together in the presidential primary. In a history-making run for the White House between democratic nominees Hillary Clinton and Barack Obama, Iowa voters rallied together at the outset of the primary to set the tone for a hitherto unimaginable race to fill the Oval Office.

As we edged toward the symbolic shoreline of the Jordan river this summer in anticipation of November's electoral crossing, it was uncertain whether or not the nomination would actually prove to be the precursor into the promised land envisioned by King that stormy night in Memphis. Would this fortieth-anniversary nomination translate into a new era of unparalleled reconciliation, as in the case of South Africa's election of Nelson Mandela following the dismantling of apartheid? Would this presidential election commence a real shift in the "levers of power" in ways that allow the marginalized to flow at a sociopolitical pace afforded by the more affluent mainstream? Would justice, in the areas of housing, health care, education, employment, and working wages, roll down like a river and righteousness like a mighty stream, or would it be business as usual with respect to the kind of class and race matters that many believed to have already been resolved and relegated to a less fortunate past? As pollsters, political pundits, and talking heads weighed in on the matter, not a few seemed bent on making the case that a vote for Obama did not necessarily reflect a shift in national consensus regarding race matters. They encouraged their readers to believe that America was as racially divided today as they were in 2000.[5]

Believing that humanity was brilliantly created with the capacity to choose, King undoubtedly would have viewed this defining moment in American history within the context of a question he raised forty years ago in his 1968 publication of "Where Do We Go from Here: Chao or Community?" The prospect of a chaotic nation and world was evoked by King some forty years ago by the frightening prospect of an unbridled armaments race, the war in Vietnam, democracy's bitter contest with communism, and the lethal mix of racism and classism that polarized, and hence paralyzed, American progress. The chaos waiting in the wings of our modern day appeared much more ominous. Complexities in the economy, energy, and the environment staggered human imagination as never before. Threats of terrorism and global unrest, complicated by conditions of gross poverty, starvation, and devastating disease further aggravated the hopes of a stable worldhouse. Indeed, where do we go from here? Would we on the fortieth anniversary of King's death learn to live together as brothers, or would we opt to perish together like fools? Robert Franklin is right to insist that African Americans must assume their role in reclaiming and rebuilding their village via the family, church, and college, in his timely work entitled "Crisis in the Village: Restoring Hope in African American Communities." He does so, however, with an eye toward King's conception of interrelatedness and interdependence, this idea that we must increasingly learn how to live together and work together as sisters and brothers. By way of forthright introduction, Franklin writes:

> . . . we must discover and implement the science and art of making better families, communities, and we hope a better nation and global community. This is the work that Dr. King referred to as building the "beloved community." It is the work that will require the collective efforts, cooperation, and investment of the entire nation.[6]

In contemplating the fractured state of our current socioeconomic environment, King would have suggested that the root of our crisis, at bottom, is a reflection of our estrangement from God and our stubborn alienation from, and at times against, each other as fellow human beings created in the image of God. In the final analysis, it has been our moral failure to embrace the path of authentic reconciliation that has ushered us down the slippery slope toward national and global chaos. In this fortieth year, however, following King's tragic assassination, America has discovered the courage and moral fortitude to emerge from the social injustices of the past with brand-new human resolve to experience the triumph of beloved community. As a public theologian, King would have applauded this novel awakening of America's moral and spiritual center, a common ground not politically defined by the creation of "purple states" for the sake of constituents but one that is already inherently common by virtue of having been created in the image of God with "certain inalienable rights." In what proved to be a parting word King wrote,

> We are now faced with the fact that tomorrow is today. We are
> confronted with the fierce urgency of now. In this unfolding
> conundrum of life and history there is such a thing as being too late.
> Procrastination is still the thief of time. Life often leaves us standing
> bare, naked, and dejected with a lost opportunity. . . . We still have a
> choice today; nonviolent coexistence or violent coannihilation. This
> may well be mankind's last chance to choose between chaos and
> community.[7]

The election was certainly a hopeful indicator of the latter. Given his keen theological sense of humanity's interrelatedness, King would have insisted that much more was at stake than the mere election of the next president; the redemption of a nation's soul was being weighed in the balance. King would have been elated to have seen that many of the pundits were sadly mistaken in their sociological assumptions. More profoundly for King, the election of November 4, 2008, more than a vote for an African American presidential candidate, would have reflected an affirming vote for human capacity at its best. For King, the election numbers would have represented that long-awaited moral shift which announced the commenced healing of a nation, and America's deliberate choice to exit the wilderness of subtle separatisms in favor of their entrance to the promised land of a society that has become increasingly intolerant of the superficial biases that withheld opportunity on the basis of class, creed, and color.

King's theological anthropology provides a lasting testament of his belief that humanity possesses this innate ability to responsibly determine where we go from here. Humanity can choose to travel the high road of altruism or opt to traverse the low road of self-indulgence and self-destruction. Forty years ago Dr. Martin Luther King Jr. imagined a transformed nation, a people created in the image of God that would one day make it to the promised land. In what seemed to be a conversational continuum, president-elect Obama's first speech resonated with that of King's last as he explained, "The road ahead will be long. Our climb will be steep. We may not get there in one year or even in one term. But, America, I have never been more hopeful than I am tonight that we will get there." Given the possibility of promised land participation, advocates of beloved community certainly cannot help but remain hopeful that our journey "there" will now be infinitely more abbreviated than previously imagined.

Notes

1. Chappell seeks to minimize the authenticity of King's beliefs by suggesting that his student papers merely reflected an attempt to patronize his professors. "Some scholars suggest that the leading Personalist, Edgar Sheffield Brightman, is the culmination and synthesis of King's intellectual influences, the closest thing to a single intellectual model. But there is reason to doubt this. The Personalists graded King every semester." See David L. Chappell, *A Stone of Hope: Prophetic Religion and the Death of Jim Crow* (Chapel Hill: University of North Carolina Press, 2004), 53.

2. Lewis V. Baldwin, *The Legacy of Martin Luther King, Jr.: The Boundaries of Law, Politics, and Religion* (Notre Dame, Ind.: University of Notre Dame, 2002), 149.

CHAPTER I

1. "Antislavery was not a living presence in the 1950s and 1960s; it was rediscovered largely by academics and not by men and women centrally involved in agitation." Ronald Walters, "The Boundaries of Abolitionism," in *Antislavery Reconsidered: New Perspectives on the Abolitionists*, ed. Lewis Perry and Michael Fellman (Baton Rouge: Louisiana State University Press, 1979), 8; see also pages 7–9.

2. Martin Luther King Jr., "Bold Design for a New South, 1963," in *A Testament of Hope: The Essential Writings of Martin Luther King, Jr.*, ed. James Melvin Washington (New York: Harper and Row, 1986), 116.

3. King, "An Address before the National Press Club, 1962," in *A Testament of Hope*, 104.

4. Aristotle's pro-slavery sentiment is forthrightly expressed in *Politics*, in which he states that "it is clear that there are certain people who are free and certain people who are slaves [by nature], and it is both to their advantage, and just, for them to be slaves." See David Brion Davis, *In the Image of God: Religion, Moral Values, and Our Heritage of Slavery* (New Haven, Conn.: Yale University Press, 2001), 128.

5. Ibid., 130.

6. Ibid., 132.

7. According to Davis, "By the 1760's the antislavery arguments of Montesquieu and the Scottish philosopher Francis Hutcheson were being repeated, developed, and propagated by many of the intellectuals of the enlightened world, including such thinkers as Burke and Diderot. John Locke, "the great enemy of all absolute and arbitrary power," had been the last major philosopher to seek a justification for absolute and perpetual slavery." Ibid., 131–133.

8. Historians such as Ronald Walters generally agree that abolitionists were roughly defined by at least three primary schools of thought that emerged in the 1830s (Garrisonians, evangelicals, and political abolitionists), although the actual dynamics were much more complex and interwoven. The Garrisonians were most notably affiliated with the work of the American Anti-Slavery Society and, while denouncing direct political action, called for the discontinuance of the union between North and South. Protestant evangelicals, who had their roots in eighteenth-century revivalism, parted company with the Garrisonians during the mid-1840s to organize their American and Foreign Anti-Slavery Society, a group characterized by its "conventional revivalistic Christianity." Political abolitionists were typified by their attempts to address the issues of antislavery through their political involvements and founded the Liberty Party as a means of facilitating their efforts. While this kind of grouping into abolitionist categories is helpful, Walters also acknowledges the complex distinctions: "There are just too many exceptions to every rule—too many evangelicals who did not become abolitionists, too many men and women of rising status who did, too many family backgrounds similar to the abolitionists who did not care about emancipation or black people." See Ronald Walters, "The Boundaries of Abolitionism," in *Antislavery Reconsidered*, 20.

9. Vincent Harding, *There Is a River: The Black Struggle for Freedom in America* (New York: Harcourt Brace Jovanovich, 1981), 42.

10. Ira Berlin, *Many Thousands Gone: The First Two Centuries of Slavery in North America* (Cambridge, Mass.: Harvard University Press, 1998), 220.

11. Dan McKanan, *Identifying the Image of God: Radical Christians and Nonviolent Power in the Antebellum United States* (New York: Oxford University Press, 2002), 19.

12. "As the American slave system became increasingly profitable, the moral doubts of the Revolutionary generation gave way in the South to strong religious, economic, and racial arguments that defended slavery as a "positive good." See Davis, *In the Image of God*, 134.

13. Berlin, *Many Thousands Gone*, 223.

14. David M. Reimers, *White Protestantism and the Negro* (New York: Oxford University Press, 1965), 11.

15. Samuel May, in his work entitled *Some Recollections of Our Anti-slavery Conflict*, recounts the 1835 purchase of a church pew by a colored parishioner that so outraged fellow members that the door of his pew was nailed shut in protest of his presence among the white membership. Samuel J. May, *Some Recollections of Our Anti-Slavery Conflict* (Boston: Fields, Osgood, & Co., 1869), 269.

16. Harding, *There Is a River*, 46.

17. Reimers, *White Protestantism and the Negro*, 3.

18. Ibid., 16.

19. Ibid., 18.

20. Ibid., 19.

21. Ibid., 6.

22. Ibid., 9.

23. Berlin, *Many Thousands Gone*, 223.

24. Ibid., 4.

25. Martin Luther King Jr., *The Papers of Martin Luther King, Jr.*, vol. 2, *Rediscovering Precious Values*, ed. Clayborne Carson (Berkeley: University of California Press, 1994), 108.

26. Berlin, *Many Thousands Gone*, 220.

27. "At the beginning of the 1830's there were some 50 local and national, predominantly white, abolitionist groups, and these often depended upon Black churches for meeting places." See Harding, *There Is a River*, 124.

28. McKanan, *Identifying the Image of God*, 13.

29. While Darwinism pointed to human evolution as a natural law, pseudosciences were concurrently developed in the nineteenth century to heighten and confirm societal phobias that justified the institution of slavery by further denigrating Afro culture and life as a result of its suggestion that slaves and those of African descent were biologically and therefore inherently inferior.

30. Henry Highland Garnet, "Urges Slaves to Resist, August 1843," in *African-American Social and Political Thought 1850–1920*, ed. Howard Brotz (New Brunswick, N.J.: Transaction, 1999), 296.

31. Eddie S. Glaude, Jr., *Exodus: Religion, Race, and the Nation in Early Nineteenth-Century Black America* (Chicago: University of Chicago Press, 2000), 131.

32. William Whipper, "1873 Address to the American People," in *Exodus*, 131.

33. Reimers, *White Protestantism and the Negro*, 28.

34. Frederick Douglass, "What Are the Colored People Doing for Themselves? (December 1, 1850)," in *African-American Social and Political Thought 1850–1920*, 217.

35. James Cone, *Black Theology and Black Power* (New York: Orbis Books, 1997), 137–138.

36. Eugene D. Genovese, "The Legal Basis for Mastery," vol. 1, in *Major Problems in African American History*, ed. Thomas Holt and Elsa Brown (New York: Houghton Mifflin, 2000), 227.

37. Ibid., 226.

38. Adeleke Tunde, *UnAfrican Americans: Nineteenth-Century Black Nationalists and the Civilizing Mission* (Knoxville: University Press of Kentucky, 1998), 34.

39. McKanan, *Identifying the Image of God*, 7.

40. Harding, *There Is a River*, 242.

41. Ibid., 309.

42. Reimers, *White Protestantism and the Negro*, 36.

43. The U.S. Constitution declared that persons of African descent were only three-fifths human.

44. King, "The American Dream" (1961), in *A Testament of Hope*, 211.

45. Reimers, *White Protestantism and the Negro*, 10.

46. Martin Luther King Jr., "A Mass Meeting Address in Montgomery dated January 28, 1956", in *The Papers of Martin Luther King, Jr.*, vol. 3, *Birth of a New Age*, ed. Clayborne Carson (Berkeley: University of California Press, 1997), 108.

47. King, "I Have a Dream" (1963), in *A Testament of Hope*, 217.

48. C. Eric Lincoln, *Race, Religion, and the Continuing American Dilemma* (New York: Hill and Wang, 1999), 273.

49. King, "The Ethical Demands for Integration" (1962), in *A Testament of Hope*, 119.

50. Martin Luther King Jr., *Where Do We Go from Here: Chaos or Community?* (Boston: Beacon Press, 1968), 180.

51. Chapter 2 shall examine the influence of Personalism upon King's theological outlook regarding *imago Dei* and its relationship to human capacity.

52. King, "A Christmas Sermon on Peace" (1967), in *A Testament of Hope*, 255.

53. Martin Luther King Jr., *Strength to Love* (Philadelphia: Fortress Press, 1963), 124.

CHAPTER 2

1. David J. Garrow, "Martin Luther King, Jr.," in *Martin Luther King, Jr.: Civil Rights Leader, Theologian, Orator*, 3 vols., ed. David J. Garrow (New York: Carlson, 1989), 441.

2. King, "An Autobiography of Religious Development" (1950), in *The Papers of Martin Luther King, Jr.*, 1:360.

3. L. Harold DeWolf, Garrow, "Martin Luther King, Jr., as Theologian" in *Martin Luther King, Jr.: Civil Rights Leader, Theologian, Orator*, 264.

4. King, "An Autobiography of Religious Development," 1:363.

5. Martin Luther King Jr., *Stride toward Freedom* (New York: Harper and Row, 1958), 20.

6. Ibid., 91.

7. Ibid., 19.

8. Ibid.

9. Ibid., 20.

10. King, "An Autobiography of Religious Development," 1:360.

11. King, *Stride toward Freedom*, 90.

12. King briefly shares a few of these vivid childhood recollections: "I had grown up abhorring not only segregation but also the oppressive and barbarous acts that grew out of it. I passed spots where Negroes had been savagely lynched and watched the Ku Klux Klan on its rides at night. I had seen police brutality with my own eyes

and watched Negroes receive the most tragic injustice in the courts." See King, *Stride toward Freedom*, 90.

13. King, "An Autobiography of Religious Development," 1:362.

14. King, "The Negro and the Constitution" (1944), in *The Papers of Martin Luther King, Jr.*, 1:110–111.

15. The term "black church" is used loosely with an understanding that the black church, far from the monolithic sense in which it is often depicted, represented a broad range of positions and voices often developed in response to the regional and historical situation. While many would agree that little dichotomy is observed between secular community and sacred congregational life, their understanding of the church's affirmation of resistive versus accommodationist tendencies varies in scope and degree. Frazier offers a view that leans toward an accommodationist position and seemingly reads black church life as one bearing the hallmark of caution and conservatism with little to recommend it to notions of radicalism. Lincoln and Mamiya are less static, conceiving of varied possibilities that may exist between the poles marked by diametrically opposed responses in support of a dialectical model of church life. Within this rather dynamic spectrum, the church may have opted for one of several positions at any given time. As such, they recognized the blend of both resistive and accommodationist characteristics. Higginbotham expands the interpretative boundary in her conception of a dialogical model that allows for the widest range of possible discourses and responses, offering additional breadth and height to one's interpretative understanding of the black church and its historical evolution, particularly as that progression relates itself to the question of nonviolent resistance as an embraced movement methodology. A less vigorous discussion of resistance versus accommodationism runs the risk of oversimplifying an extremely complex question that rarely fits into the nice, neat categories that we sometimes prefer for the sake of historical analysis.

16. The National Baptist Convention, then under the leadership of the Reverend J. H. Jackson, represented the most significant contingent of black Baptist churches in the nation. Daddy King and his Ebenezer Baptist Church were longtime members of the organization. The convention's 1961 split, resulting in the founding of the Progressive National Baptist Convention, offered King and the civil rights movement an alternative national platform.

17. Gayraud S. Wilmore, *Black Religion and Black Radicalism: An Interpretation of the Religious History of Afro-American People* (New York: Orbis Books, 1983), 179.

18. Albert J. Raboteau, "African Americans, Exodus, and the American Israel," in *Religion and Culture: A Reader*, 2nd ed., ed. David G. Hackett (New York: Routledge, 2003), 83.

19. Glaude, *Exodus*, 109.

20. Raboteau, "African Americans, Exodus, and the American Israel," 83.

21. Ibid., 77.

22. Ibid., 80.

23. Harding, *There Is a River*, 61.

24. Raboteau, "African Americans, Exodus, and the American Israel," 81.

25. Ibid., 84.

26. Ibid., 80.

27. King, "Letter to Samuel D. Proctor, October 1954," in *The Papers of Martin Luther King, Jr.*, 1:297.

28. Samuel Dewitt Proctor, *The Substance of Things Hoped For: A Memoir of African-American Faith* (New York: Putnam, 1995), xxiii.

29. Ibid., 31.

30. Ibid., 147.

31. King, *Stride toward Freedom*, 96.

32. Mordecai Wyatt Johnson, 1927 Inaugural Address, *in Education for Freedom* (Washington, D.C.: Moorland-Spingarn Research Center, 1976), 23, 24.

33. King, "The Sources of Fundamentalism and Liberalism Considered Historically and Psychologically" (1949), in *The Papers of Martin Luther King, Jr.*, 1:237.

34. Ibid., 239.

35. Samuel DuBois Cook, "The American Liberal Democratic Tradition, the Black Revolution, and Martin Luther King, Jr.," in *The Political Philosophy of Martin Luther King, Jr*, ed. Hanes Walton (Westport, Conn.: Greenwood, 1971), xxxiii.

36. King shares a brief summary of the insights provided by Personalism: "Personalism gave me metaphysical and philosophical grounding for the idea of a personal God, and it gave me a metaphysical basis for the dignity and worth of all human personality." See King, *Stride toward Freedom*, 101.

37. King, *The Papers of Martin Luther King, Jr.*, 1:363. Interestingly, Reinhold Niebuhr would experience a similar kind of return to the ideals that he grew up under as well: "Although Richard later destroyed all his correspondence, Fox has found sufficient evidence to suggest that Reinhold was vulnerable to his brother's remonstrance that Moral Man was still 'too romantic' about human nature and the promise of controlling historical change. Prodded by Richard's perceptive criticisms and by a fear that he had nearly forsaken his father's Biblical heritage, Niebuhr's interest gravitated toward theology and the goal of finding a Christian alternative to the illusory hopes of communism."

38. Garrow, "Martin Luther King, Jr.," 437.

39. McKanan, *Identifying the Image of God*, 13.

40. See also chapter 2 of this book.

41. Reinhold Niebuhr understands sectarian Protestantism as moving along at least two distinct paths; one points to the virtues of individual piety while the other is more social and eschatological: "Though the sects of the Reformation define salvation in essentially Renaissance and Perfectionist terms, rather than in terms of the Reformation, they do retain the Christian concept of grace. The Pietist sects believe that grace is required for the realization of individual perfection; and the apocalyptic sects depend upon the interposition of divine providence for the culmination of the whole historical process in an ideal society." See Niebuhr, *The Nature and Destiny of Man*, vol. 2, *Human Destiny* (New York: Scribner's 1964), 154.

42. Ibid., 152.

43. Ibid., 181.

44. McKanan, *Identifying the Image of God*, 18.

45. King, "The Sources of Fundamentalism and Liberalism Considered Historically and Psychologically," 1:239.

46. King, *Stride toward Freedom*, 21.

47. King explains the obligatory desire when he writes, "We never wanted to be detached spectators. Since racial discrimination was most intense in the South, we felt that some of the Negroes who had received a portion of their training in other sections of the country should return to share their broader contacts and educational experience in its solution. Moreover despite having to sacrifice much of the cultural life we loved, despite the existence of Jim Crow which kept reminding us at all times of the color of our skin, we had the feeling that something remarkable was unfolding in the South, and we wanted to be on hand to witness it. The region had marvelous possibilities, and once it came to itself and removed the blight of racial segregation, it would experience a moral, political, and economic boom hardly paralleled by any other section of the country." See King, *Stride toward Freedom*, 21–22.

48. Stephen B. Oates, "The Intellectual Odyssey of Martin Luther King," in *Martin Luther King, Jr.: Civil Rights Leader, Theologian, Orator*, 717.

49. King's first address as the newly appointed president of the Montgomery Improvement Association, given from the pulpit of the Holt Street Baptist Church, Montgomery, Alabama, December 5, 1955.

50. King, "Annual Recommendation to the Church" (1954–1955), in *The Papers of Martin Luther King, Jr.*, 2:290.

51. Robert M. Franklin, *Liberating Visions: Human Fulfillment and Social Justice in African-American Thought* (Minneapolis, Minn.: Fortress Press, 1990), 139.

CHAPTER 3

1. King, "An Autobiography of Religious Development," 1:361.

2. Allan Boesak, "Coming In Out of the Wilderness," in *Martin Luther King, Jr.: Civil Rights Leader, Theologian, Orator*, 86.

3. Reinhold Niebuhr, *The Nature and Destiny of Man*, vol. 1, *Human Nature* (New York: Prentice Hall, 1964), 158.

4. Dan McKanan discusses the evolution of Christian traditions into nineteenth-century concepts of *imago Dei*: "Liberal theology revolved around the doctrine of the *imago Dei*. This, of course, was no innovation of the 19th century. It placed the reformers in a long, if somewhat discontinuous, tradition. In Genesis, God creates humanity 'in our image, after our likeness' (1:26). In the context of the Hellenistic world, this teaching fits nicely with the Platonic doctrines that each human soul is a seed or spark of divinity, and that likeness is the basis of love. Christian Platonists taught that the essential kinship between God and the soul allowed humans to grow steadily in likeness to God, ultimately achieving full divinization. Various schools of esoteric and mystical Christianity have preserved this view through the centuries." See McKanan, *Identifying the Image of God*, 13.

5. One of the several nagging questions put to Augustine dealt with the origin and source of evil. If all is good, how then does one understand the reality of evil in the world?

6. Davis, *In the Image of God*, 232.

7. Unlike the common *Webster's* definition conveying the thought of a traditional story dealing with supernatural ancestors or a person/thing of unverifiable or imaginary existence, a myth, for Niebuhr, represented "a story, the origin of which is generally forgotten, which serves to explain the basis of a religious practice or belief. The myth is an artistic attempt to give depth to history." See *The Papers of Martin Luther King, Jr.*, 1:275.

8. King, "The Theology of Reinhold Niebuhr" (1954), in *The Papers of Martin Luther King, Jr.*, 2:274.

9. King, "Qualifying Examination Answers, Theology of the Bible" (1953), in *The Papers of Martin Luther King, Jr.*, 2:209.

10. Martin Luther, *Luther's Commentary on Genesis*, ed. J. Theodore Mueller. (Grand Rapids, MI: Zondervan, 1958), 121.

11. Ibid., 30.

12. As Reinhold Niebuhr explains, "Luther's extravagant descriptions of the state of perfection before the Fall are so obviously prompted by the desire to accentuate man's present state of sin, misery, and death; and they are, compared with both Augustine and Calvin, so inexact that his thought is not very helpful in interpreting the real import of the Christian conception of the image of God." See Niebuhr, *The Nature and Destiny of Man*, 1:161.

13. Luther, *Luther's Commentary on Genesis*, 73.

14. King, "How Modern Christians Should Think of Man" (1949), in *The Papers of Martin Luther King, Jr.*, 1:275.

15. Calvin, *Calvin's Institutes*," vol. 1, 208.

16. Ibid., ii.17.

17. Ibid., iii.5.

18. King, "A Comparison and Evaluation of the Theology of Luther with That of Calvin" (1953), in *The Papers of Martin Luther King, Jr.*, 2:190.

19. King, "The Place of Reason and Experience in Finding God" (1949), in *The Papers of Martin Luther King, Jr.*, 1:236.

20. Ibid., 236.

21. Ibid., 232.

22. King, "Notecards on Books of the Old Testament" (1952), in *The Papers of Martin Luther King, Jr.*, 2:166.

23. King comments on the inadequacy of William E. Hocking's philosophy: "I cannot see how Hocking can insist upon a theoretical rather than a "practical" certainty in the whole field of scientific inquiry. It seems that he fails to take seriously the significance of the particular and the contingent with which the natural sciences have to deal. Moreover, he fails to take seriously the fact that all truth, including religious, is based on the assumption that the human mind is valid and that the cosmos is rational." See King, "*A Comparison and Evaluation of the Philosophical Views Set Forth in J. M. E. McTaggart's Some Dogmas of Religion, and William E. Hocking's The Meaning of God in Human Experience with Those Set Forth in Edgar S. Brightman's Course on 'Philosophy of Religion'*" in *The Papers of Martin Luther King, Jr.*, 2:90. King

also points to the science of archaeology as a valid critique against the staunch claims of fundamentalism in an essay prepared during his first semester at Crozer: "A group of competent scholars came on the scene, who were both curious and discontent. They were not willing to accept those things which appeared to be mythological and legendary as historical truths. They dared, in the face of a world of fundamentalists, to apply the scientific method to a study of the Old Testament." See King, in *The Papers of Martin Luther King, Jr,* 1:163.

24. Richard Lischer, *The Preacher King: Martin Luther King, Jr., and the Word That Moved America* (New York: Oxford University Press, 1995), 208.

25. Niebuhr, *The Nature and Destiny of Man,* vol. 2, 172.

26. Niebuhr acknowledges the role of Catholicism in the formulation of Renaissance philosophy: "Franciscan theologians mediated both the individual perfectionist urge and the hope of historical fulfillment of the Renaissance." Ibid., 162.

27. Ibid., 166.

28. Reinhold Niebuhr is extremely helpful in drawing a distinction between the various sects found under the general heading of sectarian Protestantism: "In order to explore the genius of sectarianism more fully, it is advisable to distinguish between two types of sects, or at least between two impulses in sectarianism: (a) The impulse towards the perfection of the individual life expressed in the pietistic sects and (b) the impulse towards the fulfillment of history expressed particularly in the Anabaptist and socially radical [eschatological] sects." Ibid., 170.

29. Ibid., 176.

30. Troeltch distinguishes between eschatological sects that awaited the ushered-in kingdom and those who were willing to engage the enemy to assure its arrival. Ibid., 176.

31. Walter Rauschenbusch, *A Theology for the Social Gospel* (New York: Macmillan, 1917), 87.

32. Niebuhr, *The Nature and Destiny of Man,* vol. 2, 179.

33. King, "The Sources of Fundamentalism and Liberalism Considered Historically and Psychologically," 1:240.

34. Carson, *The Papers of Martin Luther King, Jr.,* 2:3.

35. King, "How Modern Christians Should Think of Man," 1:278.

36. King, "The Place of Reason and Experience in Finding God," in 1:239.

37. King, "Notecards on Books of the Old Testament," 2:166.

38. King, "Contemporary Continental Theology" (1952), in *The Papers of Martin Luther King, Jr.,* 2:138.

39. King recalls the racially motivated incident involving the discontinuance of a relationship with his childhood playmate, in addition to a number of personal and observed experiences.

40. Stephen Oates, *Let the Trumpet Sound: The Life of Martin Luther King, Jr.* (New York: Harper and Row, 1982), 30.

41. King, "Contemporary Continental Theology," 2:137.

42. Boesak, "Coming In Out of the Wilderness," 67.

43. Reinhold Niebuhr, cited in Stephen Oates, *Let the Trumpet Sound,* 34.

CHAPTER 4

1. King, "Six Talks in Outline" (1949), in *Papers of Martin Luther King, Jr.*, 1:245.

2. Niebuhr, *The Nature and Destiny of Man*, 1:245.

3. King, "The Answer to a Perplexing Question," *Strength to Love*, 132.

4. King, "How Modern Christians Should Think of Man," 1:277.

5. A detailed description of King's Personalist view is provided in chapter 3 of this book.

6. Otis Turner, "Nonviolence and the Politics of Liberation," in *Martin Luther King, Jr.: Civil Rights Leader, Theologian, Orator*, 1000.

7. King, "The Significant Contributions of Jeremiah to Religious Thought" (1948), in *The Papers of Martin Luther King, Jr.*, 1:185.

8. It is not altogether surprising that Stephen Tempier, the archbishop of the Paris church, would also condemn Aquinas's writings following his death, considering his reliance upon Aristotle both dangerous and heretical. Renick explains, "Aquinas's intellect was of such a high order and his work was so challenging and complex, that it took a little time for Christian leaders to realize that Aquinas's ideas represented a defense of the church rather than a threat to it." See Timothy M. Renick, *Aquinas for Armchair Theologians* (Louisville, Ky.: Westminster John Knox Press, 2002), 12.

9. Renick explains, "Aquinas integrated the ideas of the Bible; Aristotle (whom Aquinas calls simply 'the Philosopher' throughout), Augustine, Jerome, and other earlier Christian authors; the great Jewish philosopher Maimonides; Muslim thinkers such as Averoes and Avicenna; and countless others. If Christianity was to be, as it claimed, the universal church with the universal truth, it must not limit its debate to Christians. It should listen to great minds of Judaism, Islam, and even the pagans. It should learn from the wise wherever they can be found. The novelty of Aquinas in the history of early Christianity is that he did just that." See Renick, *Aquinas for Armchair Theologians*, 10.

10. Aquinas, *The Summa Theologica*, Pt. 1, Third Number, q. 85, Art. 1.

11. Law professor John Finnis explains, "Harmony with the transcendent source of the universe's existence and order is a good which Aquinas judges basic and the object of natural inclination." See John Finnis, *Aquinas* (Oxford: Oxford University Press: 1998), 85.

12. Renick, *Aquinas for Armchair Theologians*, 35.

13. Aquinas writes, "Now the intellect or mind is that whereby the rational creature excels other creatures; wherefore this image of God is not found even in the rational creature except in the mind; while in other parts, which the rational creature may happen to possess, we find the likeness of a trace, as in other creatures to which, in reference to such parts, the rational creature can be likened. . . . So we find in man a likeness to God by way of an image in his mind; but in other parts of his being by way of a trace." See Aquinas, *The Summa Theologcia*, Q. 93, Art. 6, Pt. 1.

14. King, who often reminded his listeners that "each of us have certain basic rights that are neither derived from nor conferred by the state," resorts to Aquinas to substantiate this claim in his famous "Letter from the Birmingham City Jail." King explains, "How does one determine when a law is just or unjust? A just law

is a manmade code that squares with the moral law or law of God. An unjust law is a code that is out of harmony with the moral law. To put it in the terms of Saint Thomas Aquinas, an unjust law is a human law that is not rooted in eternal and natural law. Any law that uplifts human personality is just. Any law that degrades human personality is unjust." See King, "Letter from Birmingham City Jail" (1963), in *A Testament of Hope*, 293.

15. Aquinas explains, "Although the eternal law is unknown to us accordingly as it is the Divine Mind: Nevertheless, it becomes known to us somewhat, either by natural reason which is derived therefrom as its proper image; or by some sort of additional revelation." See Thomas Aquinas, *The Summa Theologica*, q. 19, Art. 4, A. 3, Pt. 1-11.

16. Aquinas, *The Summa Theologica*, q. 19, Art. 3, A. 1, Pt. 1-11.

17. Renick writes, "While accepting God's existence as an article of faith (i.e., because the Bible or the church says so) is to be valued, a deeper (or at least different) understanding comes when we establish God's existence by rational means—precisely because we are, by design, rational creatures." See Renick, *Aquinas for Armchair Theologians*, 21.

18. King, "A Comparison and Evaluation of the Theology of Luther with That of Calvin," 2:190.

19. Oates, "The Intellectual Odyssey of Martin Luther King," 717.

20. King, "Six Talks in Outline," in 1:249.

21. Ibid.

CHAPTER 5

1. King, "The Negro and the Constitution," 1:109.

2. Cited in Baldwin, *The Legacy of Martin Luther King, Jr.*, 126.

3. Ibid. Also see Michael E. Dyson, *I May Not Get There with You: The True Martin Luther King, Jr.* (New York: Free Press, 2000), 38–39.

4. "Having studied the social contract theories of Thomas Hobbes and John Locke, King found in the Enlightenment ideals of Tolerance, Reason, and Natural Law much of the context for his appreciation of the Declaration of Independence and the Constitution. Moreover, King discovered in these founding documents, and in the Emancipation Proclamation, the same basic values that permeated African American religion, literature, and art." See Baldwin, "American Political Traditions and the Christian Faith," in *The Legacy of Martin Luther King, Jr.*, 222.

5. Richard Lischer provides helpful insights into the centrality of King's use of scripture: "The Constitution protects all people and, lest African Americans not be included in the legal definition of 'people' (as historically they were not), King reminds his listeners that the Bible contains the true definition of 'people.' The Bible says a person is a creature who is capable of a relationship with God. All people were created for this relationship in the image of God."

6. As McKanan explains: "The 'politics of identification' had deep but paradoxical roots in the culture of the early United States. Politically, its proponents were inspired

by the words of the Declaration of Independence: 'We hold these truths to be self-evident: that all men are created equal; and that they are endowed by their creator with certain unalienable rights; that among these are life, liberty, and the pursuit of happiness.' To promote identification among free and equal individuals, reformers could plausibly argue, was to fulfill the nation's central vision. Yet they also knew that the United States Constitution denied voting rights to women and many poor people and sanctioned the enslavement of blacks. The Constitution assumed, moreover, that the nation would be held together not by identification, but by military force and judicial coercion." See McKanan, *Identifying the Image of God*, 4.

7. King, *Stride toward Freedom*, 190.

8. King, "Facing the Challenge of a New Age" (1956), in *A Testament of Hope*, 137.

9. King, "I See the Promised Land" (1968), in *A Testament of Hope*, 280.

10. Rufus Burrow Jr., "Personalism, the Objective Moral Order, and Moral Law in the Work of Martin Luther King, Jr.," in *The Legacy of Martin Luther King, Jr.*, 241.

11. King, "The Ethical Demands for Integration," 119.

12. Luther Ivory explains, "The genuine worth of human beings was to be measured by a standard other than human. Consequently, King used the *imago Dei* to appeal to the white conscience. He urged whites, on theological grounds, to acknowledge the sacredness of black beings and the humanity and equal worth of black folk as brothers and sisters in the one, large family of God. King also used *the imago Dei* to issue appeals to blacks to overcome a sense of nobodiness and to develop a healthy self-love and a sense of Somebodyness. King argued that this change in racial self-perception represented, perhaps, the movement's greatest achievement." Luther D. Ivory, *Toward a Theology of Radical Involvement: The Theological Legacy of Martin Luther King, Jr.* (Nashville, Tenn.: Abingdon Press, 1997), 58.

13. Garth Baker-Fletcher analyzes the civil rights movement theme of human dignity captured in the notion of "Somebodyness" often used by King. See Garth Baker-Fletcher, *Somebodyness: Martin Luther King, Jr. and the Theory of Dignity* (Minneapolis, Minn.: Fortress Press, 1993).

14. Cited in Cook, "The American Liberal Democratic Tradition, the Black Revolution and Martin Luther King, Jr.," xxviii.

15. King, "The American Dream," 208.

16. King, "A Christmas Sermon on Peace," 255.

17. "Every person is of inestimable value to God. This necessarily implied for King the obligation of persons to treat self and others with respect. The idea of an inborn ideal of worth is prominent in the ethical system of Bowne, the black church, and the Jewish-Christian traditions, each of which influenced King." See Burrow, "Personalism," 222.

18. Ibid., 283.

19. Ibid., 281.

20. King, "The Ethical Demands for Integration," 119.

21. Historian Taylor Branch is correct in describing the ways in which Niebuhr's views on sin served to curb King's acceptance of liberalism's *extreme* views on pacifism. He fails, however, to indicate the important ways in which King critiques

Niebuhr, leaving the reader to erroneously assume that King remained "enamored" with Niebuhr and/or somehow became theologically indecisive following his encounter with neo-orthodoxy. Taylor writes, "After Niebuhr, King experienced for the first time a loss of confidence in his own chosen ideas rather than inherited ones. . . . King devoted much of his remaining graduate school career to the study of Niebuhr, who touched him on all his tender points, from pacifism and race to sin." See Taylor Branch, *Parting the Waters* (New York: Simon and Schuster, 1988), 81–87. Richard Lischer provides a much more accurate account when he writes, "King was chastened by his encounter with Niebuhr but he never converted." See Lischer, *The Preacher King*, 61. While admittedly appreciative of Niebuhr's Christian Realism, King also clearly indicates the degree to which he disagreed with Niebuhr's assessment of human nature, preferring the tenets of a slightly more optimistic anthropology instead. King explains, "At first, Niebuhr's critique of pacifism left me in a state of confusion. As I continued to read, however, I came to see more and more the shortcomings of his position. . . . True pacifism is not unrealistic submission to evil power, as Niebuhr contends. It is rather a courageous confrontation of evil by the power of love, in the faith that it is better to be the recipient of violence than the inflictor of it, since the latter only multiplies the existence of violence and bitterness in the universe, while the former may develop a sense of shame in the opponent, and thereby bring about a transformation and change of heart. . . . While I still believed in man's potential for good, Niebuhr made me realize his potential for evil." As opposed to retreating from pacifism altogether, King writes, "After reading Niebuhr, I tried to arrive at a realistic pacifism. . . . It was at Boston University that I came to see that Niebuhr had overemphasized the corruption of human nature. His pessimism concerning human nature was not balanced by an optimism concerning divine nature." See King, *Stride toward Freedom*, 97–101. King's nuanced theological anthropology, an indication of his *preference for* his chosen ideas as opposed to inherited ones, is subtle yet critical to our understanding of where King stood theologically.

22. Lischer says of King: "Martin Luther King was the last of the great liberals in America to identify the purposes of social reform with those of Christianity." See Lischer, *The Preacher King*, 148.

23. During his studies at Boston University, King examined Reinhold Niebuhr's theology and as such was not unaware of the distinctions Niebuhr made with respect to individual and group dynamics. In an essay describing Niebuhr's theology, King writes, "One of the first problems to oppress Niebuhr was the terrible contrast between 'moral man and immoral society,' between the relatively decent, good behavior of man as an individual, and man as society. His analysis of this contrast led him to the roots of the contradiction of human nature. He cogently states, 'Individual men may be moral in the sense that they are able to consider interests of others than their own in determining problems of conduct, and are capable, on occasion, of preferring the advantages of others to their own. . . . But all of these achievements are more difficult, if not impossible, for human societies and social groups." See King, "The Theology of Reinhold Niebuhr," 2:271.

24. Fanon, a mid-twentieth-century liberationist writer from Martinique, authored a work entitled *The Wretched of the Earth* that addressed the plight of

oppressed Algerians and their struggle for freedom and decolonization. This book, widely read by a more radical contingent within the civil rights movement, included violence as a viable means of securing one's liberation, a position that King emphatically refuted in his critique of Fanon: "These are brave and challenging words; I am happy that young black men and women are quoting them. But the problem is that Fanon and those who quote his words are seeking 'to work out new concepts' and 'set afoot a new man' with a willingness to imitate old concepts of violence. Is there not a basic contradiction here? Violence has been the inseparable twin of materialism, the hallmark of its grandeur and misery. This is the one thing about modern civilization that I do not care to imitate." See King, *Where Do We Go from Here?* 65–66.

25. Henry H. Mitchell, *Black Church Beginnings* (Grand Rapids, Mich.: Eerdmans, 2004), 16.

26. C. Eric Lincoln contends that the lines of black secular culture and black sacred life are, in fact, blurred and that the degree to which they overlap as black sacred cosmos is far more significant than attempts to understand each as separate and wholly distinct social realities. E. Franklin Frazier, however, insists that much of this interchange receded by the mid–twentieth century, due to the church's increased reliance on organizations such as the NAACP and the Urban League to address its lingering sociopolitical affairs. Hence, while it could be said that King stood within the scope of the earlier tradition in the manner described earlier, he distinguished himself from many of his contemporaries by continuing to bring "political affairs into the pulpit," a view less frequently embraced. See also chapter 3.

27. Although Lischer compares King to the more conciliatory examples provided by preachers such as Richard Allen and Daniel Coker (*The Preacher King*, 33–34), these northern elites may not have reflected the level of suspicion that may have typified black church life, particularly among the nonelite masses.

28. Cited in Albert J. Raboteau, *Slave Religion: The "Invisible Institution" in the Antebellum South* (New York: Oxford University Press, 1978), 310.

29. Lischer explains, "Finally, liberalism and the black gospel tradition were optimistic about the human future but on entirely different grounds. Liberals viewed history as a continuum that could not be thrown askew by divine interventions because history was itself governed by divinely sanctioned laws. The primary source of these laws, however, was not the particular message of any religion but a more general revelation manifest not in burning bushes or inspired prophets but in the noblest ideals of thinking people everywhere (the West). The so-called laws of history, by which liberals really meant to indicate their moral prescriptions for the future, were nothing but tentacles of human nature. . . . King had been raised on hope, though in his seminary years he referred to it as 'optimism'" and attributed it not to the black church's profound trust in the providence of God but to his own psychological makeup. In one of his student term papers he wrote, "Also my liberal leaning may root back to the great imprint that many liberal theologians have left upon me and to my ever present desire to be optimistic about human nature." See Lischer, *The Preacher King*, 57.

30. Ibid.

31. Cited in Carol George, "Widening the Circle," in *Antislavery Reconsidered*, 88.

32. McKanan, *Identifying the Image of God*, 4.

33. As King proceeds with his analysis of human nature, he does so not unaware of the liberal view, with its secular suggestion of human progress. King writes, "The so-called Enlightenment of the 18th century, which had its roots in the Renaissance, had made a new appearance in the easy optimism of the first three decades of the 20th century. Man was viewed as the measure of all things. History was to witness a quick and steady progress to Utopia. Man had only to be educated and put in agreeable environments in order that the kingdom of heaven might be realized on earth." See King, "The Theology of Reinhold Niebuhr," 2:271.

34. George, "Widening the Circle," 92.

35. Franklin, *Liberating Visions*, 110.

36. King did not view the achievement of justice as an end; instead, it was a necessary means to a greater end, beloved community. Franklin explains, "If King's social vision had been limited to fulfilling the demands of procedural justice, probably he would not have spent his public ministry trying to urge the United States and the international community to redirect their energies and resources away from violence toward creating the beloved community. King saw the limits of focusing exclusively on power or procedural justice as a means to achieving ideal society." See Franklin, *Liberating Visions*, 135.

37. King affirmed a concept of inevitable human progress; it is, however, emphatically distinguished from liberalism's theory of inevitability in that he placed God, not man, at the center of humanity's progress. Although human nature is necessarily endowed with the capacity to desire and to do that which is socially *good* as a means of cooperation with God, ultimately it is God, not a particular personality, that initiates social advancement. King explains, "The Montgomery story would have taken place if the leaders of the protest had never been born . . . . Whatever the name, some force labors to create a harmony out of the discords of the universe. There is a creative power that works to pull down mountains of evil and hilltops of injustice. God still works throughout history His wonders to perform. It seems as though God had decided to use Montgomery as a proving ground for the struggle and triumph of freedom and justice in America." See King, *Stride toward Freedom*, 51. The implication, of course, is that God initiates, recruits, and sustains great social movements; if Martin Luther King Jr., R. D. Nesbitt, Fred Gray, Judge Johnson, Ralph Abernathy, Virginia Durr, E. D. Nixon, Joanne Robinson, Rosa Parks, and others were not available, God would have orchestrated the movement with another cast of individuals. Of the reformer Martin Luther, he writes, "The Reformation was inevitable. . . . The significance of the individual in such a period of history is that he stands in the midst of the ongoing social movement and gives it guidance and direction." See King, "A Comparison and Evaluation of the Theology of Luther with That of Calvin," 2:175.

38. Franklin says of King: "Personally, he embodied the virtues of liberal Christianity, black folk culture, and the American political tradition of human rights and pragmatism. Symbolically, he was a man for all seasons and people, who managed to combine his African-American cultural and political agenda with his quest for an inclusive, universal identity." See Franklin, *Liberating Visions*, 103.

39. Lischer alludes to this tendency in King's preaching when he explains: "Given the theological climate in which King was trained, his own analytical step back from the text frequently led him to the authority of psychology. The Baptist tradition in which he was brought up had dwelt upon the motives and gradations of the individual's response to God, to the point that evangelism had become a science of conversion. By the mid–20th century, psychology had become the secular successor of pietism and had established itself as an objective science of human behavior. The laws of psychology were premised upon an *idealized essence* of humanity that can be known apart from the authority of biblical revelation. This is the credo of liberalism, and, insofar as King was a participant in that theological subculture, it is discernable in many of his sermons." See Lischer, *The Preacher King*, 208.

40. King, *Stride toward Freedom*, 106.

41. Ibid. A close read of King reveals the degree to which his theological anthropology was supported by aspects of his Christology, ecclesiology, pneumotology, and eschatology.

42. Lischer writes, "The church does not imagine its own future by extrapolating from human ideals but by relying on God's intervention. King knew both views and unconsciously superimposed one upon the other until toward the end of his career the liberal optimism was blown away, exposing once again the bedrock of black eschatology." See Lischer, *The Preacher King*, 57.

43. Raboteau explains, "Old Testament prophecies of the destruction of Israel's enemies easily and naturally fit the slave's desire that whites suffer just retribution for the brutality of slavery. Biblical prophets had spoken in images violent enough to suit the most vengeful feelings. Mary Livermore, a New England governess on a Southern plantation, was astonished by the prophetic terms which Aggy, the normally 'taciturn' housekeeper, used to express her outrage at the beating her master had given her daughter: Thar's a day a-comin'! Thar's a day a-comin'. . . . I hear de rumblin' ob de chariots! I see de flashin' ob de guns! White folks' blood is a runnin' on de ground like a riber, an' de dead's heaped up dat high! . . . Oh, Lor'! Hasten de day when de blows, an de bruises, an de aches, an de pains, shall come to de white folks, an de buzzards shall eat 'em as dey's dead in de streets. Oh, Lor'! Roll on de chariots, an gib de black people rest an' peace. Oh, Lor'! Gib me de pleasure ob livin' till dat day when I shall see white folks shot down like de wolves when dey come hungry out o' de woods!" See Raboteau, *Slave Religion*, 312.

CHAPTER 6

1. Ralph Luker provides an explanation of Josiah Royce's approach to beloved community. Royce identified with a universal human condition: fallen, divided by false centers of loyalty, in need of reconciliation and redemption. This universal human community was, nonetheless, beloved of God; and his love and loyalty were made known to us in Jesus Christ. In this way, Royce reinterpreted Saint Paul's understanding of the church as the body of Christ and extended Paul's metaphor to include all humanity as the "Beloved Community." It was, he said, "an ideal community of all faithful, which was to become the community of all mankind, and

which was to become someday the possessor of all the earth, the exponent of true charity, at once the spirit and the ruler of the humanity of the future." See Ralph Luker, *The Social Gospel in Black and White* (Durham: University of North Carolina Press, 1998), 281.

2. McKanan, *Identifying the Image of God*, 15.

3. As noted in chapter 2, while the black church rarely if ever embraced liberal notions of human progress from a purely humanistic view, it did appropriate, as in the case of Christianity, nuanced notions of freedom and Jeffersonian egalitarianism through the filter of the black church's experience of enslavement and human suffering. While the liberal overtones of the Declaration of Independence obviously did not take on the same meaning originally intended by its framers, the idea of God granting individual rights was undoubtedly appropriated and ideologically adjusted to include them. In this sense the early black church represented an eclectic mix of African tradition, Christian faith, and versions of sociopolitical aspirations born of nineteenth-century Protestant liberalism, each recast in the service of African emancipation. In some respect even so-called metaphysical categories (though certainly not called by that name) offered temporary refuge and some degree of transcendence above the toils of their indefinite term of human hardship, as in the case of Saint John's Isle of Patmos experience. Faith declared something beyond!

4. Boesak, "Coming In Out of the Wilderness," 86.

5. John H. Cartwright, "The Social Eschatology of Martin Luther King, Jr.," in *Martin Luther King, Jr.: Civil Rights Leader, Theologian, Orator*, 166.

6. Walter E. Fluker, *They Looked for a City* (Boston: University Press of America, 1989), 113.

7. Charles Marsh, "The Civil Rights Movement as Theological Drama: Interpretation and Application," *Modern Theology* 18 (April 2002): 233.

8. Ibid.

9. Burrow, "Personalism," 227.

10. Henry, Charles P., "Delivering Daniel: The Dialectic of Ideology and Theology in the Thought of Martin Luther King, Jr." *Journal of Black Studies* 17 (1987): 327–345.

11. Booker T. Washington, "Atlanta Exposition Address, September 18, 1895," in *African-American Social and Political Thought 1850–1920*, 358.

12. Cartwright, "The Social Eschatology of Martin Luther King, Jr.," 166.

13. Charles Marsh, *The Beloved Community: How Faith Shapes Social Justice, from the Civil Rights Movement to Today* (New York: Perseus Books, 2004), 50.

14. Cook, "The American Liberal Democratic Tradition, the Black Revolution, and Martin Luther King, Jr.," xxx.

15. Tera Hunter illustrates this relationship in her essay entitled "The Politics of Labor." "By the late 19th century, upper class (Atlantan) whites in large numbers had moved out to ostentatious suburbs and had begun to escape regular interaction with the unattractive sites that the inequitable distribution of city resources typically bred. Yet these white suburbanites continued to hire black household workers from such malodorous neighborhoods. White anxieties about the contaminating touch of black women reflected the ambivalence of a tension between revulsion and attraction to the worker who performed the most

intimate labor, e.g., taking care of children." See Thomas Holt and Elsa Brown, eds., *Major Problems in African American History*, vol. 2 (New York: Houghton Mifflin, 2000), 119.

16. See King, "Love, Law and Civil Disobedience," November 16, 1961, in *A Testament of Hope*, 48.

17. James H. Cone, "Martin and Malcolm," in *Religion and American Culture: A Reader*, ed. David G. Hackett (New York: Routledge 2003), 402.

18. Baldwin, *The Legacy of Martin Luther King, Jr.*, 90–91.

19. Roger Lloyd, *The Beloved Community* (New York: Macmillan, 1937), 178.

20. Ibid., 177.

21. Maggie Walker, a successful black female entrepreneur from Richmond, Virginia, chided the black church leadership for its civic inactivity and lack of social engagement: "And yet with the loss of citizenship . . . the destroying of Negro business enterprises, the refusal of employment to Negroes; the attempt to drive out the Negro barbers, and Negroes from every other occupation, with hostile legislation on the increase—there are still those who believe that we should look to the Lord and keep our mouths shut." Holt and Brown, *Major Problems in African-American History*, vol. 2, 163.

22. Baldwin, *The Legacy of Martin Luther King, Jr.*, 94. In all fairness to Jackson, he did, as president of the National Baptist Convention and pastor of his local Chicago congregation, offer to assist King monetarily ($1,000 from each institution was offered) and otherwise at the outset of the Montgomery bus boycott, which perhaps suggests that this later development in their relationship may have had as much to do with in-house convention struggles as with Jackson's heartfelt theological convictions. See "Letter from J. H. Jackson" (1956), in *The Papers of Martin Luther King, Jr.*, 3:155.

23. King, *Stride toward Freedom*, 28.

24. Ibid., 35.

25. Cone, "Martin and Malcolm," 403.

26. Baldwin, *The Legacy of Martin Luther King, Jr.*, 83–84.

27. Lloyd, *The Beloved Community*, 175.

28. Baldwin, *The Legacy of Martin Luther King, Jr.*, 77.

29. Lewis Baldwin provides an insightful citation regarding King's contrast of the church with other world religions. King obviously experienced an intellectual struggle around the issues of religious pluralism and tolerance on a global scale. In 1958, he described Christianity as "an expression of the highest revelation of God"—as "the synthesis of the best in all religions." At times, however, his tendency to refer to the United States as "becoming a Christian nation" did not go unchallenged, experiences that led him in 1961 to declare that "it is my sincere conviction that no religion has a monopoly on truth and that God has revealed Himself in all of the religions of mankind." See Martin Luther King Jr., "Advice for Living," *Ebony*, September 1958, 68. Also see "From Martin Luther King, Jr. to Bernard Resnikoff" (September 17, 1961), in Martin Luther King, Jr. Papers, Special Collections, Mugar Memorial Library Boston: Boston University, 1–2; and Baldwin, *The Legacy of Martin Luther King, Jr.*, 292.

30. Ivory, *Toward a Theology of Radical Involvement*, 92.

31. King, "Six Talks in Outline," 1:250.

32. As McWilliams notes, "The highest possibility and the lowest co-exist alike, and the latter are always more likely. But likelihood is never the sole language of humankind. Some minds turn to, and other voices speak, the old language of community, and that is testimony to the fact which the idea expresses: that community is a need because, at a level no less true for stretching beyond human imagining, all persons are kin, each to the other." See W. C. McWilliams, *The Idea of Fraternity in America* (Berkeley University of California Press, 1973), 622–624.

33. Howard Thurman, *The Luminous Darkness* (New York: Harper and Row, 1965), 113–114.

34. At the time of his death in 1981, Howard Thurman was dean emeritus of Marsh Chapel, Boston University, and chairman of the board of trustees of the Howard Thurman Educational Trust in San Francisco. He also served as dean of Rankin Chapel, Howard University, Washington, D.C.; as professor at Howard University School of Religion; and as director of religious life at Morehouse College and Spelman College, Atlanta. Founder of the Church for the Fellowship of all Peoples in San Francisco, the first interracial, interdenominational church in the United States, he was honorary canon of the Cathedral of Saint John the Divine, New York City.

35. King, "The Ethical Demands for Integration," 122.

36. Enoch H. Oglesby, "Martin Luther King, Jr., Liberation Ethics in a Christian Context," in *Martin Luther King, Jr.: Civil Rights Leader, Theologian, Orator*, 731.

37. Cited in Luker, *The Social Gospel in Black and White*, 324.

38. Burrow, "Personalism," 242.

39. King, "The Ethical Demands for Integration," 124.

40. Ibid., 123.

41. Ibid., 124.

42. Niebuhr, *The Nature and Destiny of Man*, 2:252.

43. One long-distant observer of the boycott who contemporaneously recognized this was Reinhold Niebuhr. "King," Niebuhr wrote, "scrupulously avoids violence and calls his strategy the 'way of love.' It is the most effective way of justice. . . . One cannot help but question that the definition of the boycott was the 'way of love.' Love is a motive and not a method. Love must always be intent on justice, and the boycott is one of the methods of establishing justice. It is justice, rather than love, which becomes relevant whenever one has to deal with conflicting interests." See "The Way of Nonviolent Resistance," *Christianity and Society* 21, no. 3 (Spring 1956). Also see James E. Sellers, "Love, Justice, and the Nonviolent Movement," *Theology Today*, January 1962, 422–434, 452, 726–727.

44. Paul R. Garber, "King Was a Black Theologian," in *Martin Luther King, Jr.: Civil Rights Leader, Theologian, Orator*, 407.

45. Niebuhr, *The Nature and Destiny of Man*, 2:257.

46. Cited in William R. Miller, *Martin Luther King, Jr.: His Life, Martyrdom and Meaning for the World* (New York: Avon Books, 1968), 66.

47. King, *Stride toward Freedom*, 106.

48. King, "Give Us the Ballot, We Will Transform the South" (1957), in *A Testament of Hope*, 199.

49. King, *Where Do We Go from Here?* 180.

50. King, "If the Negro Wins, Labor Wins" (1961), in *A Testament of Hope*, 207.

51. Martin Luther King Jr., "The Days to Come," in *Why We Can't Wait* (New York: Harper and Row, 1963), 151–152.

52. Niebuhr, *The Nature and Destiny of Man*, 2:245.

53. McKanan, *Identifying the Image of God*, 9.

54. Garrow, "Reformer to Revolutionary," in *Martin Luther King, Jr.: Civil Rights Leader, Theologian, Orator*, 428.

55. "The search for community was the defining motif of Martin Luther King Jr.'s life and thought. From his early childhood until his death, there is a progression in his personal and intellectual understanding of the nature and goal of human existence, which he refers to as 'the beloved community.' King's search for community was characterized by an insatiable thirst for truth and a deep seated religious faith that began in his early years in the intimate contexts of his family, the black church, and the larger black community of Atlanta, Georgia. . . . After his formal education and training, his experiences as pastor and spokesman for the black community in Montgomery served as a 'proving ground' for his embryonic, theoretical formulation of community that would be refined in the praxis of the civil rights movement." See Fluker, *They Looked for a City*, 81–82.

56. Samuel DuBois Cook, "Is Martin Luther King, Jr. Irrelevant?" in *Martin Luther King, Jr.: Civil Rights Leader, Theologian, Orator*, 293.

57. C. Eric Lincoln, "Martin Luther King: The Magnificent Intruder," in *Martin Luther King, Jr.: Civil Rights Leader, Theologian, Orator*, 616.

58. King, *Why We Can't Wait*, 96.

CHAPTER 7

1. King, *Where Do We Go from Here?* 106.

2. King, "Where Do We Go from Here?" in *A Testament of Hope*, 246.

3. Fairclough, "Was Martin Luther King a Marxist?" in *Martin Luther King, Jr.: Civil Rights Leader, Theologian, Orator*, 304.

4. King, *Where Do We Go from Here?* 152.

5. Turner, "Nonviolence and the Politics of Liberation," 1008.

6. King, *Where Do We Go From Here?* 37.

7. King, "Where Do We Go from Here?" 247.

8. Ibid., 317.

9. Niebuhr, *The Nature and Destiny of Man*, 2:255.

10. King, *Where Do We Go from Here?* 43.

11. King, "Where Do We Go from Here?" 317.

12. Cook explains, "Integration did not mean for Dr. King a new and refined method of the subordination of black humanity to white humanity. It meant, rather, a free, pluralistic, and open society in which lives equality of shared power, purpose, opportunity, and fulfillment. He clearly rejected the form of integration as a new and subtle way of white domination and as a one-way street. Integration is a river that flows both ways and involves shared meaning, participation, respect, and power.

Integration is as possible and desirable under black leadership and control as under white leadership and control. Genuine integration involves not the glorification of white men or black men but of men, all men. It is saturated with justice and equality." See Cook, "Is Martin Luther King, Jr. Irrelevant?" 245.

13. King, "Black Power Defined," in *A Testament of Hope*, 303.

14. Robert Michael Franklin Jr., "An Ethic of Hope: The Moral Thought of Martin Luther King, Jr.," in *Martin Luther King, Jr.: Civil Rights Leader, Theologian, Orator*, 354.

15. King, "Where Do We Go from Here?" 246.

16. Niebuhr, *The Nature and Destiny of Man*, 2:265, 266.

17. King, "Black Power Defined," 312.

18. Fairclough, "Was Martin Luther King a Marxist?" 306, 307.

19. Franklin, "An Ethic of Hope," 351–352.

20. Cook, "Is Martin Luther King, Jr., Irrelevant?" 245.

21. Hanes Walton Jr., *The Political Philosophy of Martin Luther King, Jr.* (Westport, Conn.: Greenwood, 1971), 18.

22. Ibid., 61.

23. Paul Garber, "Black Theology: The Latter Day Legacy of Martin Luther King, Jr.," in *Martin Luther King, Jr.: Civil Rights Leader, Theologian, Orator*, 414.

24. Martin Luther King Jr., *The Trumpet of Conscience* (New York: Harper and Row, 1968), 54.

25. Niebuhr, *The Nature and Destiny of Man*, 2:245.

26. Ibid., 247.

27. Ibid., 265, 266.

28. King, "Where Do We Go from Here?" 247.

29. Niebuhr, *The Nature and Destiny of Man*, 2:244.

30. Ibid., 249.

31. King, "Where Do We Go from Here?" 592.

32. King, *Where Do We Go from Here?* 142.

33. King, *The Trumpet of Conscience*, cited by Vincent Harding, "Recalling the Inconvenient Hero: Reflections on the Last Years of Martin Luther King, Jr.," in *Martin Luther King, Jr.: Civil Rights Leader, Theologian, Orator*, 536.

34. King, "Where Do We Go from Here?" 251.

35. Ibid., 585.

36. Ibid., 247.

37. King, *Where Do We Go from Here?* 138.

38. King, "Where Do We Go from Here?" 589.

39. Cook, "Is Martin Luther King, Jr., Irrelevant?" 244.

40. Cook, "Is Martin Luther King, Jr., Irrelevant?" 244

41. King, "Six Talks in Outline," 1:272.

EPILOGUE

1. CNN reporter Ashely Fantz reported, "Since September, nooses have been found in a Coast Guard office, a suburban New York police station locker room, a North Carolina high school, a Home Depot in New Jersey and on the campus of the

University of Maryland. A Brooklyn, New York, high school principal, who is black, received one in the mail recently, along with a letter that read, 'White Power Forever,' *The New York Times* reported. In mid-October, a noose was discovered outside a post office at New York City's 'Ground Zero,' just days after a noose was hung on the office door of a black Columbia University professor." CNN Web site, http://www.cnn.com/2007/US/11/01/nooses/index.html#cnnSTCText?iref.

2. In 1991, Rodney Glen King, an African American resident of Los Angeles, California, was stopped while driving and brutally beaten and tasered by four LA police officers while four to six additional officers stood by as onlookers. The act of police brutality, which was videotaped by a nearby eyewitness, was forwarded to the media for broadcast. The Los Angeles riots followed the 1992 acquittal of the officers, prompting Rodney King's appeal for civil order.

3. Josephine Hearn, "Black Lawmakers Emotional about Obama's Success," June 4, 2008, http://www.politico.com/news/stories/0608/10858.html.

4. Frank Sesno, "Analysis: Obama a Symbol of Progress, Change," June 4, 2008, http://www.cnn.com/2008/POLITICS/06/04/obama.history/index.html.

5. An article by Adam Nagourney entitled, "Poll Finds Obama Isn't Closing Divide on Race," concluded, "Indeed, the poll showed markedly little change in the racial components of people's daily lives since 2000, when The Times examined race relations in an extensive series of articles called 'How Race Is Lived in America,'" July 16, 2008, http://www.nytimes.com/2008/07/16/us/politics/16poll.html.

6. Robert M. Franklin, *Crisis in the Village: Restoring Hope in African American Communities* (Minneapolis, Minn.: Fortress Press, 2007), 3.

7. King, *Where Do We Go from Here?* 191.

Bibliography

PUBLISHED SOURCES

Abernathy, Ralph David. *And the Walls Came Tumbling Down*. New York: Harper and Row, 1989.

Ansboro, John J. *Martin Luther King, Jr.: The Making of a Mind*. Maryknoll, N.Y.: Orbis Books, 1982.

Aquinas, Thomas. *The Summa Theologica*. 3 vols. New York: Benziger Brothers, 1954.

Armstrong, A. Hilary. *St. Augustine and Christian Platonism*. Villanova, Pa.: Villanova University Press, 1967.

Augustine. *Confessions*.

———. *De Trinitate*.

———. *The City of God*.

Baer, Hans A., and Merrill Singer. *African-American Religion in the Twentieth Century: Varieties of Protest and Accommodation*. Knoxville: University of Tennessee Press, 1992.

Baker-Fletcher, Garth. *Somebodyness: Martin Luther King, Jr. and the Theory of Dignity*. Minneapolis, Minn.: Fortress Press, 1993.

Baldwin, Lewis V. *There Is a Balm in Gilead: The Cultural Roots of Martin Luther King, Jr.* Minneapolis, Minn.: Fortress Press, 1997.

———. *The Legacy of Martin Luther King, Jr.: The Boundaries of Law, Politics, and Religion*. Notre Dame, Ind.: University of Notre Dame, 2002.

Barth, Karl. *Protestant Theology in the Nineteenth Century: Its Background and History*. Grand Rapids, Mich.: Eerdmans, 2002.

Battenhouse, Roy W., ed. *A Companion to the Study of St. Augustine*. New York: Oxford University Press, 1955.

Bennett, John. "Love and Justice." In *Theology and Change: Essays in Memory of Alan Richardson*, ed. Ronald Preston, 128–142. London: S. C. M. Press, 1975.

Bennett, Lerone, Jr. *What Manner of Man: A Biography of Martin Luther King, Jr.* Chicago: Johnson, 1968.

Berlin, Ira. *Many Thousands Gone: The First Two Centuries of Slavery in North America.* Cambridge, Mass.: Harvard University Press, 1998.

Boer, Harry, R. *An Ember Still Glowing: Humankind as the Image of God.* Grand Rapids, Mich.: Eerdmans, 1990.

Branch, Taylor. *Parting the Waters.* New York: Simon and Schuster, 1988.

Brotz, Howard, ed. *African-American Social and Political Thought 1850–1920.* New Brunswick, N.J.: Transaction, 1999.

Burner, David. *Making Peace with the 60's.* Princeton, N.J.: Princeton University Press, 1996.

Burns, Stewart. *To the Mountaintop: Martin Luther King, Jr.'s Sacred Mission to Save America.* New York: HarperCollins, 2004.

Calvin, John. *Calvin's Institutes.* 2 vols.

———. *Commentary on the Book of Genesis.*

Cannon, Katie G. *Black Womanist Ethics.* Atlanta, Ga.: Scholars Press, 1988.

Cauthen, Kenneth. *The Impact of American Religious Liberalism.* New York: Harper and Row, 1962.

Chappell, David L. *A Stone of Hope: Prophetic Religion and the Death of Jim Crow.* Chapel Hill: University of North Carolina Press, 2004.

Charry, Ellen T. *By the Renewing of Your Minds: The Pastoral Function of Christian Doctrine.* New York: Oxford University Press, 1997.

Colaiaco, James A. *Martin Luther King, Jr.: Apostle of Militant Nonviolence.* New York: St. Martin's, 1988.

Cone, James. *Black Theology and Black Power.* New York: Orbis Books, 1997.

———. *God of the Oppressed.* New York: Seabury Press, 1975.

———. *Martin and Malcolm and America: A Dream or a Nightmare.* New York: Orbis Books, 1992.

Cornelius, Janet D. *Slave Missions and the Black Church in the Antebellum South.* Columbia: University of South Carolina Press, 1999.

Cushman, Robert E. "Faith and Reason." In *Companion to the Study of St. Augustine,* ed. Roy Battenhouse. New York: Oxford University Press, 1955, 287–314.

Davies, Alan T. *Infected Christianity: A Study of Modern Racism.* Kingston, Ont.: McGill-Queens University Press, 1988.

Davis, David Brion. *In the Image of God: Religion, Moral Values, and Our Heritage of Slavery.* New Haven, Conn.: Yale University Press, 2001.

Davis, Harry, and Robert Good, eds. *Reinhold Niebuhr on Politics.* New York: Scribner's, 1989.

Duffy, Regis, and Angelus Gambatese, eds. *Made in God's Image: The Catholic Vision of Human Dignity.* New York: Paulist Press, 2003.

Dyson, Michael E., *I May Not Get There with You: The True Martin Luther King, Jr.* New York: Free Press, 2000.

Evans, Sara. *Personal Politics: The Roots of Women's Liberation in the Civil Rights Movement.* New York: Vintage Books, 1980.

Evans, Zelia S., with J. T. Alexander. *The Dexter Avenue Baptist Church, 1877–1977.* Montgomery, Ala.: Dexter Avenue Baptist Church, 1978.

Fairclough, Adam. *To Redeem the Soul of America: The Southern Christian Leadership Conference and Martin Luther King, Jr.* Athens: University of Georgia Press, 1987.

Farmer, Herbert H. "The Bible: Its Significance and Authority." In *The Intepreter's Bible,* ed. George Arthur Buttrick. Vol. 1. Nashville, Tenn.: Abingdon Press, 1952.

Felder, Cain Hope. *Stony the Road We Trod: African American Biblical Interpretation.* Minneapolis, Minn.: Fortress Press, 1991.

Fernandez, Eleazar S. *Reimagining the Human: Theological Anthropology in Response to Systemic Evil.* St. Louis, Mo.: Chalice Press, 2003.

Finnis, John. *Aquinas.* New York: Oxford University Press, 1998.

Fisher, Miles Mark. *Negro Slave Songs in the United States.* Ithaca, N.Y.: Cornell University Press, 1953.

Fluker, Walter E. *They Looked for a City.* Boston: University Press of America, 1989.

Franklin, John Hope. *From Slavery to Freedom: A History of Negro Americans.* New York: Knopf, 1994.

Franklin, Robert M. *Liberating Visions: Human Fulfillment and Social Justice in African-American Thought.* Minneapolis, Minn.: Fortress Press, 1990.

Franklin, Robert M. *Crisis in the Village: Restoring Hope in African American Communities.* Minneapolis, Minn.: Fortress Press, 2007.

Frazier, E. Franklin. *The Negro Church in America.* New York: Schocken Books, 1963.

Fullinwider, Robert, and Claudia Mills. *The Moral Foundations of Civil Rights.* Lanham, Md.: Rowan and Littlefield, 1986.

Garrow, David J. *Protest at Selma.* New Haven, Conn.: Yale University Press, 1978.

———. *The FBI and Martin Luther King, Jr.* New York: Norton, 1981.

———. *Bearing the Cross: Martin Luther King, Jr., and the Southern Christian Leadership Conference.* New York: Morrow, 1986.

———, ed. *Martin Luther King, Jr.: Civil Rights Leader, Theologian, Orator.* 3 vols. New York: Carlson, 1989.

Gilby, Thomas. *The Political Thought of Thomas Aquinas.* Chicago: University of Chicago Press, 1958.

Glaude, Eddie S., Jr. *Exodus: Religion, Race, and the Nation in Early Nineteenth-Century Black America.* Chicago: University of Chicago Press, 2000.

Gray, Fred. *Bus Ride to Justice: Changing the System by the System.* Montgomery, Ala.: Black Belt Press, 1995.

Hackett, David G. *Religion and American Culture: A Reader.* 2nd ed. New York: Routledge, 2003.

Hallett, Garth L. *Christian Neighbor-Love: An Assessment of Six Rival Versions.* Washington, D.C.: Georgetown University Press, 1989.

Harding, Vincent. *There Is a River: The Black Struggle for Freedom in America.* New York: Harcourt Brace Jovanovich, 1981.

———. *Martin Luther King: The Inconvenient Hero.* New York: Orbis Books, 1996.

Harrison, Carol. *Beauty and Revelation in the Thought of Saint Augustine.* New York: Oxford University Press, 1992.

————. *Augustine: Christian Truth and Fractured Humanity*. New York: Oxford University Press, 2000.

Hauerwas, Stanley. *A Better Hope: Resources for a Church Confronting Capitalism, Democracy, and Postmodernity*. Grand Rapids, Mich.: Brazos Press, 2001.

————. *With the Grain of the Universe: The Church's Witness and Natural Theology*. Grand Rapids, Mich.: Brazos Press, 2001.

Henry, Charles P., "Delivering Daniel: The Dialectic of Ideology and Theology in the Thought of Martin Luther King, Jr." *Journal of Black Studies* 17 (1987): 327–345.

Herskovits, Melville. *The Myth of the Negro Past*. New York: Harper and Row, 1941.

Heschel, Abraham. *The Prophets*. 2 vols. New York: Harper and Row, 1962.

Hoitenga, Dewey J., Jr. *John Calvin and the Will: A Critique and Corrective*. Grand Rapids, Mich.: Baker Books, 1997.

Holt, Thomas, and Elsa Brown, eds. *Major Problems in African American History*. 2 vols. New York: Houghton Mifflin, 2000.

Hughes, Philip Edgcumbe. *The True Image: The Origin and Destiny of Man in Christ*. Grand Rapids, Mich.: Eerdmans, 1989.

Ivory, Luther D. *Toward a Theology of Radical Involvement: The Theological Legacy of Martin Luther King, Jr*. Nashville, Tenn.: Abingdon Press, 1997.

Johns, Vernon. *Human Possibilities: A Vernon Johns Reader*. Washington, D.C.: Hoffman Press, 1977.

Johnson, Mordecai Wyatt, "1927 Inaugural Address," in *Education for Freedom*. Washington, D.C.: Moorland-Spingarn Research Center, 1976.

Jones, Major J. *Christian Ethics for Black Theology: The Politics of Liberation*. New York: Abingdon Press, 1974.

Kegley, Charles W., ed. *Reinhold Niebuhr: His Religious, Social and Political Thought*. New York: Pilgrim Press, 1984.

Kierkegaard, Søren. *Works of Love*. New York: Harper and Row, 1962.

King, Coretta Scott. *My Life with Martin Luther King, Jr*. New York: Holt, Rinehart and Winston, 1969.

King, Jr., Martin Luther. Advice for Living. *Ebony*, September 1958, 68.

————. *Stride toward Freedom*. New York: Harper and Row, 1958.

————. *The Measure of a Man*. Philadelphia: Christian Education Press, 1959.

————. *Strength to Love*. New York: Harper and Row, 1963.

————. *Why We Can't Wait*. New York: Harper and Row, 1963.

————. *Where Do We Go from Here: Chaos or Community?* New York: Beacon Press, 1968.

————. *The Trumpet of Conscience*. New York: Harper and Row, 1968.

————. *A Testament of Hope: The Essential Writings of Martin Luther King, Jr.*, ed. James Melvin Washington. San Francisco: Harper and Row, 1986.

————. *The Papers of Martin Luther King, Jr.* Vol. 1, *Called to Serve*. Ed. Clayborne Carson. Berkeley: University of California Press, 1992.

————. *The Papers of Martin Luther King, Jr.* Vol. 2, *Rediscovering Precious Values*. Ed. Clayborne Carson. Berkeley: University of California Press, 1994.

————. *The Papers of Martin Luther King, Jr.* Vol. 3, *Birth of a New Age*. Ed. Clayborne Carson. Berkeley: University of California Press, 1997.

———. *The Papers of Martin Luther King, Jr.* Vol. 4, *Symbol of the Movement.* Ed. Clayborne Carson. Berkeley: University of California Press, 2000.

Lewis, David. *King: A Critical Biography.* New York: Praeger, 1970.

Lincoln, C. Eric. *Martin Luther King, Jr.: A Profile.* New York: Noonday Press, 1984.

———. *Race, Religion, and the Continuing American Dilemma.* New York: Hill and Wang, 1999.

Lincoln, C. Eric, and Lawrence Mamiya. *The Black Church in the Afro-American Experience.* Durham, N.C.: Duke University Press, 1990.

Lischer, Richard. *The Preacher King: Martin Luther King, Jr., and the Word That Moved America.* New York: Oxford University Press, 1995.

Lloyd, Roger. *The Beloved Community.* New York: Macmillan, 1937.

Lovin, Robin W. *Reinhold Niebuhr and Christian Realism.* New York: Cambridge University Press, 1995.

Luker, Ralph *The Social Gospel in Black and White: American Racial Reform, 1885-1912.* Chapel Hill: University of North Carolina Press, 1991.

Luther, Martin. *Christian Liberty.* Philadelphia: Muhlenberg Press, 1947.

———. *Luther's Commentary on Genesis.* Ed. J. Theodore Mueller. Grand Rapids, Mich.: Zondervan, 1958.

———. *Luther's Works.* Ed. Jaroslav Pelikan. St. Louis, Ill.: Concordia Press, 1986.

Marsh, Charles. *God's Long Summer: Stories of Faith and Civil Rights.* Princeton, N.J.: Princeton University Press, 1997.

———. "The Civil Rights Movement as Theological Drama: Interpretation and Application." *Modern Theology,* April 2002.

———. *The Beloved Community: How Faith Shapes Social Justice, from the Civil Rights Movement to Today.* New York: Perseus Books, 2005.

Mays, Benjamin E. *Dr. Benjamin E. Mays Speaks: Representative Speeches of a Great American Orator.* Ed. Freddie C. Colston. New York: University Press of America, 2002.

McKanan, Dan. *Identifying the Image of God: Radical Christians and Nonviolent Power in the Antebellum United States.* New York: Oxford University Press, 2002.

McNeill, John, T. *Calvin: On God and Political Duty.* Indianapolis, Ind.: Bobbs-Merrill, 1950.

McWilliams, W. C. *The Idea of Fraternity in America.* Berkeley: University of California Press, 1973.

Miller, William R. *Martin Luther King, Jr.: His Life, Martyrdom and Meaning for the World.* New York: Avon Books, 1968.

Mitchell, Henry H. *Black Beliefs: Folk Beliefs of Blacks in America and West Africa.* New York: Harper and Row, 1975.

———. *Black Church Beginnings.* Grand Rapids, Mich.: Eerdmans, 2004.

Mitchell, Henry H., and Nicholas Cooper-Lewter. *Soul Theology: The Heart of American Black Culture.* Nashville, Tenn.: Abingdon Press, 1986.

Morris, Ronald Elliot. "The Black Experience as Expressed in Contemporary Thought and Theology." Unpublished ms. Richmond, Va.: Union Theological Seminary, 1974.

Moses, Greg. *Revolution of Conscience: Martin Luther King, Jr. and the Philosophy of Nonviolence.* New York: Guilford Press, 1997.

Niebuhr, Reinhold. *Beyond Tragedy: Essays on the Christian Interpretation of History.*
New York: Scribner's, 1940.

———. *Christianity and Power Politics.* New York: Scribner's, 1940.

———. *Moral Man and Immoral Society: A Study in Ethics and Politics.* New York:
Scribner's, 1940.

———. *The Irony of American History.* New York: Scribner's, 1952.

———. *Christian Realism and Political Problems.* New York: Scribner's, 1953.

———. The "Way of Nonviolent Resistance." *Christianity and Society* 21, no. 3
(Spring 1956).

———. "The Problem of a Protestant Social Ethic." *Union Seminary Quarterly Review*
15 (1959).

———. *The Nature and Destiny of Man.* Vol. 1, *Human Nature.* Upper Saddle River,
N.J.: Prentice Hall, 1964.

———. *The Nature and Destiny of Man.* Vol. 2, *Human Destiny.* New York:
Scribner's, 1964.

———. "Walter Rauschenbusch in Historical Perspective." In *Faith and Politics,*
ed. Ronald H. Stone. New York: George Braziller, 1968.

Oates, Stephen B. *Let the Trumpet Sound: The Life of Martin Luther King, Jr.* New York:
Harper and Row, 1982.

Oates, Whitney J., ed. *Basic Writings of Saint Augustine.* New York: Random House,
1948.

O'Connell, Robert J. *The Origin of the Soul in St. Augustine's Later Works.* Bronx, N.Y.:
Fordham University Press, 1987.

Outka, Gene. *Agape: An Ethical Analysis.* New Haven, Conn.: Yale University Press,
1972.

Paris, Peter L. *The Social Teaching on the Black Churches.* Minneapolis, Minn.: Fortress
Press, 1985.

Payne, Charles. *I've Got the Light of Freedom: The Organizing Tradition of the Mississippi
Freedom Struggle.* Berkeley: University of California Press, 1995.

Perry, Lewis, and Michael Fellman. *Antislavery Reconsidered: New Perspectives on the
Abolitionists.* Baton Rouge: Louisiana State University Press, 1979.

Powell, Adam Clayton, Jr. *Marching Blacks: An Interpretive History of the Rise of the Black
Common Man.* New York: Dial Press, 1945.

———. *Riots and Ruins.* New York: Richard R. Smith, 1945.

Powell, Adam Clayton, Sr. *Against the Tide: An Autobiography.* New York: Richard R.
Smith, 1938.

Proctor, Samuel Dewitt. *Samuel Proctor: My Moral Odyssey.* Valley Forge, Pa.: Judson
Press, 1989.

———. *The Substance of Things Hoped For: A Memoir of African American Faith.*
New York: Putnam, 1995.

Raboteau, Albert J. *Slave Religion: The "Invisible Institution" in the Antebellum South.*
New York: Oxford University Press, 1978.

Rauschenbusch, Walter. *Christianity and the Social Crisis.* Boston: Pilgrim Press,
1907.

———. *A Theology for the Social Gospel.* New York: Macmillan, 1917.

Reimers, David M. *White Protestantism and the Negro.* New York: Oxford University Press, 1965.

Renick, Timothy M. *Aquinas for Armchair Theologians.* Louisville, Ky.: Westminster John Knox Press, 2002.

Roberts, Samuel K. *African American Christian Ethics.* Cleveland, Ohio: Pilgrim Press, 2001.

Robinson, Jo Ann. *The Montgomery Bus Boycott and the Women Who Started It: The Memoir of Jo Ann Gibson Robinson.* Knoxville: University of Tennessee Press, 1987.

Royce, Josiah. *The Sources of Religious Insight.* New York: Scribner's, 1912.

———. *The Problem of Christianity.* Chicago: University of Chicago Press, 1913.

Savage, Barbara Diane. *Broadcasting Freedom: Radio, War, and the Politics of Race 1938–1948.* Chapel Hill: University of North Carolina Press.

Sellers, James E. "Love, Justice and the Nonviolent Movement." *Theology Today,* January 1962: 422–434.

Sernett, Milton C., ed. *Afro-American Religious History: A Documentary Witness.* Durham, N.C.: Duke University Press, 1985.

Smith, Kenneth, and Ira Zepp Jr. *Search for the Beloved Community.* Valley Forge, Pa.: Judson Press, 1974.

Stone, Ronald. "Liberty and Equality." In *Faith and Politics,* ed. Ronald Stone. New York: George Braziller, 1968.

Suchocki, Marjorie Hewitt. *Divinity and Diversity: A Christian Affirmation of Religious Pluralism.* Nashville, Tenn.: Abingdon Press, 2004.

Thurman, Howard. *Deep River.* New York: Harper and Row, 1945.

———. *Jesus and the Disinherited.* New York: Abingdon Press, 1945.

———. *The Inward Journey.* New York: Harper and Row, 1961.

———. *The Search for Common Ground.* New York: Harper and Row, 1961.

———. *The Luminous Darkness.* New York: Harper and Row, 1965.

Tillich, Paul. *Love, Power and Justice.* New York: Oxford University Press, 1954.

Tunde, Adeleke. *UnAfrican Americans: Nineteenth-Century Black Nationalists and the Civilizing Mission.* Knoxville: University Press of Kentucky, 1998.

Vaughn, Wally, and Richard Wills. *Reflections of Our Pastor: Dr. Martin Luther King, Jr. at Dexter Avenue Baptist Church.* Dover, Mass.: Majority Press, 1999.

Walton, Hanes, Jr., ed. *The Political Philosophy of Martin Luther King, Jr.* Westport, Conn.: Greenwood, 1971.

Washington, Joseph R. *Race and Religion in Mid–Nineteenth Century America, 1850–1877.* 2 vols. New York: Edwin Mellen Press, 1988.

West, Cornell. *Race Matters.* New York: Penguin, 1997.

———. *Democracy Matters: Winning the Fight against Imperialism.* New York: Penguin, 2004.

Wilmore, Gayraud S. *Black Religion and Black Radicalism: An Interpretation of the Religious History of Afro-American People.* New York: Orbis Books, 1983.

Wimbush, Vincent, L. *Stony the Road We Trod: African American Biblical Interpretation.* Minneapolis, Minn.: Fortress Press, 1991.

———. *The Bible and African Americans: A Brief History.* Minneapolis, Minn.: Fortress Press, 2003.

Yoder, John Howard. *For the Nations: Essays Public and Evangelical.* Grand Rapids, Mich.: Eerdmans, 1997.

Zepp, Ira G., Jr. *The Social Vision of Martin Luther King, Jr.* New York: Carlson, 1989.

ARCHIVES, COLLECTIONS, AND RECORDINGS

Alabama Department of Archives and History, Montgomery, Alabama.

Auburn Avenue Research Center on African-American Culture and History, Atlanta, Georgia.

Black Studies Collections, Wilder Library, Virginia Union University, Richmond, Virginia.

Burke Library, Union Theological Seminary, New York, New York.

Dexter Avenue Baptist Church, Private Archives, Montgomery, Alabama.

Norman Walton Papers. Private collection, Montgomery, Alabama.

Schomberg Center for Research in Black Culture, Harlem, New York.

Special Collections Library, Alderman Library, University of Virginia, Charlottesville, Virginia.

Special Collections Library, Morton Library, Union Theological Seminary, Richmond, Virginia.

Thelma Rice Papers. Private collection, Montgomery, Alabama.

INTERVIEWS

The following interviews were conducted during my tenure as senior pastor of Dexter Avenue Baptist Church:

Mr. Clarence Bozeman, Mr. Warren Brown, Dr. Ralph Bryson, Mrs. Dorothy Calhoun, Mrs. Johnnie Carr, Mrs. Claressa W. Chambliss, Mr. Osborne C. Chambliss, Ms. Verdie Davie, Mrs. Minnie Woods-Dixon, Deacon Zelia Evans, Deacon John Feagin, Sr., Deacon John Fulgham, Deacon William B. Gary, Mrs. Myrtle Pless Jones, Deacon Richard Jordan, Mrs. Viola H. Jordan, Mr. Rufus Lewis, Mr. Nelson Malden, Deacon Robert Nesbitt, Sr., Mr. Robert D. Nesbitt, Jr., Dr. John Porter, Mrs. Dorothy Posey, Mrs. Thelma Austin Rice, Mr. David Ross, Mrs. Maggie Shannon, Deacon Richmond Smiley, Mrs. Jean Smiley, Mrs. Althea Thompson-Thomas, Mr. Wiley Thomas, Mrs. Jimmie P. Walton, Mrs. Bertha P. Williams, Deacon Robert Williams.

Also see *Reflections of Our Pastor: Dr. Martin Luther King, Jr. at Dexter Avenue Baptist Church.* Dover, Mass.: Majority Press.

Index

Made in United States
Orlando, FL
01 December 2021